Wildwood Days

Wildwood Days

Francesca Wright

iUniverse, Inc.
New York Lincoln Shanghai

Wildwood Days

Copyright © 2006 by Francesca Wright

All rights reserved. No part of this book may be used or reproduced by any means, graphic, electronic, or mechanical, including photocopying, recording, taping or by any information storage retrieval system without the written permission of the publisher except in the case of brief quotations embodied in critical articles and reviews.

iUniverse books may be ordered through booksellers or by contacting:

iUniverse
2021 Pine Lake Road, Suite 100
Lincoln, NE 68512
www.iuniverse.com
1-800-Authors (1-800-288-4677)

ISBN-13: 978-0-595-38959-9 (pbk)
ISBN-13: 978-0-595-83343-6 (ebk)
ISBN-10: 0-595-38959-7 (pbk)
ISBN-10: 0-595-83343-8 (ebk)

Printed in the United States of America

To My Mother—Lillian Dean Ingram Wright

Childhood days,

Wildwood days,

Songs of birds and bees;

Tho you left me alone,

Still you're my own,

In my beautiful memories. *

* Author unknown

Contents

Foreword................................ xi

CHAPTER 1	I Remember the Day I Was Born 1
CHAPTER 2	Lily of the Hills 9
CHAPTER 3	John Wright the Painter 21
CHAPTER 4	The Reaper is Death 35
CHAPTER 5	Granny and Her Corncob Pipe 41
CHAPTER 6	The Seat of Knowledge is Mighty Hard.......... 51
CHAPTER 7	Young Sprouts............................. 61
CHAPTER 8	The Sweet Smelling Boy 81
CHAPTER 9	Drought but Christmas Anyway 86
CHAPTER 10	Little Pearl............................... 98
CHAPTER 11	I Help Father Make A Coffin 110
CHAPTER 12	Meeting In A Brush Arbor................... 118
CHAPTER 13	The Years of the War....................... 127
CHAPTER 14	Day is Done 139
CHAPTER 15	How Strange It Seems...................... 149
CHAPTER 16	Try, Try Again 162
CHAPTER 17	Hands Along The Way 171
CHAPTER 18	The Hay Balers 181

CHAPTER 19	The Hills Close In	190
CHAPTER 20	The Ghost With a Wet Tongue	200
CHAPTER 21	Escape	208
CHAPTER 22	My Irish Rose	214

About the Author 235

Foreword

As a little girl, Francesca Wright followed at her father's footsteps through the Ozark hills as he gathered bark and berries to mix paint for his paintings. Francesca soon became an artist and a student of nature. After studying art at Washington University in Missouri she moved to New Mexico in 1942. From that time on she has created more than one thousand original oil paintings that are in private and corporate collections of art lovers in every state of the United States and throughout the world.

Francesca was one of the founders of the New Mexico Art League and the All Faiths Home, a refuge for underprivileged children. Through the years she has donated innumerable paintings for charitable causes. Along with her family, she has created two award winning restaurants, built seven homes of her own unique design, composed a collection of original poetry and written this story about her life as a girl of the hills.

Francesca is a colorist and a creator of impressionistic paintings. The eyes of her portraits gaze at you with love and understanding; the reality is vivid, as you reach to touch a petal in her romantic still-lifes. The beautiful vistas of the Southwest have been the inspiration for many of her ethereal and mystical landscapes. The Indian people of these lands say that God paints through her hands.

All of the story which follows, with the exception of its final chapter, was originally hand written by Francesca Wright—copied in her own hand seven times—more than thirty five years ago. It was finally transcribed for publication in 1998, with Francesca dictating the final chapter at the age of 87. Her memory of the events described herein is still as vivid and sure as it was when she first recorded her thoughts. Today, as this story goes to press, Francesca is 95 years of age, and eagerly anticipating its publication.

1

I Remember the Day I Was Born

On a tender day in mid-April, 1911, in the foothills of the Missouri Ozarks, I was born in a log cabin. The humidity was so enervating it made one long to drop everything and succumb to a delightful case of spring fever. Swift showers played hide and seek with the sun, washing the pale new leaves and softening the buds that burst forth from the lowest buckbrush and paw paw patches to the highest chinkapen oak. The showers left the air alternately cool as well water, or hot as a kitchen at canning time. The sky was full of birds. Martins with clipping black wings circled a tiny birdhouse that brother Jim had build for them on a pole, clattering to each other joyfully at finding a new home. A petite wren, her bill stuffed with feathers and sticks, was busily weaving her own nest in the pocket of an old coat thrown carelessly over the paling fence. Blue jays squawked, darting in and out amongst the cedar trees. Crows cawed in the cornfields. Robins nearly fell over backwards tugging at long worms in the plowed garden. In the hollow below the house, wild doves wooed each other, and a sexy mockingbird trilled love-lust notes to a lady bird who was already willing.

Contrasts were everywhere. Forests and valleys, beautiful and promising, were splashed with redbud, wild crabapple, dogwood and plum blossoms. But the high ridges, with the pale bones laid bare by wind and weather, frowned down on us. The tall walnut and sycamore trees below the house and along the spring that flowed towards Dean's Creek were lush compared to the puny scrub oak that stubbornly sought to creep into the plowed fields and close-cropped pastures. Along the creek, hazelnuts, sassafras and wild blackberry fought constantly the naked bluffs above and the gravel beaches below.

Such a beautiful day to be born in, even in a log cabin, whose shake-shingled roof sat slightly awry like a rakish hat. The windows, like sleuthful eyes, peered from underneath.

The four rooms of the cabin, two upstairs and two down, were sparsely and poorly furnished, but cozy nonetheless. They were permeated with the odor of dry straw from the homemade mattresses that crumbled and sifted on to the floor underneath the beds. Usually three of us children slept in a bed, snuggled together like rabbits in a burrow. A few things spoke of better days, such as the immense oak table in the kitchen with beautifully turned legs, and the grand old cooking stove with elaborate nickel trim. In winter we would move the table closer to the stove at mealtime and the children would line up on benches on opposite sides of the table. Our parents sat in cane-bottomed chairs at the head and foot and reigned over us like a king and queen in an impoverished kingdom.

On a washstand against the wall rested a blue porcelain water bucket, dipper and washpan. The bucket caused many a heated argument over whose turn it was to go to the well for water. Above the washstand hung an oval mirror with coarse towels on wooden pegs beside it. Every day on inspecting our faces and hands Mother declared we never used either of them

A hideous big cupboard with tin doors, to hold dishes, pots, pans, and staples, filled an entire corner. It wouldn't have looked so bad if someone hadn't tried to pretty it up with aluminum paint instead of scrubbing the grime off it. Mother must have turned one of us loose with a paintbrush when Father was away.

The front room was shut off by a green door with a convenient wide crack in it through which we peeked at what was going on in there. Through the crack Father spied on the girls courting. Mother helped. The boys spied on the girls courting. I spied on the girls courting. And the girls spied on each other.

Mother's and Father's bed, beautifully carved in a daisy pattern occupied one whole corner of the front room. The King heater in the middle of the room, got more attention in the winter than we children did, as it constantly had to be fueled and stoked. An old clock with wagging pendulum rested on a shelf. Alongside it was the family bible. Through the years Father, in searching for the answers to life's perplexities, made many a notation in the margins of its pages.

When the family gathered in the front room in the evening to sew, study, play the violin and banjo, or just talk, we sat on rockers and settees made of hickory wythe. Father cut and bent the limbs while green to form their curved backs and arms. When the wood seasoned the nails often fell out, and many was the time the chairs and settees collapsed and eased us laughing to the floor. It was no laughing matter, though, when the neighbors came to call on Sundays and unsuspectingly flopped down in them. We would hold our breaths and brace ourselves in fearful anticipation, but I don't recall anything ever happening. Mother aged a lot over it though.

A rather fancy old dresser with a mottled mirror graced the far corner. Father's shaving strap and mug, and the coal oil lamp to light the room at night rested on its marble top. The dresser drawers held our Sunday-go-to-meeting clothes, a fine damask tablecloth and a small red velvet chest containing a bone-handled mirror and brush that Grandpa Ingram brought from Scotland many years previous.

By the window stood mothers pride and joy—a Climax sewing machine. Every time she passed it she polished it lovingly with the tail of her apron.

The two rooms upstairs were the boys' and girls' rooms. The boys' room had two big beds and a cherry chiffonrobe made by Grandfather Wright. Two round-topped steamer trunks filled with Mother's and Father's wedding clothes and beautiful old albums and love letters stood against the wall. We children used to put pillows on the trunks, straddle them and pretended they were galloping horses.

The girls' room also had two beds and a chest of drawers nestled under the sloped ceiling. Above it was a mirror decorated with pincushions, hair-ribbons and old valentines.

This was the house I was born in, filled with the people I loved, and for that reason, I will always call it home.

Like a small frog on a lily pad gulping flies, I swallowed every story my brothers and sisters used to tell me. They all had a little different version of what happened on the day of my birth, but time, place, and people being what they were, most of what they said had to be the truth.

There was only one of them who might have added a bit of embroidery to her crocheting. That was Goldie. Being only two and one-half years old on that day it is hard to understand how she came to remember so many of the details. But not for the world would I accuse her of fibbing since it was her version that was best remembered.

The day I was born Mother lay moaning on the big bed in the front room. Green window shades were drawn to cool the room from the sun's hot rays and to keep the light out of mother's eyes.

Sixteen year old Garsy hitched our team of horses to the wagon that was already loaded with rail ties to sell in order to pay the doctor. Desperately he drove over the hill towards Richland, many miles away. As he whipped the horses to a full gallop, Father shouted. "Don't forget to stop and call the doctor from the nearest phone. Hurry, now, you hear!"

Mother had her heart set on having a real doctor deliver her baby this time. Father had helped all the others into the world except once, when she managed alone. Now he eagerly adhered to her wishes. In truth, anxious to avoid the whole mess, he had resolved to take off for the bushes the minute the neighbor ladies arrived. Father knew they would flock around as soon as Jim, who had been sent to notify them, hollered out the news at their gates. Jim was only ten years old, but fast on his feet, and the word spread in no time at all.

Up and down hills, across the creek, the neighbor women hurried towards our house. Faces hidden deep in slat bonnets, starched aprons flying in the breeze, they resembled pioneer women heading for a gold rush. Birth, almost as exciting as death, was something a body oughtn't to miss. It would give them something more interesting than the weather, gardens and sewing to talk about.

They came bearing gifts—everything they could spare, each with an eye to outshine the other.

Mrs. Rowden was too poor to bring anything other than a Mason jar of wild flowers—sweet William, waxy cowslips and fragrant wood violets.

This gift from the heart and from the earth lay treasured in mothers memory. She loved flowers.

Grandma Abbott everyone called her, the oldest woman around, arrived first, a small patchwork quilt for the baby under her arm. She creaked her ancient bones down the hill, across the creek and up another long hill to our house, hoisting her feet along as if she were on crutches. Her lips puckered around the corncob pipe she smoked all the way. Upon arriving she ordered the oldest girls, Annie and Nellie, to gather chips and start a fire in the kitchen stove. Also to fetch water from the well to put on to boil so that the doctor could sterilize his instruments. This done she sat down in the rocker by the bed to time mother's pains, watching the clock on the shelf. Lighting up her pipe again, she nearly stifled mother with its smoke. Grandma was a love though, and it was to her house I went on my first night away from home.

Frail cousin Laura, an old maid who lived over the hill to the north of us, came, although she was terrified of the whole affair. She tried to hide her fears by laughing at everything the others did whether amusing or not. She adored my mother and badly wanted to help, but was too distressed to enter the dark shade room where mother lay. Instead, she hovered by the door wringing her thin hands in anxiety. Then she took the broom and swept the porches at least a dozen times without stopping.

Mrs. Thornsberry came only for the lark, and to moon at my handsome father's black wavy hair, violet eyes and flaming mustache. He didn't know she existed. That her ample bosom flopped and her rear cheeks pummeled each other under her one garment when she walked bothered him not at all. Her gift of huckleberry cobbler was obviously for him only. He stuffed down a huge piece of it, clomped on his straw hat, and took off for the brush in a dead run after a thick swarm of bees that swept past the house. Set on finding the bee tree with its hollow full of honey, he left poor Mrs. Thornsberry to pucker pretty lips over his paintings and gave her nary a thought. Mother, knowing she had a crush on him, smiled quietly to herself.

Mrs. Willougby lived way to the north of us and must have been very tired when she arrived. Walking primly, she came down the hill, a big basket on her arm containing boiled squirrel and dumplings and melon rind preserves. A woman determined to pay mother back for all she had done for her. Hadn't mother held her in her arms when her little boy was thrown from a horse and killed? For her, mother had also braved criticism by the other neighbors who would not accept her because she was of the Mormon faith and did not attend our Church of Christ. Hurt at their sideways glances she stubbornly insisted on helping Mother in her travail. She wrung out cold cloths for Mother's hot brow, fanned her, and tidied the bed and room.

Mrs. Traw was a bottom-lander. She brought peach preserves and three loaves of light bread. Fixing a lunch for the children, she sent them off to play in the sawdust piles down where an old mill had once stood. Years later, on one of my rare trips back, I came upon her putting flowers on Mother's grave.

Aunt Frances Monismith outdid them all. She came bearing a most beautiful crocheted cap in blue thread done in a shell pattern with white satin ribbon bows. Mother was overcome with joy and repaid her with the promise that she would name me after her if I was a girl, and she did. Aunt Frances was no more an aunt than Grandma Abbot was our grandma, but was called Aunt out of affection and respect. In addition to the cap she brought along a big black satchel containing thread, scissors, receiving blanket and a wooden spoon for mother to clamp between her teeth when the pains came hard. Big boned and apple-cheeked, with large scrubbed hands, she appeared capable of arising to almost any situation. Actually, she was the midwife of our community and proud of it. When she heard there was to be a real doctor in attendance she was chagrined, scolding, "Lily, you hadn't oughta done a thing like that there. Why, I brung a army of younguns into the world and could have spared you all that expense." Deprived of the leading role, she willingly set about being a useful helper. On discovering there was no wood for the stove she went out to the woodshed. Swinging the axe like a man, she soon chopped a pile of wood waist high.

Doctor Clark finally arrived in a mud-splattered surrey. He whoa'd the proud roans to a stop at our gate, bounced from the seat like a ball of yarn, tied up the horses, and bag in hand marched on short fat legs straight to the front door. With one shoo of chubby paws he waved the women out of the room, then scrubbed his hands in the kitchen basin, felt mother's brow, told her to stick out her tongue, counted her pulse, and after examining her ever so gently, covered her, left the room and eased himself into the rocker on the front porch. He unlaced tight shoes, undid his belt, propped his feet on fathers toolchest, took out a plug of Beeswax tobacco, bit off a chaw and rolled it around to get the saliva flowing before beginning to chew. To gain complete comfort, he leaned back, put his hat over his eyes to shade the sun, and folded his hands over an ample stomach. Every now and then he would disrupt this tableau by turning to spray tobacco juice on mother's scarlet climbing rosebush.

The sun came out, a rainbow arched over the hill to the east, and yellow butterflies floated silently past his nose. A patient man, Doctor Clark sat prepared to wait, his ear tuned to the intensity of the moans of the woman in the darkened room. He admired the woman whom he was about to deliver of child. He knew her strength and character; had stood gazing at her across more than one deathbed; had seen her sitting patiently through the night beside the ill; and now for the first time he had come to help her. They were friends.

In her last moments of delivery his words were soft as he encouraged her. His hands were swift and sure, and his voice as elated as if I were the first born instead of the ninth when he declared, "Its a girl, Lillian, a fine girl."

Later he treated Father for bee stings. Father had found the tree and the bees had objected. With little coaxing from the womenfolk, Doctor Clark refreshed himself by eating some of the honey on thick slices of yeast bread. He returned the favor by passing out cough syrups, pills, salves and purgatives to the women gathered about him, and advised how to use home remedies for emergencies like snakebite, scours, and pineworms. Over Ethel, my oldest sister who had been addled since she fell from a tree at the age of eight, he just shook his head sorrowfully. He lined up the other children, had them stick out their tongues, and listened in on their chests, remarking that they were a healthy looking lot.

Father grew embarrassed because Garsy had not yet returned with the cash to pay. The doctor merely shrugged his shoulders and accepted a young pig and four chickens for his services. He drove off over the hill, the pig squealing and the chickens squawking in the back of his surrey.

2
Lily of the Hills

Mother's dreams were of gossamer stuff, but to her they never floated out of reach. She wanted for her children noble things: knowledge as well as an education, goodness as well as cleverness, godliness as well as righteousness, strength to open our own doors and courage to hold them open against all odds. Garsy must be a great violinist; Annie and Nellie, teachers; Jim, an engineer; Paul a preacher; Ruth, an actress; Goldie, a writer; and me, an artist like Father.

Mother was thirty-nine when I was born. By the time I could see beyond her breasts she had lost most of her teeth, and her hair was streaked with silver. Still she possessed an unconscious loveliness that made her every gesture, whether it was planting corn or tending the sick, an act of grace and dignity. The little wrinkles of laughter around her expressive gray eyes and the short curls on her neck that escaped her tight French roll are two things I especially remember about her. She had an arresting mannerism, that of tossing her head ever so slightly when about to assert herself, indicating that she had a definite view on the subject at hand and one had ought to stop, listen and take heed.

The burden of raising us children and running the farm rested on her slim shoulders, since father had to be gone so much on painting trips to earn the cash we so sorely needed. It was her decision when to plow, when to plant, and when to harvest. She loved the earth. To her seeds were living things. It gave her infinite pleasure to nourish them to their fulfillment. "It's like helping the Lord to create," she told us. She was keenly attuned to nature and ever so aware of its miracles. She would hold a green leaf before us, and through her eyes we marveled at Gods handiwork. She would often stand on the hill above our house and with one glowing gesture transform our poor farm into an Eden. She discovered diamonds in little stones and convinced us that the dewdrops in a petal were in truth gleaming pearls.

Even the frost on our windowpanes through her imaginative eyes became beautiful fairy landscapes. Her personality was mirrored in the words by William Blake:

To see the world in a grain of sand
And heaven in a wild flower
Hold infinity in the palm of your hand
And Eternity in an hour.

Certain that an education was the way out of the hills for her children, mother took on added chores, saying: "Let me finish the milking. Run along to school or you'll be tardy. Study your lessons and mind the teacher. Now don't get a whippin' or you'll get a bigger one when you get home."

When she talked of what we would become when we grew up, the bone-weariness that usually bent her shoulders lifted, and a glow came over her face renewing it with beauty and vitality.

The people who came to our door, whether young or old, friend or stranger, were taken in, fed, bedded down, and encouraged to pour out their troubles into her sympathetic ear. Her good sense, her warmth and hospitality reached out to everyone.

Her passion for cleanliness gave the impression that if we stood still for very long we would get scrubbed with strong lye soap. Once upon a time this idiosyncrasy of hers backlashed, and gave us all some bad moments.

Almost every year an ancient tramp preacher invaded our hills. I can see him now coming down the path; his silver white hair and beard blowing in the wind, looking like a prophet newly risen from the dead. Tall and gaunt he was, and ragged beyond belief. His trousers were held up by nails that pierced galluses of rope crossing his shoulders. His shoes, worn through to the uppers, had soles padded with cardboard and laced with binder twine. His white shirt, now gray and with only one button to hold it together, hung like a rag on a coat hanger. Red flannel underwear showed underneath, and his feet were bare of any socks at all. In his hand he carried a worn bible, the key that opened all doors. Ours was no exception. When mother held out her hand to welcome him, he bent low over it, brushing it with his flowing beard.

"Mrs. Wright," he purred, "in all my journeys since I was called to spread the gospel, nowhere do I receive such a warm and gracious welcome as here. You and your beautiful children are like a fresh breath of life to me. You renew my faith, reward my perseverance, and inspire me to go on."

He might have added that we also fed him.

Mother felt duty bound to feed and shelter this man of God even though we suspected he couldn't read a line of the book he carried. She spread a feast before him that made us children think we might not have another square meal for a month. Three chickens were slaughtered, potatoes dug, string beans snapped, biscuits popped in the oven, walnut kernels picked out to stir into a molasses cake big enough to feed a threshing crew. While all this was going on the old tramp preacher snored softly behind his opened bible as he slept in the big rocker in the front room.

At last the table was set with a snow-white cloth, our only one, and loaded with all the lovely food. His Reverence was asked to say grace. While we children waited hungrily and impatiently, he blessed the house and each of us in turn, and asked the Lord to forgive us our sins. Then he prayed for the crops and that the rains would come just right; prayed for our country, for our government, and on and on until I though I would faint from hunger. We all sighed when he closed with "…and may His mercy shine down on my hostess, who, from the goodness of her heart has set such a bounteous feast before a disciple of God. Amen."

"Amen!" we chorused as we seated ourselves quickly.

The preacher was served first. He was the fastest and most skillful eater I had ever seen. His nimble fingers hardly seemed to move as he became fenced in by chicken bones. The biscuits and butter never got to our end of the table, he was so constantly reaching for more. Defeated, we gave up trying to fill our own plates, and just sat and watched, fascinated by his propensity for stowing it away and still looking gaunt as ever.

Finally satisfied, the preacher licked all his fingers carefully, took a quill from his pocket and picked his yellow teeth one by one. Then smacking his lips and sucking on his mustache, he reached for his back pocket and pulled out the filthiest handkerchief imaginable to wipe the crumbs and gravy from his beard.

"Thank you, Mrs. Wright!" he beamed contentedly. "A lovely meal fit for a king and He will reward you a thousand fold."

Mother was flattered, but his dirty rags nearly drove her out of her mind. The girls were sent scurrying to the well for water to fill a washtub in the smokehouse, the boys ordered to dump the preacher in it, and while he was soaking in suds to lop off some of his hair and trim his beard—then to scrub the hide off him. We threw his clothes in the old brass boiler on the stove to boil. Pretty soon the old man emerged wrapped in father's overcoat, shiny and red as a canned tomato. The boys, proud of his gravy-bowl haircut, hustled him into the front room to wait for his clothes to be washed, ironed and patched. So delighted was the preacher from all this attention, tears actually stood in his eyes. "Bless you, bless you," he kept saying. Relaxed, he began to nod, and when he nearly fell out of the chair a couple of times, mother told the boys to tuck him in bed and let him rest.

Things began to quite down. We children tiptoed around and mother stood stirring the clothes in the boiler with a broom handle. Then, lo and behold, Aunt Loretta was seen bouncing down the hill. Now Aunt Loretta was not related to us, and we were glad this gossipy and whiny old busybody was not our real aunt. She lived with our cousins, the Simpsons, to the north of us. I think she was their aunt.

"There'll be no keeping her out of the front room," mother moaned in a voice of panic. "She's bound to see the preacher and spread it all over the county that I had a man other than your father in my bed." Rushing to the front room, she piled bedclothes and pillows on top of the sleeping tramp preacher until he was completely buried beneath them, but he slept on.

"Well just have to pretend the bed isn't made. Pull down the shades, Annie, so it'll be dark in here. The rest of you children kinda stand in front of the bed so she can't see past you. And do try to act as if nothing's wrong. She'll want to sit in the rocking chair, so face it toward the front door and maybe she wont notice the bed. I'll blister the first one who dares to giggle."

Puffing and perspiring, Aunt Loretta entered the darkened room, took off her slat bonnet and fanned herself. Easing her broad bottom into the rocker, as mother predicted, she then began to whimper and whine.

"Oh, my back. I don't know why I risk my health to visit people who don't appreciate it no-how. Bring me a pillow, Francie. Oh! My back! I ain't slept a mite fer weeks, it pains me so dreadful."

She peered over the glasses on the end of her nose and quickly spied the tumbled bed behind us.

"Lily! For pity's sake! Why don't you teach them thar big lazy, grownup girls to make the beds in the morning?"

Mother weakly replied, "They were busy carrying water from the well to do the washing."

"Tsh, Tsh! You oughta get things like that done the first of the week, I always say. I do mine on Monday. Then it's tooken care of fer the whole week."

Then she stared at us children.

"Ruth, don't you ever wash your feet? Them black toes look pert near rotten, if ye ast me."

"Nopes," said Ruth with her usual flippancy. "I just let the dirt wear off. And I didn't ask you."

Aunt Loretta chose to ignore that sassy answer and turned to me. "Francie's that a ragdoll you have there? Why, when I was your age I could cook and sew better'n most grownups." And she smacked her puckered lips against toothless gums with, "Tsh, tsh."

Mother fluttered nervously from the kitchen to the front room, hinting that she simply must get busy and get her work done. Suddenly a muffled sneeze came from the bed. Instantly mother said, "Excuse me!" and put her hand over her mouth coughing politely.

Aunt Loretta scolded, "Lily, you ought to do something about that cold. Many a body is layin' cold in the grave from a cough like that. I've got a mighty good recipe for horehound cough syrup."

She went on and on in her whiny voice. The world was goin' to the dogs. Young folks was no more 'count than ever. Her hens were moultin' and hardly laid an aig these days....

She took out her knitting, definitely intending to stay a while. We stood like storks in front of the bed, nerves as taunt as a barbed-wire fence.

Without warning, she popped out of her chair. "Lily, I don't think you've ever teached them younguns how to make a bed proper. Here, let me learn 'em." And she began to tug at the bed covers. There was a horribly tense moment. In panic, Mother rushed up and took her arm forcefully and hurried her to the front porch.

"Oh, don't do that, dear Aunt Loretta. They'll learn soon enough. You might hurt your back. Come now and see my peonies out in front. They are the prettiest things you every laid eyes on."

Mother, persuasively but firmly, steered her outside. The day was saved. A few moments later she left. Goldie helped her up the hill so she would have someone to lean on to save her aching back. When we were sure she was gone, we exploded with laughter.

"Whew!" said mother. "That old lady is as cranky as a hounddog with a gnat in its ear, and as troublesome as a black snake in a chicken coop."

Even the preacher, awake now, laughed in a restrained sort of way, and kept repeating, "Praise the Lord! Praise the Lord!"

I'm sure no French bedroom farce was enacted with greater skill. Mother laughed until the tears rolled.

"That was a narrow escape," she gasped. "With father gone the past week, if Aunt Loretta had found the preacher in my bed my reputation would have been no better'n Jezebel's. Why I'll bet my name would have been crossed off the church book."

The tramp preacher understandably left in a hurry.

Shortly after that, one day when Ruth and I were coming home from school, Mother met us at the well and announced, "The tramp preacher is here again." Ruth kicked the well bucket, began to cuss and said, "Dammed if I'm going to help cook a feast for that old bastard!" Mother only smiled and picked up the water bucket and walked back to the house. I followed her into the kitchen and peeked through the crack in the green door into the darkened front room and saw an old man sitting in the rocker, holding a Bible in front of his face. Mother told me to go into the front room and get the table cloth out of the dresser drawer. Doing so, I glanced up into the mirror over the dresser and saw the man's head from the back; it was bald! This was no tramp preacher, this was my mother's only brother, Uncle Oliver. I adored him and was so excited that I threw myself upon him, kissed his cheek, and started searching through his coat pockets, knowing they would be full of gum and candy for all of us. Everybody then began to gather around and laugh at Mother's joke. Ruth hugged him so hard I thought she might kill him. He had tramped miles from the town of "Mary's Home" to visit my mother, his baby sister. He adored her and always made her laugh. Mother scolded him because he hadn't brought his son, Crate and daughter, Lucy. He promised, "Next time."

Mother was practical.

The Thornsberrys, our neighbors, had a fat, friendly cow named Old Reddy, who was loved and petted by their children and us as well. We led her around by her ears and rode her as if she were a horse. Though gentle as a lamb, she had a terrible habit. She jumped or maneuvered herself over and around any fence ever built, and would clean up whole patches of grain.

One spring night, on one of her sallies, she devoured a field of our wheat and half of our garden. We found her the next morning standing among the ruins, mildly chewing her cud, looking serene and innocent. Father was so angry he threatened to blast Mr. Thornsberry with buckshot. Mr. Thornsberry said, "I'll skin you alive and hang your hide on the fence, if you do."

Mother easily persuaded father not to shoot. Eager for a brawl, we were disappointed. We reckoned father could lick him any day.

The feud was settled one morning. We were wakened by a loud plaintive bellowing and hurried towards the sound. It had poured down rain all night and we found Old Reddy buried up to her belly in the soft clay at the foot of the hill just below our house. Mr. Thornsberry was already there, and father joined him in efforts to free her. Ropes and chains were used in the rescue attempt, but Old Reddy's struggling thwarted any success and she sank deeper and deeper in the mud.

It was finally decided that the cow had to be killed. Somehow, she had injured herself and was slowly bleeding to death, anyway. Heartbroken we pleaded for her life, and hid our tearful faces as the gun was fired.

At mothers suggestion the men laid planks across the mud to get to the carcass. "One doesn't waste good red meat," she declared.

Mr. Thornsberry graciously offered us a hindquarter. Not to be outdone, mother invited him and his family to our house for a beef dinner that night. When dinner was ready, no one rushed to table as was usually the case, and no one made a dive for, or eyed, the piece of his choice. To relieve the tenseness, I quipped:

I had a little calf.
I fed it on clover.
When it died,
It died all over.

That went unappreciated.

Father and Mr. Thornsberry helped themselves generously and the platter then started around the table.

When it came to Goldie, she turned a little green around the mouth. In a wavering voice, she blurted, "I'd feel like a cannibal if I ate any of Old Reddy."

When it was passed to Ruth, she shook her head and handed it on to Paul while tears stood in her eyes. Paul sounded a warning retch, put his hand over his mouth and rushed from the room.

Ruby and Lee Thornsberry openly bawled. Ruby wailed, "She was so cute and now we cain't ride her."

By the time the platter reached me, my eyes were popping and my mouth overflowing with saliva and anticipation. Intimidated by the angry looks of my brothers and sisters, I found myself whispering, "I don't want any of Old Reddy, either."

It was too bad. We children passed up the only time in our young lives to feast on fresh beef. Cattle were scarce and needed for milk and butter. Also for cash. So we never slaughtered them.

Mother was courageous.

There was a story mother used to tell that filled us with pride at her courage. It was about the time she took out in the dead of night after a chicken thief.

"It happened on a night in February," she began. "Your pa was away on a painting trip. There had been a fierce blizzard, leaving deep drifts of snow and terrible cold. The country was mighty pretty to look at but downright dangerous to be out in.

"We had been in bed and asleep for hours when I heard a racket coming from the direction of the henhouse. Thinking a fox or weasel was killing our chickens, I flew out of bed, put on my brogans and mackinaw and grabbed the shotgun. Slowly and carefully I sidled out the door.

"Plowing through drifts I circled around to the henhouse in time to see a man sneak out of the shed clutching my finest fat hens by their legs. I raised my gun to fire and then decided I hadn't the heart to shoot a human being. He hadn't seen me at all and went trompin' off towards the west, clutching the squawking birds before I could get my mouth open. Too mad to realize what I was doin', I followed after him. 'Low down chicken thief,' I kept saying to myself. 'I'll follow him and give him a piece of my mind. He'd better return my hens or I'll fill his britches full of buckshot.' Anyway, I was curious as to who he might be and where he was going.

"He climbed the long hill the other side of Dean's Creek and went on down to the Glaze where a big square log held by chains crossed the stream. I couldn't catch up with him, although I did manage to keep him in sight. He then followed a narrow path around a bluff that seemed to lean out over the water below. I lost my footing time and again and except for the underbrush to hold on to, would've plunged into the icy creek. It was scary. I followed him for about a quarter mile along the bluff till he reached the mouth of a big cave, a hundred foot above the stream, all lit up by a fire just inside it. The fellow went on in. I snuck up for a better look. Hiding behind a big rock, I was able to peer directly inside.

"He was greeted loudly by a bunch of mean looking, bearded fellows. They'd been playing cards and drinking corn squeezings, the no good skunks. While they crowded around the chicken thief, admiring my hens, I noticed that one fellow remained behind and I saw him scoop the folding money left on the table into his overall pocket. Upon discovering the loss they began to quarrel and accuse each other of stealing. The guilty one was as positive as the others in passing the blame. Shouting and cussing, they began to push and shove until one of them hauled off and knocked a feller clear across the cave. Then the fighting started in earnest. They all dived in. Knife blades flashed in the glow of the fire and I couldn't tell one body from another in that mess of swinging arms and legs.

"They milled closer and closer to the mouth of the cave and the sheer drop below. Soon it was a cinch they might all go over if something didn't happen to stop them. Hardly knowing what I was doing, I raised the shotgun and fired a blast into the air. The roar stopped them dead in their tracks. There's no imagining their astonishment when I stepped out from behind the rock holding a double barreled shotgun on them.

"'I want my chickens back or I'll shoot you down like dogs.' It was all talk, of course, but I was real mad. 'Now, I'll make a deal with you,' I caught myself saying. 'If you make that chicken thief return my hens, I'll tell you who's got the money. Is it a bargain?'

"They hesitated, watching one another out of the corners of their eyes. Finally one burly fellow said, 'Hits a bargain.' The guilty fellow, knowing he was trapped, shelled the money out. The fighting almost started all over again, but by shouting and raising my gun again, I nipped it in the bud with the help of the burly one who seemed to be the leader. I guess he was the one who really quieted them down. Turning to me, he said, 'Thankee, Mrs. Wright. Were much obliged. We'd be still more obliged fer ye not to mention what ye see'd here tonight to our womenfolk.'

"'I would be too ashamed to tell anyone what I saw here. All I want is my chickens back. If they're not in my henhouse by mornin' I'll come back and blow this place to thunder.'

"Turning to go, I noticed one man lying on the floor, bleeding from a slash clear across his chest. I just had to patch him up. The fellows held him while I sewed him up with the needle and thread that I always carry in my apron pocket. By this time, I had the rascals eating out of my hand. One even offered to see me home. The nerve of him!

"They promised the hens would be returned come morning. The next day, on counting the chickens, I found that not only were my hens returned, but, bless Pat, there were a dozen more than I'd ever had. I nearly died laughing. There'd be just no trying to find their owners. A thing like that could get embarrassing.

"Every now and then through the years one of these men would come by with an offering—sometimes a string of bass, a fat possum, or a bucket of wild blackberries. One even offered to plow the field for spring planting. I told him to go ahead and do it." She chuckled thinking about it.

Although so much of our hill country was farmed out, slashed with gullies and ridges—the top soil washed away, there were a few areas that were so precious and dear to the families that lived there that as the seasons rolled by, these areas were visited year after year. There were great patches of wild plum, wild cherry, wild strawberries, wild onion and garlic, dewberries and blackberries, and wild mushrooms always to be found on the north side of an oak tree after a rain. These wonderful gifts from nature were enjoyed by everyone. People came from far and wide during canning season to gather this bounty. We were blessed with a field of wild strawberries a couple of miles north of us. We tramped barefoot through a cool stream onto a meadow where we gathered the berries that were as thick as grass. Later, Mother would make a shortcake and cover it with thick cream and the berries for our supper.

Also to the north of us, was a tremendous wild blackberry patch, maybe covering a fourth of an acre. Blackberry cobbler was a tradition on the Fourth of July in our family. There was usually a catch of catfish by the boys, and we would have a catfish fry with the cobbler for desert. Mother sent Ruth and I off to the patch with buckets to gather the berries. Ruth and I were picking carefully. We wore long stocking-tops on our arms to avoid the thorns of the berry bushes, and bonnets to shade our eyes. Ruth had a bucket full of berries and I was reaching for a limb of large ripe ones, when Ruth's arch-enemy, "Bertha," a girl she often fought with, scratching and biting and pulling hair—an activity they engaged in quite often—arrived at the patch with her little sister, who was my age, in tow. They carried buckets meaning to help themselves to our blackberries. "Little sister" immediately marched up and grabbed my limb of blackberries out of my hand. I turned on her without pausing and spit on her face. Bertha grabbed me by the hair and yelled at Ruth, "Make her lick it off! Make her lick it off!" Without hesitation, Ruth dumped her own bucket of blackberries over Bertha's head. Then she grabbed me by the arm and we ran for home.

After Mother finished laughing at our story, she said, "I still want to make blackberry cobbler; Paul, you and Jim are big enough to stand up to Bertha." She handed them each a bucket and they tromped off looking very persecuted.

Mother was like a piece of satin fabric—closely woven of stout thread and oh, so lovely to touch.

3

John Wright the Painter

Father was many things.

He was a gleaner in a field gathering sheaves of wisdom; a visionary on a hilltop with far reaching eyes; sometimes withdrawn as a monk in penance; and other times so talkative that his words went on and on and on, like a swift stream circling boulders of interruption. He was like rugged terrain—with heights, and depths, and shadows.

As I said, he was an artist. No one lays his soul so bare to scrutiny as an artist. To look at the artist's work is to know the man. His was alternately elusive and strong, but always imaginative.

Sometimes he wrote poetry and prose that to me was reminiscent of the nineteenth century. Here is a verse from one of his poems:

The round log cabin
With puncheon floor.
The stick and clay
Chimney and batten door.
The sweet gourd dipper
As of yore.

Since he was forty-eight when I was born, writing about a round log cabin may have been recent history for him, but it was ancient history as far as I was concerned.

Once he built a printing press by hand. His brother, James, ran the county paper in Tuscumbia with it for years. It was an improved model, but father never had the money to have it patented.

He painted houses, hung wallpaper, built churches, and in the quiet winter evenings, scraping and shaving with a sharp knife, he made axe handles of tough hickory limbs. Always busy reading, creating, talking. He seemed bigger than life to me and sometimes not so very real.

Without the money he made away from the farm, we would not have been able to survive on our eighty acres, of which less than thirty was under cultivation

His homecomings were big events in our lives. He might arrive at dark, or sundown or even earlier. The day he was to arrive we scurried about our chores of milking, feeding the chickens, slopping the hogs and bringing fresh water from the well. Every little bit we would turn our eyes to the horizon above the house from where we would first get a glimpse of him

He would appear on the crest of the hill, straw hat on the back of his head, a new painting slung over his shoulder, with his paint box of precious colors in one hand and his coat, rolled up and tied with a rope, in the other. My heart beat fast in anticipation. I could hardly wait to see him and his new painting.

The hounds rushed out from under the house, baying and tails wagging happily. Mother stood shy, but happy, self-consciously brushing back strands of hair from a moist forehead. All of us children lined up along the paling fence, watching his approach. He had walked perhaps twenty miles that day from the house he had just finished painting. Being a fast walker, he had made it home before dark.

We all greeted him warmly. I gave him the bear hug he always expected.

It had been a hot day. He was fanning himself with his straw hat while waiting for Annie to bring a pan of water so that he could bathe his tired and swollen feet. His coal black hair shone against the untanned brow where his hat had shaded him. Violet eyes looked keenly around at us, at mother, and around the house. He was happy and contented. We hovered around him, eager for news from the "outside."

At dinner, we waited respectfully for his short prayer and for him to be served first. After the meal was over we heard more news and old-timer yarns spun of more fiction than truth, I suspect. Later, father and the boys got out their banjos and fiddles and stirred the night with music. While the boys stomped their feet to the rhythm, father danced a jig. It was years later that I found out that my father had been an entertainer on a Mississippi River boat.

The next day, father and mother would wander arm in arm through the fields, orchard, and garden. If it was a good year, father would walk with pride, shoulders straight and head high, and talk of what they would do with the money—plaster the inside of the house, put on a new roof, build a new front porch. All this they did in due time. If the crops were poor, he would wander helplessly about, predicting that the end of the world was at hand. This was his homecoming through the years.

My parents were very much in love. Once on a mellow evening after a hot day in July, mother and father stood on the hill above our house where you could look out over the farm to the purple horizon in the distance. We were on our way home from the new field they had just finished clearing of oak sprouts. "Well," said Father proudly, "That'll give us another cornpatch and we ought to raise some pretty good crops on it, being newer ground and all. I been worried as to whether we could raise enough corn to tide us through the winter, the way it's been turning yellow, shriveling up and dying in the other fields cause the ground is gettin' so poor."

Mother looked out over the farm, and shaded her eyes with her hands. "Yes, it seems like every year we have to turn another field over to the weeds. Seems a shame. Wish we knew some way to build up the soil. We never have enough barnyard manure to do any good."

They stood there quietly for a spell, then Mother said, "John, you ain't sorry you stayed on the farm, are you?"

"Why, no," he answered, meditatively. "No, Reckon not. Why should I be? I got time on my long treks to think, to study nature, and to paint. I'm free to come and go as I please and I got a fine little woman to come home to. No. I ain't got nothin' to complain about. But what about you? You got a hard row to hoe here along with the younguns, when I am away."

"You don't hear me complaining, do you? A woman is happy as long as she knows she is loved by her man. The only thing that worries me is that the children are getting to talk and act like the other hill children around here. I been noticing lately how backwoodsy they are. Look at Francie now."

I sat barefooted, in a ragged dress, on a rock, chewing on a stem of grass. Whatever was wrong with being backwoodsy I didn't know, so I pulled down my dress modestly as if to cover up my shortcomings.

"Don't worry about the young folks," father said. "We'll send them off to school and chances are they will get married and never come back. In the long run they'll probably thank us for raising them in the country where they could learn about the soil and animals and how to use their hands. Those are good things to know, whether you plan on being a farmer or not."

"You're probably right, John. Anyway, don't worry about me none. The important thing is we have each other."

"Lillian, my beloved. Without you my feet would have no light to quicken them."

Mother's face became radiant. "John, my love!" And she went into his outstretched arms. They tenderly kissed while their lengthened shadows stretched past me, mingling like kindred drops of water.

The sun was setting and the sky was a vault of crimson overhead. From my seat on the rock I looked up at their dark forms outlined against the sky. The blazing light had turned their garments to flame, and mother's hair had fallen loose to her waist, the soft wind lifting and tossing it gently like a veil.

Among my souvenirs of memory across the trailing years, this mural of love is still the most beautiful picture I have ever seen.

"Painter John" he was called, but to me who followed his every move with wide-eyed admiration, he was an artist. His paintings were primitive. I aimed to follow in his footsteps, so day by day I watched, listened, and learned from him. He would stand on the hill with the wind in his black hair and point. "Watch the clouds, see how light and airy they are. They Float. They move and moisture determines the nature of them.

"Now," he said, "look down at your feet. See how the light gets lighter and the dark gets darker." I looked down at the grass and rocks and trunks of trees and saw them through his eyes. He pointed with one hand and stroked his red mustache with the other.

"Don't ever forget the reflected lights," he said. "It's not so strong as that from above, but the earth does send back reflections on the shady side of trees, rocks, and limbs, making them look round and molded." We stood by deep pools along Dean's Creek and he pointed out the beauty of nature around me.

"Paint deep water still and dark with reflections. See how the colors vibrate? There is the green reflection of trees, blue reflection of sky, brown reflection of bark, and hard, clear, reflection of rocks. Look up at the giant, white sycamore. See how the limbs twist and turn to the sky. One must know the nature of a tree to paint it right. Each kind grows in its own way and in its own way reaches for the sky."

We trudged in winter on a day following a heavy snow. The sun sparkled on it like a million diamonds.

In the fall when we would be looking for bark and berries for him to make paints for his primitive painting he would declare, "What contrast! That's what makes for beauty. Hot and cold colors, light and dark, rough against smooth. Blue sky, yellow hickory nut trees, red sumac. There is russet, there gold, there green and brown. My, what a master artist Mother Nature is!"

In the clean washed freshness of spring, he took my hand and squatted to show me at eye level how to look at the world about me. "The leaves are delicate, dainty, and new. Everything looks misty with pale fresh colors against gray trunks, clear and yet somehow soft. See the rosebud, like splotches of flame in the forest? The white dogwood looks almost like a cloud against the green hill. Spring is lovely beyond compare. No wonder the poets write of it. Summer is a time of fulfillment. Look, nearly every stalk of corn is grown and the melons are ripening and the peaches are turning rosy. Colors are stronger now, but the sky seems more dense, more dull; storms hover over the horizons. See the thunderheads billowing up? How like a puff of cotton almost too heavy to float. What a heavenly day!"

He showed me the veins in rose petals and leaves and the stamen in flowers where bees supped their honey; and the frost flowers in winter and woodbine in the fall. I drank as of a great thirst. A longing tugged at me to put down on canvas these things of beauty so that forever and ever they might remain lovely to the sight.

Thus he taught me to see, those first years of my childhood. Is it any wonder I looked upon my teacher with reverence? Next to God I placed him, but next to God he could not stay, and I could not always see life through his eyes. Growing up was painful for me, growing old was painful for him. What a pity it had to be so.

Ah, but Father lacked Mother's sense of humor.

One fall day Father was putting up the stove in the front room. I followed his every step, anxious to help. (Every spring we took down the giant King heater and stored it in the smokehouse so we would have more room, and every fall we carried it back in and set it up again.) Directly in the middle of the room, the stove sat, with the pipe going straight up through the room above. He joined the pipes neatly downstairs, then carrying the sawhorse to stand on, he went upstairs. No matter how carefully he put the pipes together they kept slipping apart. "Francie," he said, "run out to the tool shed and fetch me a piece of wire from on the work bench." I left him standing on the sawhorse, straining to reach the ceiling to hold the pipes together. Aware of his precarious position, I ran on flying feet. Sure enough, under the workbench I found the wire but under the workbench also was an old hen in a nest of shavings, in the strenuous effort of laying an egg; her efforts aroused my maternal instincts. I found myself actually grunting for her, and forgetting Father completely, I decided to see her through her ordeal. Finally the pink egg dropped. She went off cackling, not in the least appreciative of my help.

Gathering up the warm egg and the wire, I proceeded dreamily to the house, marveling at Mother Nature. Leaving the egg in the kitchen, I sauntered upstairs, singing absentmindedly:

I'll eat when I'm hungry,
I'll drink when I'm dry.
And if a tree don't fall on me,
I'll live till I die.

I was cut short by Father yelling, "Frances!" in a tone of utter vexation. Jerked to reality by the sting of his voice, I flew up the stairs. There was

Father, just as I had left him, stretched on his toes on the sawhorse, holding the pipe. His face was purple with rage and exertion. "Where in tarnation have you been?" he bellowed.

I held the wire up meekly, but because of his lofty position he couldn't quite reach it. Eager to redeem myself, I then put a foot on the sawhorse to climb up and help. That bit of added weight tipped the sawhorse, and Father, losing his balance, fell with a crash. The pipes, the soot, and Father's dignity fell with him.

"Goldarn, dadburn, carnsarn," Father roared. He never swore, but those words were just as expressive. "Don't just stand thare," he shouted, "get a broom and clean up this mess. Help me up. Brush me off. Dad blame it, anyway." I fled to the stairway, threw a leg over the banister and sailed down it as if the devil himself were chasing me. I ran out to the barn, climbed into the hayloft, and nestled down with my family of cats to wait out the storm.

So much did I love my Father, and so filled with curiosity was I at every fascinating thing he did, that I was willing to go in a dead run on every little errand to please him. Sometimes I was in for trouble when I did. Calamity often dogged our footsteps when we were together. Another of these happenings I shall never forget, and I'm sure he never did, either.

The night was cold; the family was sitting around the big noisy heater which was red-hot. It cracked and popped and seemed fairly to dance around the room. I was drawing on my slate while Goldie was trying to get me to play tic-tac-toe. Knowing that she would beat me, I refused. Annie was tatting, the shuttle flying in and out between her nimble fingers. Nellie was ironing; Paul and Ruth were scuffling on the settee where they were supposed to be doing their lessons. Mother was mending. Jim was stretching a possum hide tight on a board. Garsy was shelling corn.

Accompanying himself on the banjo, Father was singing his favorite songs, the tunes dear to our hearts over the years: Listen to the Mockingbird, The Yellow Rose of Texas, Oh, Them Golden Slippers, Maggie Darlin', The Last Rose of Summer, and Johnny Sands, the one that never ceased to amuse me.

There was a man named Johnny Sands

Who married Betsy Haig.
Although she brought him gold and wealth,
She proved a terrible plague.
Says he, "I think I'll drown myself,
The river runs below."
Says she, "Pray do, you silly oaf.
I wished it long ago.
Oh, Oh, I wished it long ago.
"For fear that I may courage lack,
And try to save my life,
Pray tie my hands behind my back."
"I will, replied his wife."
She tied them tight as you may think
And when securely done,
She stood him there upon the bank
As she prepared to run.
Down the hill his blushing bride
Then ran with all her force
To push him in; he stepped aside,
And she fell in, of course.
Now splashing, dashing like a fish,
"Oh, save me Johnny Sands!"
"I can't my dear, so much I'd like,
For you have tied my hands.
"Oh, Oh, Oh, for you have tied my hands."

Father, seemingly restless, put aside his banjo, glanced at Mother, and very deliberately donned his coat and cap and walked to the door. Pausing with his hand on the doorknob, he announced, "Lily, think I'll go possum huntin'."

Mother nodded without looking up. On impulse, I jumped up. "Can I go, too? Please, pretty please." I held my breath.

After what seemed an eternity, he said, "All right, get your coat on." Diving for my coat and stocking cap, I tore after him.

It was a still night with a tiny harvest moon in a star-studded sky. The air was crisp and clear. I imagined the eyes of wild animals were watching us from behind every tree, curious and fearful. My heart trilled with adventure. Gradually my eyes became accustomed to the night, and my body was soon warm from the exertion of trying to keep up with Father's long strides. The dogs rustled the leaves as they ran industriously among the trees searching for scent of game, noses to the ground. Every little bit Father would stop and listen for the sounds of the dogs, and in the quiet I could hear my heart beat from excitement. Abruptly, piercing the stillness of the night, rose the wild sounds of baying and barking dogs.

"They've treed somethin'," Father shouted. "let's go. Hurry or it'll get away."

When we located the hounds they were running in circles around a persimmon tree, leaping up on its trunk to get at what was in its branches, and making enough noise to arouse the dead. Peering into the tree, Father shouted, "It's a possum, a big one. You're little, shinny up the tree and shake it down."

I climbed the tree in a flash. There, on a limb, was the largest possum I had ever seen, grinning like—well, grinning like a possum. As I put out my hand it snapped at me. Pulling back, I called, "I can't get him down."

"Grab him by the tail," yelled Father. I did just that and the possum suddenly let go and I swung it hard away from me. Its tail slipped out of my hand and it went crashing through the branches and landed squarely on Father's head. Father was felled like a clubbed ox. The excited hounds attacked with joyous ferocity and Father, possum, and hounds thrashed on the ground in wild pandemonium.

I slid down as fast as I could, and with much tugging and pulling, managed to hold the dogs off long enough for Father to stagger to his feet, holding tenaciously to the possums tail. He was so furious he could hardly speak. Spitting out leaves, dirt and words at the same time, he said, "Dad gum the goldarn luck. What did you have to do that for? Can't you learn to be a mite more careful? Every time you're around somethin' happens. Carnsarn it anyway."

He started for home, carrying the possum by its tail. I followed at a respectful distance, dying to laugh but not daring to. As we entered the house Mother looked up, saw the state he was in and exclaimed, "John you look as if you've been in a wild cat fight! What happened?"

"Cat fight, nothin'," said Father, glaring, "your daughter clomped me over the head with a possum an nearly killed me, that's what happened."

"That's a shame, John, now, isn't that too bad? Francie do be more careful." Unable to repress her mirth any longer, she burst out laughing. We all laughed until the tears rolled, while Father fumed and blew angrily through his mustache, unable to see the humor in it all. Finally we were able to divert his wrath by bragging on the big fat possum.

Father was hard put to keep his family and his community on the straight and narrow. Sometimes the job was almost too large for even his broad shoulders to bear. On Sunday he prayed and preached and threatened and quoted the Good Book right and left. He instigated prayer meetings and singings for the young people. They came in droves, but not all would come into the little church he had built across Dean's Creek. There were those who would hang around outside, drink White Mule, get into fights, and when church was out, follow the girls home with intentions far from honorable. Out of the goodness of his heart, Father tried to bring the young folks closer to God by offering music lessons. While he hummed with his tuning fork and wrote the notes on the blackboard, the young folks would disappear two at a time, causing Father to suspect that a bit of fornication went on in the bushes outside. Father felt they were bound for perdition and that never had the devil spawned such a crop of wild ones.

Finally, at his wits end, to civilize the younguns, he decided that perhaps they would find freedom of expression in more wholesome entertainment such as square dancing. He and Mother decided to give an old fashioned barn dance and candy pulling, which they would chaperon at our house for our barn had no floor in it. They fondly hoped that some good, clean innocent fun would lure the young folks into the fold.

The night of the party Father had trouble with his own young ones, as well as with the others, and his knack for rising to a situation failed him this time. The family had an early supper of cornbread and warm milk.

Water was brought from the well and heated on the cookstove. The big tub in the smokehouse was filled with it for our baths, and we all lined up to take our turn in the tub. When it was Ruth's turn and she saw how dirty the water was, she began to swear and pound on the door, "If someone don't fetch me clean water I'll come out without a stitch on an get it." Paul, the saintly one, hurried to the well.

After we were all bathed, Mother lined us younger ones up to inspect our neck and ears. She had to stand on tiptoe to check Paul, who's ears she found crusty. Trying to be tactful, she said, "Paul, I reckon you ought to do 'em again. They are still a mite dirty." Paul, ever sensitive, blushed to the roots of his hair, but obediently went and scrubbed them good. We all crowded around the dresser in the front room and primped while Father stormed that he couldn't shave, and wanted to know who had been using his razor to sharpen pencils again. Of course, we all looked innocent, and didn't tattle on Goldie whom we knew to be guilty. The brightest of all us children, she needed a sharp pencil to do her sums.

Jim was the last one to get bathed. It seemed he spent hours in the smokehouse scrubbing, all the while singing his favorite:

Old Dan Tucker was a mighty fine man.
He washed his face in the frying pan.
Combed his hair with a wagon wheel.
And died with the toothache in his heel.

I had a blue satin bow on top of my curls almost as large as my head. I was so proud of it I couldn't keep my hands off it. Mother looked like a doll in a calico dress trimmed with rickrack. Father was dressed to the teeth in a striped shirt and black wool trousers. He had absolutely no reason to blow his nose except to show off his new white kerchief. But blow it he did, and every few minutes.

The guests started arriving about dark on horseback, on foot, and in wagons. They all stood bashfully around at first, the boys leaning first on one foot and then on the other, with their big awkward hands stuffed in their pockets. They girls, looking coy, fluttered their lashes in a come hither way, till the boys, getting bolder, sidled up to them.

To get the party going, Mother said, "Let's get on with the candy pull before we start the dancing." She passed around a cloth with lard on it for everyone to grease their hands, so they could pull the molasses candy without it sticking to them. She gave each one a ball of soft candy to work with. They pulled and stretched to arms length, then folded and twisted and stretched it again until the dark amber candy became light and taffy-colored. Finally the long twists were put to cool in mother's breadpans on the backporch. When cooled they became brittle enough to be broken into sticks about six inches long. A game was played by a boy choosing a girl for his partner. Placing each end of a stick of candy in their mouths, the partners, with their hands behind their backs, were to attempt to break the stick in two. This gave the excuse for a lot of nose rubbing, squealing and laughing, and a kiss was fair if they had the courage.

After the candy pull the square dance began. Garsy played the fiddle; Jim, the banjo, and Father rattled the old black bones for rhythm. A boy named Joe was the caller. In a singsong voice he chanted:

"Lead her up and down, Rosie Betsy Liner.

Change and swing, Rosie Betsy Line…"

Some of the couples managed to stay in the dark corners, not bothering with the candy or the dancing. Then father noted, with utter fury, that couples were sneaking out one by one. Having made it his duty to keep an eye out for that sort of thing, he would no sooner bring back one embarrassed couple when another couple would disappear. In the dead of December there was no reason for anyone to go to the well, or the springhouse, or the grape arbor. But go they did, and father's temper got shorter and shorter. Mother was no help with her observation that, "Younguns will be younguns." That only increased his anger. He began to throw around loose talk about how young people were going to the dogs right and left, and he bet there'd be some shotgun weddings soon.

When the party was over and the last good-byes were said, Father returned to the house, collapsed in his chair, and moped a beaded brow. Suddenly he leaped up as if he had sat on a cocklebur, and looked around wildly. "Where in blazes is everyone?" he hollered. Five of the children were missing. Annie, Garsy, Nellie, Jim and Ruth were nowhere to be seen.

"Now, John," Mother soothed, "don't you reckon the boys walked their girls home?"

"Yes, but where are our girls hangin' out at?"

With that, he tore out the door. Nellie and her beau were innocently pulling on the well rope to get water to clean up the mess. Ruth was found swinging on the barn lot gate, her face mighty close to a boys ear. While Father rounded them up, Annie snuck in the back door and slipped upstairs to bed. Later I heard her tiptoe back down the steps. I knew she was going to meet Carl in the hollow below the house. She no sooner had time to clear the yard when I heard Father's feet hit the floor with a bang. (My trundle bed was under the stairway, so I was in a fine position to observe all that went on in the house.) He grabbed the shotgun and took after his daughter in his long-handled underwear. He stalked her for at least and hour. Then I saw Annie slip back in, carrying her shoes as she tiptoed to her room. Father came in a few moments later, chattering with cold, and crawled into bed.

"What happened?" Mother asked.

"Nothin'," Father exploded. "Not a dadburned thing. Its a good thing, too. I was gonna whale the tar out of them."

"With a shotgun?" Mother said, giggling.

"Lily, you won't think it's very funny when I tell you I think Annie and Carl are falling in love."

"Oh, no," said Mother. Surely not. If she marries a hill boy she'll never get out of here. His folks are a sight poorer than we are, and that's bad. He didn't finish the eighth grade."

"Well, I'm afraid that's what's gonna happen." Father sighed. "Our girls don't get a chance to meet boys that got anything. The bottomlanders don't allow their younguns to court us hill folk's children. Its a pity. Our girls can work for them, but ain't good 'nough to marry them." I went off to sleep with their troubled voices in my ears.

Father was a good man and Mother was a good woman and they loved each other and they loved their children and they worked hard and prayed often, but in our hills all of this was not enough.

4

The Reaper is Death

Sister Ethel, as we called her, was the oldest child in the family. She was nineteen and I was five when she died. As a child she had suffered a fall from a tree and hadn't been right since. It took all of mother's strength to hold her when, racked by convulsions, she had what we called a spell. After one of these spells I remember finding mother kneeling under a wild crabapple tree in full bloom, looking up as if imploring the blossoms above to answer her, "Why? Why?"

Sister wandered wherever her feet led her, played under the horses feet, gently picked up things like lizards and wasps, but was never hurt. It was as if fate, having already dealt her such a cruel blow, had cautioned every creature to be gentle with her. Her condition affected all of us one way or another, depending on our ability to understand.

Before her death, I remember a scene that remains clearly in my mind—a picture that revealed to me how we all felt about her then. It was one of those rare moments when a sudden shock opens your mind like the shutter of a camera, and the faces around you become so bright and clear as to forever remain a vivid memory.

It was after supper, and I had been ordered to get undressed for bed. I had backed up to Nellie and she was unbuttoning my dress. Everyone was in the front room but Paul, who was in sight at the washstand in the kitchen. Father had just lifted off the lid of the stove, and had the poker in his hand, shifting the logs. His cheeks looked ruddy, and his ginger mustache glowed in the light from the bright fire inside. Annie had leaned over to get something out of the dresser drawer, and I saw her round face and her loose hair above a gingham dress, blue checked, I think it was. Over it she wore an apron whose bib was held up with two large safety pins, and the front of it was still wet from washing dishes. Goldie, her back to me, showing her two long brown braids tied with red plaid strings, a worn dress that wrinkled up at the seat, wide ribbed stockings scootched down, and run-over shoes with heel spurs pushing through worn leather, had just started out the door to bring in the stove-wood Father wanted for the fire. Garsy in overalls knelt by his violin case on the floor and drew his bow across the resin. His knee on the floor, I noticed, was bare where the patch was worn out, and the skin looked rusty and cold. The light from the round damper in front of the stove gleamed on the dark red mahogany of the violin.

Ethel had been put to bed upstairs. Paul was at the water bucket drinking from a long-handled blue granite dipper. He whistled through his teeth and remarked the water was ice cold. Jim, in a heavy mackinaw, was unbuckling overshoes and knocking the snow off them, which I noticed made little puddles on the floor. Ruth had started to light a lamp with a torch made from a page of the catalog. She held the glass chimney in one hand, and gave the wick a turn before it would catch. The light exposed her face with its firm mouth, green eyes, and high cheekbones. Her auburn curls that had fallen over her forehead glowed as bright as the side of the red-hot King heater. I observed that there were circles under her eyes that looked almost black from the up cast shadows.

Mother hunched over the sewing machine where she had moved it over to the window to catch the last light of day. The light shone on the soft waves of her fine brown hair. She pedaled fast and furiously as if she were stamping out something she didn't like. Suddenly, she stopped and the clackety-clack of the machine ceased abruptly. She looked around her with a grim, desperate face, and voiced something that must have been on her mind for quite a spell. "All of the neighbors are saying that we had ought to send Ethel away."

The room became hushed and still. I could hear a flock of wild geese honking high overhead, and the tinkle of the cowbells far away. Father spat an amber stream of tobacco onto the fire and clapped the lid down hurriedly as if he wanted to shut out the light that would show his face for fear that we would read there that he agreed with the neighbors. Ruth dropped the paper torch and stomped viciously with her foot, to put out the fire, as she cried out, "Stuff and nonsense. There ain't nothin' wrong with Ethel. She's got more gumption than the neighbors. At least she knows how to mind her own business. Besides, 'tain't none of their affairs anyway."

The mirror reflected Annie's shocked face that was about to crumple up as if she were going to cry. "Everybody at school asks if my sister is crazy and if I take after her. Sometimes I think I can't stand it any more.

Goldie's braids seemed to stiffen, and she turned around slowly. Her dark eyes surveyed Mother with a questioning look. I thought, "She wonders if that wouldn't be the best thing to do." She was only eight, but we all knew that sister was hopeless.

Garsy put the bow back into the violin case, and carefully closed the lid while he looked anxiously up the stairway as if he feared Ethel had heard, and with a tender voice said something to the effect that he was "a'feared she was getting harder and harder to keep track of."

Jim put his overshoes back on, and I though, "He'll take the hounds hunting, but he'll walk the woods with quivering chin and worry about what to do with Sister." For so often had I seen tears spring to his eyes when she sat with folded hands staring into space.

Softhearted Paul was afraid no one would be kind to her if we sent her away. He told of horrible tales he had heard of how they were strapped to beds in small rooms with bars over the windows, and gags put in their mouths to keep them from screaming. All this while he kept wiping his nose on the back of his hand and ignored the tears that were making a clean streak down a dirty face.

The hands that were unbuttoning my dress fumbled and then became tense. Nellie's low voice, close to my neck, said firmly, "I don't care what people say. We had ought to keep her here where we can keep any eye on her and take care she don't get hurt."

I could see complete agreement in Mother's eyes, while I looked around in childish amazement, as if I had seen my family as individuals for the first time. The picture faded at that point and I can remember no more of what happened that night.

The knowledge that Ethel was not right did not come upon me all at once, but rather it came from the intuitive power of childhood perception, I guess. The responsibility we all shared in watching over her grew with every coming year. I was barely able to dress or care for myself when I learned to lead her from the heels of the horses, and to take things out of her hands that might injure her.

She was a slim, beautiful, fragile girl with large blue eyes and thick wavy brown hair which Mother always kept in loose braids. Her skin was almost transparent, and tiny blue veins showed through the skin of her slender white hands. There was an ethereal beauty about her not of this world. She looked like a lovely flower dropped from a nosegay, and left to wither in the sun. Yet, she was always smiling in an amused sort of way as if she had a secret which only she knew about. She was the gentlest of souls and permitted herself to be led anywhere, to be fed, dressed, or put to bed, all this without ever raising a hand in revolt. She would wander off when we were not about, and Mother had to be constantly on the alert lest she leave her bed in the night.

Mother rose before the sun one morning, and whispering to me to keep an eye on Ethel, gathered up a bucket full of fish the boys had caught the day before and started out over the hill to share our bounty with our cousins, the Simpsons. She had barely left the house when I was aroused by Ethel leaving her bed. She seemed to sort of drift to the window that faced the East where she leaned on the sill, looking out. The gray dawn brightened as I watched her. Life began to murmur in the chicken yard. The screech owls gave a final hoot and flew to their daytime hideout. A morning dove cooed a plaintive call to its mate, and the rustle of mice could be heard in the kitchen. Sleepily, through half closed eyes, I watched my sister. There were dewdrops on the window, and when the sun finally peeped over the hill it tinted them into rainbow colors. Standing there in a long, white gown against the golden light, I thought Ethel looked like an angel in a biblical painting I had seen in the large leather-bound Bible on the shelf by the clock.

Suddenly she fell as if she had been struck from behind. The upper part of her body crashed through the glass of the window. Her knees were relaxed, yet she stood half-erect, hanging by a huge jagged point of glass stuck directly into her face.

The next thing I remember was that I was in Jim's arms and he was running as fast as his legs would carry him down the path to the big cherry trees. Here he sat me down and wiped my sister's blood from my face and hands while his own hands trembled. Gasping for breath, he leaned against a tree-trunk and retched. There we sat for what seemed hours watching the house. We saw someone rush up the hill after Mother. Then saw them return together accompanied by our cousins. Hours later we saw the doctor arrive in a horse-drawn buggy, and then saw people hurry to and from the well. Then we heard awful screams from the house, and Jim held his hands over my ears. After an eternity of waiting we saw the doctor leave. It was then we summoned enough courage to go back to the house.

Mother was pacing back and to in the yard with her apron over her eyes and her shoulders trembling.

Father came home late that night from a painting trip. Mother told him everything. Ethel was cut from the bottom of the right eye down through the cheek to the left corner of the mouth and through to the teeth. The doctor had sewn her up without a drop of anesthetic.

Way into the night I heard them talking.

"We must send her away, Lily. This is too much for you here alone with the children. I never have a moments peace when I'm away."

"No, John. Don't ask me to do such a thing. I simply can't. Nobody'll care for her like I do."

Father went on. "There's an asylum in Fulton. She will have good medical care. Lily, she's getting no better."

"She's no trouble, John, except when she has these spells. I can bear it as long as I can have her with me. Oh, John, how could you let her go. She's our first baby. NO! I'll fight this thing. She'll die there. I know it. No one will love her there and care for her the way I do."

Unable to stay awake any longer, I fell asleep.

Mother finally gave in, however, and in a few weeks preparations were made for the journey to Fulton. Since our only means of transportation was by horseback or by horse and wagon, a light buggy was hired from a neighbor. Before Father, Mother and Ethel rode off over the hill, we all lined up at the gate to wave goodbye. Mother bent down and whispered to Ethel who looked up with a smile, as sweet as an infant's, and blew us a kiss. It was the last time we saw our sister. She died shortly after entering the hospital, from a fall from which she never regained consciousness. She was buried there. When Mother and Father, looking sad and worn, came home, they brought a wilted flower from her grave and put it in the Bible on the shelf by the clock. Mother gathered up Ethel's pitiful little clothes to give away. As Jim carried the bundle out the door, Mother covered her face with her apron and wept. And we all wept with her.

5

Granny and Her Corncob Pipe

Childhood recollections are seldom consecutive. They are more like a collection of small and large events strung on a long chain of days.

Each time my horizon widened I was seized with unforgettable excitement at the unknown and my feet longed to wander further and further, and learn about people and their ways. The first adventure away from home was on a June Sunday when I visited Grandpa and Grandma Abbott. They were no relations really, and Grandpa and Grandma just seemed to be their names. I was around five years old on this lovely day.

The sun was warm, the leaves were waxen in their freshness, and the air was filled with the twittering of birds and chirping of crickets. The summer sounds hovered around us without seeming to disturb the quiet as the family filed down the path to Glover's Chapel, the little church that nestled in a growth of black oak on the side of the hill above Dean's Creek. Annie, Nellie, Goldie and I were carrying our shoes and stockings so they wouldn't get wet with dew or muddy when we crossed the creek bottom. Just before turning up the hill to the church, we would, of course, sit down on stumps and logs, dry our feet on cloths brought along for that purpose, don our stocking and shoes and walk with pride into the church.

This was one of the many days that Ruth was in a pout. She hated her faded old dress, she had thrown her hair-ribbons away, and she didn't "give a damn" how she looked. In fact, "I don't want to go to church; I aim to go to Hell anyway," she said. We all ignored her, determined not to let her spoil our Sabbath, the most lovely day of the week: the day of worship when we saw and visited with the other people; the day we donned our Sunday-go-to-meetin' best, starched and ironed and combed. We mingled with other folks and later we ate fried chicken and light bread, a feast compared to the side meat or possum and sweet 'taters we lived on the rest of the week.

Ruth strode ahead, whistling sassily, and flipping her skirts high as she climbed over the wire fence. Mother walked nervously from the front to the rear of the procession, giving my hair ribbons a final touch, brushing powder from Annie's collar, tying Goldie's shoelaces, smoothing back Garsy's, Jim's and Paul's hair, and using great restraint in not boxing Ruth's ears. The boys lagged far behind, uncomfortable in their starched overalls, no doubt wishing they were home playing mumble-peg in the shade.

Father, in his Panama hat and light trousers, herded us along, determined our souls should not be neglected. Mother herself looked like a China doll, done up in a white lawn blouse and alpaca skirt she had brought with her to the farm years ago. So down the hill, through the woods and clover field, and across the creek we trailed on a summer Sunday. I was in a happy mood that day. The scolding bluejay that followed us struck me as very funny. I went into ecstasies over a robin's egg found in the path. I made little sallies to gather wild flowers, while Mother cautioned me to look out for snakes. A squirrel swung friskily from the bough of one sycamore tree to another, flaunting its tail and sending me into gales of laughter.

I was frisky myself because I had plans. In order to do what I wanted, I schemed to be especially nice to everyone, so that Mother would notice and be hard put to refuse my wishes. I held the wire down with my foot for everyone to crawl through the fence, and even waited for the Simpsons to come up, and made a show of holding down the wire for them. I refrained from giggling when I noticed that Cousin Laura had her new mail order hat on backwards. I further restrained myself when I saw, as she was squeezing through the fence, that the top of her black stockings had fallen sloppily over her string garters. I didn't even tattle to Mother, as I had in the past, when I saw Cousin Wilford coming down the path clutching his Bible in one hand and picking his nose with the other, a habit she always scolded him for. I offered to carry Mother's Bible and Goldie's shoes, and held the foot log steady while everyone crossed. And I was ever careful not to let branches fly back into the face of the one behind me. In fact, I was so obviously gracious that Mother caught on. She could always read me like a book, anyway. When I slipped my hand in hers on the final stretch, she remarked with a knowing smile, "Penny for your thoughts. Wait, don't tell me. Let me guess. You want to go home with somebody today, don't you?"

"Well, I hadn't thought of it," I lied. "Could I please? Pretty please!" We were now climbing the steps of the church entrance. "We'll see," she whispered. "Ssh, they're singing."

Pandemonium always seemed to break loose when our large family of ten entered the church. People paused in their singing, turned around and looked, and no matter how quiet we tried to be, the sound of our shuffling feet seemed to echo in the rafters. I always sighed with relief when we were finally seated. Only then did it seem as if we were forgiven our intrusion and the congregation would return to the service.

I was clothes-conscious even at this early age. So the first thing I always did in church before settling down to try to listen to the prayers, hymns, and sermons, was to look around and see what everybody was wearing. My little friend, Marie George, had on a pretty new dress and hat. She caught my eye and we grinned at each other. Normally, she was the one I liked to visit on Sunday, but today she was too dressed up for me. My dress was starched and ironed, but faded and old, so I decided against going to her house. Besides' she was a bottomlander and through no fault of her own she made me feel inferior. Still I had to visit someone because Mother had said I might. My eyes wandered around the room for a likely prospect and finally rested on Grandma and Grandpa Abbott. They sat meekly in the corner, apparently rapt in deep meditation at what the preacher was saying. I was fond of them. Grandma had often remarked that my curls were "purty" and that I was growing like a weed. And Grandpa observed that I was "a pert young sprout."

Grandma and Grandpa were very old. Their faces were dried and puckered up like persimmons. The little hair Grandma had left was drawn tight in a knot on top of her head, but Grandpa's white hair was unbelievably thick and heavy and hung down over his collar in the back. He wore a long handlebar mustache which he continually curled around his finger as he listened to the preacher's every word. Grandma always wore a large white apron whose belt was buried entirely between her large bosom and larger tummy. They both had snapping, merry black eyes. Grandma and Grandpa were supposedly part Indian, but that didn't worry me. To me, they looked old and friendly and very lovable.

When church was finally over, everyone shook hands and visited a long time, lingering around the church steps talking of weather, crops, rheumatism, setting eggs, tomatoes, pickles, teething babies, and all the things country folks talk of, before leaving for home. Grandma and Grandpa shook Father's and Mother's hands, saying, "Howdy, Brother Wright, Howdydo, Sister Wright. How air ye? It were a mighty fine sermon, weren't it?" Then they shook hands with every one of us. When Grandma came to me, I was too tongue-tied to speak, and it was not until the crowd was ready to disperse that I summoned up enough courage to say, "Grandma, I want to go home with you today."

Goldie kicked my shins, whispering, "It ain't nice to invite yourself." Mother reprimanded me by saying, "You better wait until you're asked."

"Let the child come," said Grandma. "We'd be might proud to have her." I could have hugged her for that. "She can spend the night," continued Grandma, "and Pa'll see her across the creek in the mornin'." Mother said I must ask Father if I might since nothing was done in our family without his say so. It took all my courage to plead with this handsome, stern man to let me spend the night away from home. Grandpa cinched it by offering Father a chaw of his own homegrown tobacco. Father bit off a cud, chewed and spit a dozen times while I stood first on one foot then on the other saying, "Please, pleas-se." Father finally nodded then said I'd have to hoe corn all the next day to make up for it.

I had never spent a night away from home and this was too good to be true. I dismissed the family with a casual wave of my hand, ignoring Goldie's glare, and walked gleefully away between Grandma and Grandpa, clinging to a hand of each.

It was a long hot trek along the road that led past the church and wound up the hill to their cabin. There was little shade here on this dusty road and the heat waves beat down to where I felt like I was being broiled under a bright lid. Grandma took off her bonnet and fanned me with it. I began to long for a cold drink of water. Not a word passed among us; they seemed deep in their own thoughts. The idea struck me that my folks were probably all home by now and had their shoes and stiff clothes off and were lolling on our cool front porch waiting for Mother to finish frying the chicken. I began to feel a little sorry that I had come, but full of excitement and too eager for adventure to be daunted by the long hot climb.

A horse and rider appeared over the top of the hill. He tipped his hat, said, "Howdy, folks," and continued on, his horse's hooves kicking up little clouds of dust and the steel shoes making ringing sounds as they struck stones.

When I thought I could bear the heat and thirst no longer, we came to a large oak tree and sat down underneath to rest in the shade. Grandma fanned me and Grandpa rested with his hat over his eyes for a little spell. There were black-eyed-Susans all around us, and Grandma picked some, made a daisy chain and hung it around my neck and laughed a toothless laugh. Grandpa rose slowly, disappeared into the brush, and returned shortly with his hat filled with hazelnuts. He cracked them on the rock, using another rock for a hammer, picked out the rich meats carefully, and laid them in my lap. Water was no longer important. I ate them, being careful to insist that they share them with me. They refused, saying simply, "We ain't got no teeth."

Then refreshed and rested, we started on the last lap. Butterflies fluttered ahead of us. I turned loose of the hands that were leading me and chased them. As I ran about I heard Grandpa say, "Hit's been a long time, Ma, since our younguns were little aren't it?" "Hit sure is, Pa." When I returned to them they both had corncobs in their mouths and were puffing placidly. I was astounded, wondering where they had kept such large pipes on their persons. I resolved to keep a sharp eye open and discover this secret. Grandma just had to have a hidden pocket, I figured.

Their log house seemed to be ready to collapse any minute, and we opened a front gate so ramshackled that it had to be reassembled after we passed through it. Then we were on a neat dirt path shaded by tall cedars, bordered with rocks and masses of flowers of every variety. There were hollyhocks, rose moss, bachelor buttons, touch-me-nots, larkspur, and cosmos. Before entering the house, we paused at the well under the grape arbor where Grandpa drew up a bucket of cold refreshing water. He offered it to me first with a kind of stiff bow like I was something special. Even though my mouth felt like dry sand, I said politely, "You go ahead, Grandpa," for I was not used to being served first. He shot me a strange look and raised the brimming dipper to his lips. When it was finally my turn, I thought I would never get enough.

It occurred to me while I was drinking that Grandpa was the most polite man I had ever seen; then I noticed that their pipes had disappeared again.

Before we entered the house, two cats and a funny little fat dog had to be removed from in front of the door where they were sleeping. Grandpa pushed them gently and carefully aside. Entering the two room cabin from the bright sunlight, it seemed almost pitch dark inside. Gradually my eyes became accustomed to the darkness and I looked around with interest. The place was as neat as a pin. The walls were papered with old magazines and hung with pretty calendars that dated back for years. An embroidered sampler of "God Bless our Home" hung in the kitchen. Here hung a bunch of bright colored corn; there, stalks of tobacco; and yonder, a string of gourds. There was a large smoke-blackened fireplace with a cap and ball rifle hanging above it on pegs along with a powder horn. The boards of the floor were worn, with wide cracks in between, but scrubbed and spotless. A bed with at least three feather mattresses stood in a corner, topped by a spotless white homespun bedspread. A spinning wheel rested on sprawling legs by a chair padded with crazy-quilt cushions.

I followed Grandma into the kitchen. She took a black checked apron from where it hung on a nail behind the door, and tied it over the clean white one she wore at church. With calm deliberation, she pulled an iron kettle from back of the stove and rekindled the dying fire under it. I was ravenous from the long walk and curious as to what we would have for dinner. I didn't have long to wait. In a flash, it seemed, the pot was boiling on the stove and Grandma had whipped some cornbread into the oven.

The three of us sat down while Grandpa said grace over the beans, green onions, thick yellow cornbread, butter and molasses and sassafras tea. Grandpa served Grandma before serving himself. This filled me with wonder and I though him a most unusual man. Completely forgetting that Mother had always cautioned me to eat lightly when I was visiting, I was hungry enough to eat anything and all I wanted was lots of it. I hadn't though of dessert, but imagine my surprise when Grandma set large pieces of golden-brown gooseberry pie swimming in thick cream before us. To this day I have never had anything taste so delicious as Grandma Abbott's pie.

After dinner I offered to help with the dishes. Grandma handed me a coarse towel to dry with. When this was finished, the old folks retired to the cool front room, and I peeked out the door to see what had become of the cats and dog. They were still asleep on the step. The fat dog, only slightly aroused, got up, walked about four steps, dropped down again and was instantly asleep.

Remembering that I hadn't solved the mystery of the corncob pipe yet, I hurried to the front room. Grandma and Grandpa sat placidly smoking their pipes, puffing ever so gently in a contented manner. I sat down on a little footstool at Grandma's feet. The stillness and lack of conversation began to bore me. I was used to noise and laughter, so I began to talk, perhaps, as Mother often said, "Just to hear my head rattle."

"We have a new cream separator," I announced. "It cost forty dollars. We bought it on the installment plan. Do you know what the installment plan is, Grandma?" I didn't pause for an answer, but prattled on. "Annie and Carl are sparking again. I guess Carl is pretty sweet on my sister. Father said he was going to chase him off with a shotgun if he didn't quit hanging around our place."

I had an uneasy feeling I was saying things I shouldn't and my folks wouldn't approve of my telling family secrets, but I couldn't seem to stop.

"Mr. Thornsberry took his fence down and moved it ten feet over on our line. Every time he does that we move it back and it's happened so many times we don't know where the real line is. Father said he was going to knock the stuffings out of him if he didn't quit moving it around." My mind flew like a butterfly from one flower of thought to another. "Mommy said she wished the Hedges would quit borrowing things from us cause they never pay anything back. They have a rich farm, but Mr. Hedges is so stingy he won't even buy a calico dress for his wife. And, gee, they're dirty people. I heard Mommy say they wash the babies diapers in the same water they wash the dishes in. I don't know which they wash first. Guess it doesn't matter. Mommy says they're going to die if they don't start being a little cleaner, but Ruth says she guesses they're used to it and it probably won't hurt 'em if they et cow turds. Aunt Effie sleeps with every man comes along, they all say. It goes on under Uncle Si's nose and he doesn't even seem to pay any attention to it."

I was now faintly aware that I had disclosed enough to start a civil war and my conscience began to smite me. I searched for other less potent things to talk about. My tongue was loose at both ends, I was afraid. Suddenly a thought that had been in the back of my mind for some time came to me. "Grandma," I blurted out, "Where am I going to sleep tonight?" Seeing only one bed in two rooms, I wondered where I would sleep. There was no answer. Turning, I found my audience fast asleep. The corncob pipes were stored neatly out of sight again. No doubt they hadn't heard a word I said. Indignantly, I sprang up and shook Grandma roughly and yelled in her ear. "Grandma, it's getting dark and where am I going to sleep tonight?" She gr-u-mped and ha-r-umped and finally peered over her fallen glasses at me.

"To be sure you'd want to know. Come with me child."

Grandpa had aroused by now, stretched himself, and said, "Guess I'd better milk Old Daisy." Grandpa do the milking? I was astounded. The women did the milking at our house. Then I remembered hearing once that Grandpa and Grandma were considered peculiar. I guessed that was the reason. He helped her with the chores. How strange. Gathering up a pail in the kitchen, he went out the door. Grandma and I stepped out to find the sunset tinting the sky pink, and chickens flying to their roosts in the cedar trees, the half grown ones fussing because they couldn't fly as high as their mothers. A cool breeze stirred the branches and gently lifted the curls on my forehead. I followed Grandma around the corner of the cabin to another log room built on to the back of the house.

"This was the girls' room," Grandma informed me. "I keep it jist as they left it."

It was a good sized room with three iron beds made up with embroidered bedspreads and folded crazy-quilts at the foot. It had a corner fireplace, cane bottom chairs, and on the wall dozens of pictures of round-faced girls and boys. Oval braided rugs were scattered about the floor. On the dresser were dainty pincushions, handmade dolls, and lace scarves. Appliqued curtains hung at the window. The room had the cozy cluttered air of happy girlhood about it. I went from one object of interest to another. "Whose was this?" I inquired and, "Which one did that belong to?" and, "Where are they all now?" Grandma answered every question patiently, so I gleaned bits of information about her thirteen children, who were all gone away, married, working, or dead.

She helped me undress, and I had to stand on a stool to climb into the high bed. I sank into the soft featherbed. Grandpa came in with a glass of warm milk fresh from the cow, and another piece of gooseberry pie and set them down on the dresser by the bed. I lolled in the luxury of so much attention; they sat down and rocked while I ate. Grandpa said, "Ye ain't afeered, air ye?" With my mouth full of pie, I shook my head. Then when I had finished, Grandma tucked me in and Grandpa said, "Do you want to blow out the light?" I extinguished it with a big puff.

I floated around on a fluffy cloud of sweet oblivion. I have a faint memory of rousing some time in the night to see the room bathed in bright moonlight and Grandma and Grandpa standing by the bed with folded hands looking down at me. I felt warm and protected and slept deeply.

They woke me early with the words, "Your Ma will be worried about you if you don't git home 'fore it gits too hot." So after a breakfast of fried turnips, gravy, biscuits, and molasses, Grandpa got his straw hat and held out his hand, and made me another stiff little bow. "It's nice having you for company," he said politely as if to a grown-up. I responded in kind and thanked him politely for the nice time and we started down the path. On an impulse I ran back and threw my arms around Grandma and hugged her tight. Her shiny black eyes twinkled when she waved goodbye. Holding on to jutting rocks, branches, bushes and trees, we slid on slick leaf mold along the precarious path down the steep wooded hillside to Dean's Creek. With trembling callused hands, Grandpa helped me across the foot log. We climbed up a mud bank and Grandpa showed me the path that led through the tall grass and under brush in the wide valley towards our house. The sun was beginning to beat down in a hot glow. Grandpa took a red polka-dot handkerchief from his pocket and tied it around my head then twirled his mustache and smiled like a gentleman in the presence of a lady.

"That'll keep the heat off," he said. Then he took out an oatmeal box with a hole in it. "Hit's a present for you. Now foller the path and don't get lost."

"What's in it?" I inquired. "Let me see." Taking off the lid I peered into the box. There was a little brown chicken inside. "Oh, goody. Thankee, Grandpa. Thanks lots. Don't worry I won't get lost. The chicken's a beauty; I always wanted a banty!"

"Wall, that's sure what it air," he said and he pulled his mustache again, pleased.

"Goodbye now, Grandpa. Thanks again. And tell Grandma thanks, too."

I ran skipping up the path. At the top of the rise I turned and waved to Grandpa. There he stood, his small figure outlined against the dark wooded hill. I remember his homespun trousers, baggy and patched; his frayed straw hat on the back of his head; and wreaths of smoke rising from the corncob pipe held exactly in the center of his handlebar mustache. He raised his hand in farewell and I blew him a kiss.

Wouldn't I have great things to tell the folks! I had actually slept in a room all by myself, and I had pie brought to me in bed. I'd hugged Grandma and she'd liked it, and I had a parting gift to show that they liked me, too.

Yes, my first night away from home had been a happy time, a pearl on a string of memories.

6

The Seat of Knowledge is Mighty Hard

The people of the hills were much preoccupied with death. It came often to visit us. Next to talking about hunting, fishing, crops and weather, death was the main subject of conversation. There was much searching in the bible, preaching and praying and singing about the after-life.

Concerning all of this, Mother was a bit of a rebel. She held that life had a purpose, other than just living 'til you die, in the hope of Paradise gained. She was liberal about what other people wanted to do with their lives, but for her children, an education and escape from the hills to where life was more abundant was the main goal to struggle towards; and to achieve it, no sacrifice was too great. If we worked hard, were faithful, good and true and tried to make something of our lives here on earth, Heaven would be our natural reward, she figured.

"First it is important for a body to decide what they are going to do with their lives," Mother said. For me there was no confusion, no uncertainty: I would be an artist like my Father. Having bowed my head and lit my candle at the altar of art, everything else in my life must be channeled in that direction. Whether or not I might know fame or fortune, or create one single picture of note, still I had to paint.

The eye sees color, form, light, shadow; the mind clutches to hold the image; and the hand trembles to transpose it onto canvas. My heart ached to share with those around me the vision of loveliness captured for a breath in time; the truth of life and love that binds people together. This gift is not acquired, nor is it born of wisdom, but rather of a motivation to create out of hope and joy an illusion of beauty that would live and endure forever. What one born and raised in the hills is supposed to do with such a gift, I did not worry about then.

It seemed a pity to me to clutter my head with reading, writing and arithmetic when I only wanted to draw people, flowers, trees and other things. Mother and Teacher had other plans for me, however. Long before I was born it seems, somebody with nothing to do had cooked up an institution called school and in cahoots with the law, had managed to make getting an education compulsory.

I was open-minded enough to think it was all right for people who wanted it, but as for me, I would rather stay home and turn the grindstone for Father while he sharpened the ax. At least while I was doing that, I could be outdoors and drink in the lovely world about me and later record it on my drawing pad. I came to feel differently about education later, but at the age of six, in the year of our Lord, nineteen hundred and seventeen, these were my sentiments and I meant to stick by them. It took drastic measures on the part of my mother, that first day, to get me started off into the field of learning. But when you once get a taste of Mother's "hickory tea," you tie in with a sort of persuasion that is down-right lasting.

The morning of that first day, Mother combed my curls carefully around her fingers until they looked like long wood shavings, slipped my blue gimp over my bleached flour sack drawers (which were not quite fully bleached, and still said visibly on them, "Eventually, why not now?"), forced my unwilling feet into shoes, and then with a gentle slap on my bottom said, "March!" She faced me towards the path that led past the well, through the meadow where the fierce bulls grazed, through the cornfields where tall stalks of corn closed over my head, over treacherous Dean's Creek on a foot log, through Pemberton's muddy corral and hog pens, up the hill through the woods where I was to watch for snakes lurking in my path, over a stile, through the tall saw grasses and so on to school.

I knew the path quite well and what awaited me at the end of the journey and liked the whole idea not at all. I was to follow my brothers and sisters who trotted swiftly along, eager to meet their schoolmates again. I sulked as I followed slowly. Coming to the rail fence beyond the well, instead of climbing over after the rest, I squatted under a peach tree in the fence corner. I was going to lean back on my haunches and balk like any mule. I wouldn't go to school and they couldn't make me, I kept telling myself. I'd simply sit here until the other children came home again.

My ruse was discovered in less time that it takes to tell it. Mother came up the path to draw water from the well and spied me right away. Without a word she broke off a peach tree limb and came and rapped me smartly across the legs. With an emphatic final whack she again pointed me towards the house of knowledge. I scampered over the fence and ran bawling along the path catching up with Jim, and showed him the marks on my legs and blubbered out how mean Mommy was. He soothed me by saying, "Don't cry. Everybody has got to get a whuppin' on their first day of school." Then he offered me a piggy-back ride. I forgot my distress and gleefully climbed onto his shoulders. He began to run like a loping horse while I laughed my tears away.

The schoolhouse was built of poured cement and nestled in a grove of huge oak and walnut trees at the edge of a tremendous pasture. A narrow and rutted lane passed its only door. It was an ugly rectangular building made less attractive by the small outbuildings around it—the leaning well houses and the boys' and girls' privies. How clearly I can still see the drab and uninspiring interior. Brown wallpaper, of a pattern so old and faded it was no longer distinguishable, hung in shreds on the wall. Blackboards covered one end of this one room affair and the teacher's desk sat squarely in front. A little to the side of this desk was a monstrous stove with its pipe hanging by wires and running almost the entire length of the room to its chimney, actually only a hole in the roof.

It was terrible punishment to plop a person down in one seat and make him sit there in a hot, stuffy room with his nose in a book when the air was fresh outside, and the swimming holes clear and inviting. Heat waves danced outside the window and flies buzzed around, making specks on my nice new Big Chief tablet. Restless feet shuffled the floor. Chalk dust flew as the eraser in the teacher's hand swished across the blackboard. I could hear the unfolding of drinking cups and smell the sweat of the boys' shirts.

Songbooks were passed out, and I can still hear the songs that rang out in utter disharmony.

There were soft voices, shrill voices, and tuneless voices that shook the wasps nests in the rafters. Loudly we sang—The Battle Hymn of the Republic, The Star Spangled Banner, Juanita, The Old Oaken bucket, and America the Beautiful. The singing over, the teacher ordered the first grade class to rise and pass to the bench in front of her desk.

"Let's begin our lessons by learning the memory gem I have written on the blackboard," and she pointed out each word as she repeated, "If you have work to do, do it with a will. They who reach the top, first must climb the hill."

I looked at the other children on the bench beside me. I knew and liked the three girls in my class and gave them a wide grin. The four boys I wasn't much interested in, except one, and this one, Hank, was downright revolting. He sat next to me and I appraised him out of the corner of my eye. He smelled of skunk. His blond curly hair was uncut, dirty, and matted, and I could see nits and lice in it. His face was rusty with dirt; only his mouth had a clean rim around it where he kept it licked with his tongue. He had tremendous feet, with black split toenails, and sore toes that flies buzzed around and nibbled on. I sidled away from him. Then a bedbug crawled across his britches, over my skirt and onto my open primer. The teacher said, "What did I say the word was, Frances, that I wrote on the board?" I slammed my book shut, squashing the bug, and in disgust said, "Bedbug." I wasn't trying to be a smart-aleck, but it was a spontaneous reflex.

Hank was about six years older than I and already feeling his oats. He had never been promoted from the first grade because he refused to study. But from that day on through our school years, whenever I raised my eyes from my books, he was staring hungrily at me. He did everything he could think of to torment me. He would slip me love notes which the other children would snitch and titter over. He whispered loudly that he admired my "purty blue eyes and yallar curls." Worse of all, he bragged to the other children that we were going to get married when we grew up. To my horror, he now began to study so that the teacher promoted him and he continued to be in my class until we both graduated. From the first day of school till the night I was fifteen, I feared, loathed and hated this boy.

I soon began to develop complexes. There were no funds available for textbooks so parents had to buy schoolbooks for their children. The lowlanders could afford books. The ridge children could not. The brand new primer Mother got me that first year was the last book I was to own until by a strange circumstance I was able to get some my last year. Of this, I shall write later, for it is an unusual story indeed, but until then if I wanted to study I had to wait until a more fortunate child finished with his lessons and was gracious enough to loan me a book. Not only was this humiliating, but also it seemed I would barely start to get my lesson when the bell would ring and I would either have to stop or stay in during recess and the noon hour and study. All this left me unprepared for my class work or examinations, making me feel ignorant and inferior, ashamed and humiliated.

Sister Goldie added to my inferiority complex. I still remember the look of anxiety on her face when I was called on to recite my lessons. With her black eyes upon me and her lips forming the answer, I couldn't remember a thing I had studied, even if I had a chance to study, and so I stood mute. Sometimes when the answer did come, I just whispered it. The other pupils would hear, and quickly raise their hands to give my answer, while the teacher looked at me, scolded and threatened not to promote me if I didn't try harder.

Our school term usually began in early August so that the children would have more time to attend while good weather lasted, as shoes and warm clothes that were needed in winter were unnecessary in August. Ours was a very poor school district and usually the funds ran out before a five-month period, and then school had to close down. As a rule our teachers were very young with no more than an eighth grade education and a few months of teacher's training. Their salary varied from forty to sixty dollars a month. Many of the children never got as far as the eighth grade. Their parents had to keep them home for planting in the spring and harvesting in the fall.

Some of our neighbors, like the Brumleys, felt that education was a thing to be avoided. They were sharecroppers on Thornsberry's farm about two miles east of us. There were seven beautiful blond girls in the family, and none of them ever attended school. They lived like wild creatures, avoiding all contact with the rest of us.

They would hide in the house or bushes every time any of us approached their house. To see these children growing up without an education troubled Mother a great deal. Every summer before the school term began, she made a friendly pilgrimage to their house, bearing cakes and pies in an effort to entice them to listen to her. I went along on one of these trips in order to help open the gates, as her arms were full of gifts. When we approached their house we could see the children scrambling for safety, or perhaps to herald the news of our coming. Mother marched up and rapped resolutely on the door. It popped open, hands reached out and grabbed the parcels, and the door slammed in our faces.

Somewhat taken aback, Mother knocked again. After a long period the door opened and Mrs. Brumley peered cautiously around it. I saw a face of undetermined age, brown and dry as leather, and a mouth that was puckered and toothless. Mother began politely: "You have a lot of children who should attend school, Mrs. Brumley."

"Yup," she said, "but they ain't got no shoes." And the door banged shut again. Mother began to lose her temper and rapped loud and hard upon the door. Slowly it opened again. Mother spoke rapidly, "If I see that the children have shoes, will you send them to school?" Privately, I wondered how this miracle was to be brought about.

"Hit's too fer and hain't never no footlog 'cross the crick," said Mrs. Brumley, flatly.

Mother made a final bid for friendship by saying, "Do you happen to have a toothache? I see your jaw is all swollen."

"Nope, no toothache," said Mrs. Brumley, "I ain't got no teeth. That lump is tobaccer."

"Do you chew?" asked Mother, shocked.

"Why, shore," replied Mrs. Brumley. "I spit on one side of the bed and Pa spits on t'other."

With these remarks the door popped shut again. After that, in spite of Mother's determined banging, it did not open anymore.

I was nearly drowned in Dean's Creek that first year. On the night of this unforgettable event I learned why, come hell or high water, a body had to go to school.

Autumn had waited long and quietly behind the warm door of summer, but it was ushered in with a blast we all remembered for a long time. I recall clouds like molten lead swirling restlessly across the sky when we arose that morning, and the treetops were tossing nervously about. As the morning progressed it blew harder and harder. We hurried through our chores, anxiously watching the sky. We dreaded going to school with a storm brewing. By the time we were ready to go, the rain hadn't begun yet, so we started out at a dead run. The wind was from the east, to the back of us, and literally blew us along the path. My skirt billowed out in front of me like an umbrella. The falling leaves rose in whirlwinds in our path. Lightning danced about us and the thunder laughed loudly overhead.

By the time we entered the school building the storm was close upon us. Suddenly the heavens tilted over like a washtub and poured a solid waterfall upon the earth. Limbs and branches from the trees were flung madly against the windowpanes, like wet wash. The trees themselves bent after them as if trying to hold on to their summer skirts. The roof leaked first in one spot and then in another, and we scurried about to put dinner buckets under the leaks as they sprung. Shingles flew off like they were made of paper and it was hard to believe the roof would stay on. The wellhouse fell flat on its face where it lay and rolled around as if in agony. The din continued until about one o'clock, when, with one last blast of wind, it was suddenly over and the sun peeked brightly between scudding clouds.

With sighs of relief, and thanking Heaven we were still alive, we rushed out. The world glistened and shone like a reflection in a mirror, but the havoc of the storm was all about us. The road in front of the school was a swift muddy stream that made deep ditches and gullies wherever it went.

The air was crisp and cold as white wine. In a state of frenzy we all hurried for home. With the other children I ran swiftly down the hill, leaping over little streams that came from every direction. We were brought up suddenly to find ourselves standing on the bank of Dean's Creek, and this stream that had only been a few feet wide in the morning, was now a mighty and turbulent river. The great roar of it filled the air. Huge trees, uprooted by the flood, tumbled over and over down the stream. We were horrified to see dead cattle and pigs floating along. The waves seemed to reach out to our very feet to crowd us further and further back. I was terrified at the sight of it.

Faint, I stood there for a second with my eyes closed, and put my hand out for support. My hand came in contact with the warm tight muscles of a horse's trembling withers. I looked up to discover I was leaning against Old Prince, Mr. Willoughby's prize horse. As if guessing my feelings, Mr. Willoughby, our neighbor, reached down his hand and patted me on the shoulder. I climbed up behind him, clung to the back of the saddle and tried to still the pounding of my heart. He said something comforting to me I am sure, but because of the noise I could not hear what it was. Dozens of people had gathered on the bank, for this was a sight indeed. Dean's Creek had never been this high before.

Mr. Willoughby and I, on Old Prince, were on a soft bank close to the waters edge. Suddenly the bank collapsed underneath us, and we found ourselves plunged into the torrent. Immediately the water rose, swirling around us, leaving only Mr. Willoughby, me, and Old Prince's head and back above the flood.

Old Prince began to fight a life and death struggle while we clung to him, for only he could save us. The strong muscles of his legs pawed the water as we rose and fell with the current. We were tossed about like driftwood, but his feet and heaving body fought the powerful current to keep us afloat. Mr. Willoughby began talking to Old Prince in a soft and soothing voice. Then he started to pray. Across my mind flashed the thought that he was a Mormon; he prayed very much like other people. I had my arms tight around his waist now and shut my eyes to the tossing waves. The shore seemed miles away and eternity seemed very near. When I dared open my eyes, even a little bit, everything was murky confusion about us. Old Prince, gallant creature that he was, struggled on and on. Finally we approached the opposite bank where the shoreline rose and fell as the waves swept us forward and then pulled us back again. All at once a big wave washed us up upon the shore where we stood on solid ground.

We had come out nearly a mile below the point where we had entered the stream. Old Prince stood up on the bank and shook himself so vigorously to rid his coat of water, he nearly unseated us. We just sat there, breathing deeply, hardly able to believe we were still alive. Then we climbed down and stroked the horse's proud head. No creature seemed so dear to me as Old Prince did at that moment. We led him back up the stream opposite to where we had entered it. Mother, who had seen all that had happened, was waiting for me there. She folded me in her arms without a word; cradled and kissed me, and wept over me, while my fears flowed away as if they were nothing. Then we turned and waved to assure everyone standing on the other side of the stream that we were all right.

Mother fixed me fried chicken for supper that night, and it was the first time in my young life I had ever had all the chicken I wanted to eat. She let me sleep with her, for Father was away, and as I snuggled down in her bed I was so happy to be the center of her attention that I wished the creek would overflow every day.

In the night, however, I woke up crying, dreaming the flood was still around me and that I was drowning. "Oh, Mommy," I cried. "Don't make me go to school no more. I'm scairt of the creek, and of Pemberton's mean bulls. And their old sow chased me t'other day, and I seed a copperhead snake in my path going down the hill, and it's so fur. And I don't like to set by that stinkin' boy, Hank. I ain't got no books to do my lessons or tablet and pencils, and I broke my slate, and I get hungry at noon 'cause we got nothin to pack to eat in our dinner bucket. I don't want no learnin' that bad. I don't want to go to school."

Mother shot up to a sitting position. "Now listen here, young lady. You got to go to school. It's important. It's the only chance you got to get out of these backwoods. You don't want to live like this all your life."

I was seeing for the first time something wrong with the way we lived—that the roof leaked; that the furniture was wearing out; that we had no fit clothes to wear and barely enough food to survive on for the most part. I was beginning to notice things. I had thought everybody in the world lived that way.

Mother talked on, as she cradled me in her arms. "You must not be afraid. You must brave the creek and bulls and snakes, 'cause you got to get an education so you can go in search of the great big, beautiful, wonderful world that it talks about in them story books. Why, out there are people who do things. They paint pictures, write books, build houses and build big cities and bridges and ships and things. You mustn't miss all that. There, there, don't cry. Someday you'll be glad you went to school. You don't want to stay dumb and starve like the Woolerys. You want to learn things and to amount to something one day. You want to be an artist, and you want to be a lady and be treated like one; not just somebody who never stops workin' for nothin'. As for that boy Hank, don't you let him come near you, you hear? You have no truck with him. He ain't got no raisin' and iffen you ever mess around with the likes of him you'll never git out o' these hills, you hear? You understand?" But I didn't, not then nor for a long time.

"Yes, mommy, yes mommy."

Again, I drifted off to sleep.

7

Young Sprouts

Mother's burning ambition to educate us and send us out into the world was to consume her every moment for as far back as I can remember.

The four older children, Garsy, Annie, Nellie, and Jim, because they missed so much school in order to help on the farm, were behind in graduating from the eighth grade. The next three, Paul, Ruth, and Goldie graduated on schedule.

Father, busy with his painting, helping Roscoe teach in the church, and making whatever money possible away from home, sanctioned Mother's plans for all the children.

We were all caught up on the feverish hustle and bustle of Mother's preparations to send us out into the world, one by one. Year by year we must put our every effort into a set project. We must decide on a thing, she insisted, to do that year what would make us the most money, and do it without fail.

Garsy, the oldest, would be the first to go forth. So this year our plans to make money were for him. Garsy was a young man as I first remembered him. He was slim, dark, and slightly stooped already, like a young tree grown in too shady a place. I think now he was too heavily leaned upon as a lad. He had downcast eyes, quivering nostrils, and a bobbing Adam's Apple revealing nerves deep below the surface. He hands, though callused, were the long slim hands of a musician. They either guided the handle of a plow, or tenderly quivered over his precious violin. One never knew what was in his mind or heart. If he was angry, or sad, or hurt, he never showed it. I think, perhaps, this was the loneliest young man who ever followed in the plowed furrow of life. I did not know him then; I never will, and this saddens me.

Mother began to rack her brain as to what would be the best way to make money out of the farm this coming year. Should we put the whole farm in corn or wheat, or maybe it would be better to cut down more trees in the forest and make them into railroad ties to sell? Mother hated to cut down our trees and we didn't have enough corn to seed the whole place, so what to do? Then one morning Mother arose with her gray eyes shinning, she had a plan at last! We sat around the table at a breakfast of fried mush and apples, and listened. Instead of saving our best corn for seed, we would sell all we could spare of it, and invest our money in turkey eggs. We already had enough hens to hatch them, Mother was sure.

Raising turkeys is a hazardous business. They are subject to many diseases if they are kept penned up, and prey to wild animals if allowed to roam. They have a natural cunning way of hiding their nests in brush piles and then taking their families off in the woods as far as possible. As a rule, everyone decides to raise turkeys the same year and the market is then flooded, and the prices, of course, drop. But this was the year the neighbors decided against raising turkeys. Knowing all this, Mother kept ahead with her plans while Father and the neighbors shook their heads in disapproval and predicted failure. The boys, Garsy, Jim, and Paul sided with Mother and worked like squirrels to put her project over. Garsy said he could handle the work in the field alone, and for Jim and Paul to help Mother. The girls had all they could manage with the housework, garden, truck patch, canning and milking, in addition to helping plant the fields and hoeing the corn. The boys were up with the sun, and when through with their regular chores, they cleaned the poultry houses and yards and strung high wire around them. They set out traps for weasels and rats, and it would be past midnight before they got to bed sometimes. Every few days neighbors would drop by, and when Mother proudly showed off her flock, they would bet her anything from a plug of tobacco to a moon-eyed mule, that she wouldn't raise enough to pay for the "settin' aigs." Mother only laughed, tossed her head, and went about her business.

While everyone was busy at work, I was busy following them around for fear I would miss something. Of course, I had my tasks of feeding the chickens, carrying in stove wood, doing the churning and running errands for all. But for the most part, I fear I was just in the way. And when school stared in August, I again became bothered and annoyed by Hank. In the shuffle that went on at the beginning of every class, when we scrambled from seats to the bench in front of the teacher's desk to recite our lessons, I was sometimes able to avoid him by sliding in between some of the other children. But the odds were against me since he sought to sit by me and the others sought to avoid him. So, most of the time, Hank won. He would sit down and sidle up against me, closer than necessary and turn a glistening grin almost in my face. By now he had taken to stealing pencils and tablets and apples out of the other children's dinner buckets, which he would present, with a grand gesture, to me. My classmates caught on, and began to taunt me with: "Ya, Hank loves Frances, Frances loves Hank," and on and on and on. This began to instill in me a large capacity for hate, yet underneath it all, I had what every woman has, a love for admiration. I was both angry and flattered by Hank's puppy love.

All of this did not go unobserved by my brothers and sisters. Goldie figured that I had ought to settle it by myself with sarcasm. When he rolled up his sleeve and offered to show me his muscle, I should say, "It looks like a snake that just swallowed a frog." She bet that would shut him up. Ruth swore that if she caught him kissing me, she would kick his ass up between his shoulders. Paul told me just to ignore him, and practice brotherly love, by asking the Lord to forgive him for his thievery. Jim threatened to fill his britches full of buckshot or to rub his face in a pile of cow manure. On hearing of this last threat, Mother pleaded with Jim not to, saying, "Hank would probably never get around to washing it off." In my opinion, sweet Nellie had the best answer: "Just tie him to a tree trunk and let the buzzards eat him," but Annie haughtily tossed her head and said that she doubted if the buzzards would eat him, that he was enough to make the buzzard puke. Garsy and Father agreed that Hank was the best skunk trapper around these parts and that I oughtn't to be so high and mighty, and that someday we'd all be sorry for the way we had treated him. Piously, Father said, "Anyway, he is one of God's children." All the rest of us doubted that.

August, September, and October passed. Our flock of turkeys grew large and fat. November was finally upon us, and it was Paul who proved that nothing is really insurmountable if you set your mind to it. The poultry yard was swarming with full-grown turkeys. "It's the largest flock ever raised in our neck of the woods," Mother declared. Here we were, just a few days before Thanksgiving, and the market price was at its peak, so we had been told by a neighbor who had hurried over the hill with the good news, moaning because they hadn't raised turkeys this year.

Then tragedy. The spokes of the front wagon wheel were broken, and Father wasn't home to fix the wheel. Even if he were, it would probably have taken him days to carve new spokes out of scaly-barked hickory limbs. Mother was in a state of agitation for fear we couldn't get the turkeys to town before the market price dropped.

"I tell you what let's do," Paul said. "Let's drive them to town on foot." It was an incredible idea. Eight long miles through the brush and woods, up and down hills with turkeys, the most cantankerous and stupid creatures on earth, and the hardest to manage, since they can fly as well as run fast. "Let's try it!"

"Paul, do you reckon we could? You'd be the one to go with me, bein' fast on your feet. It'll take a heap of fast running to keep the flock together," Mother exclaimed.

Paul then became very important and full of ideas. "I'll just wear what I got on, 'cause I'll be shinnyin' up trees after 'em. I'll fill my pockets full of corn and go ahead of Mommy and throw the corn in the path, and the turkeys oughta foller right along."

Mother pinned up her skirts, donned an old pair of Father's brogans and threw a shawl around her shoulders. Paul cut long branches from our peach trees to wave at them and herd the flock along, then opened the gate to the poultry yard, and all of us shooed the turkeys out and got them started on their way. It was after midnight when they returned, exhausted, caked with mud, clothes torn, but glowing with triumph. We had waited up anxiously for them. Mother had fat rolls of bills hidden in her bosom, and Paul was the proud possessor of a pearl-handled pocketknife as his reward. Mother dropped into a chair and kicked the shoes from her swollen feet.

"You should have seen Paul," she bragged. "He clumb tree after tree to poke old gobblers out when they'd fly up on a limb and just sit there and gawk and gobble. We ran out of corn long before we got there, but he hit on the idea of picking wild berries and throwin' them along the path and the turkeys went flockin' after them. It's a good thing the creek was as dry as a bone or we'd never made it across. The whole town turned out in surprise when they seen us comin'. Highest price we ever got for turkeys, and I couldn't have done it without Paul. I'm tellin' you, he's a smart one. Fast as lightening on his feet, too."

Paul lowered his head to conceal his pleasure and shifted from one foot to another. He pretended it was nothing, but even I could detect that he was proud from the way he took his new knife firmly from Jim, as if he had held it long enough. Mother looked at Paul, as if to say as it does in the Bible, "This is my beloved son in whom I am well pleased."

Then we all sat around the big kitchen table while Mother counted the money. We were thrilled to find that there would be enough left over from what Garsy would need, to order each of us an outfit of desperately needed clothes from the mail order catalog.

"Turn up the lamp, get the catalog, and bring Paul and me a bite of somethin' to eat, and let's get busy," said Mother, her eyes sparkling.

"There's nothin' to eat but a little dab of possum and sweet 'taters," said Ruth, "and they're nasty lookin' 'nough to make a dog puke."

Nellie scolded, "Ruth, I wish you wouldn't talk so awful."

"She's probably right," said Mother, "Bring it on anyway. I'm starved." So while Mother and Paul ate, we filled out order blanks for knicker suits and tweed caps for the boys; yard goods for dresses and coats for the girls; and new shoes for all of us.

"Could I," I pleaded, "have just one, teensy, weensy, little ole box of Crayolas?" With a smile, she added them to the order. After filling out the order blank, Mother said with a happy sigh, "Isn't it wonderful that Garsy will have one whole year to study music without having to work, except perhaps on weekends." What a thrill! With excitement we all began to discuss plans for his leaving! Through all this talk Garsy's face became tighter and tighter and he avoided our eyes and did not enter into the conversation at all.

Without warning, he burst out, "Stop it! I don't want to go away to school. I don't want to become a famous musician. I just want to stay here and be me. Mama, don't send me away from here. I love the farm. Who will take care of you when Father is away? Besides, I wouldn't know how to act anywheres else. I can play the violin right here any time I want to. Father can teach me all I want to know. I appreciate you all wantin' to help an' the money you all sacrificed so much for, but I don't want it." And he looked at us in defiance.

Mother's face became deathly pale. She almost never gave vent to anger or ever touched us in punishment except perhaps a switch across the legs with a tree limb. But at this news, she jumped up and grabbed her tall son and slapped him hard across the mouth. Trembling from head to foot she shouted with emphasis on every syllable, "Listen here, young man, if you don't get away from here and go to school and learn something beside plowing corn, you ain't never gonna amount to nothin'. What are you going to do with your life? Sit on the steps, chew tobacco, and whittle, and become a first class rabbit hunter? Its a cinch you ain't gonna make a fortune on our eighty acres. You stay here and you will never have more than one pair of britches to your name or one decent meal a month. For God's sake, is that all you want out of life?"

She stopped talking; she was breathing hard and held onto the table to keep from falling. We all sat in speechless shock, unable to believe our ears. Never had we seen Mother so overwrought.

We were full of pain at the hurt in Garsy's unyielding eyes, for we all knew how he adored her. His face flushed red and tears spurted, but he said not a word. She shook his shoulders and implored in a voice of anguish: "Answer me, son, answer me!" He took her hands gently away and fled the room. Mother was so pale and shaky I thought she would collapse. We looked at her in sympathy, knowing that this was the biggest disappointment of her life. She looked at the money on the table as if she had no use for it. Then needing something to do, she picked up the water bucket and went out in the night towards the well. This one defeat for Mother only meant that the next obstacle must be approached with more vigor. Soon she was planning to send forth the next one, Annie.

Annie, healthy and sturdy, was less than a year younger than Garsy. She had a pretty, round face, tip-tilted nose, and a large but prim mouth. She had a temper just two degrees below boiling, but usually kept it under control. This everyone knew, but should you ever forget it, she had a way of reminding you.

A year passed. The money for the turkeys had melted away. For Annie's schooling Mother decided to plant wheat. "You can't know what heaven is like 'til you get down and smell the earth," Mother used to say as we worked in the fields, planting wheat.

The rains came just right this year, waiting until the grain was carefully nestled in the soil. I didn't have to get down to smell the earth as Mother suggested. The smells came to me. I remember the smell of the plowed fields as the sod, brown and shining, was turned up. In the forest, the redbud, black haw, crab apple, and dogwood flung their bright colors and sweet fragrance to the wind. The spicy fragrance of sassafras down by the springhouse hung heavy above the stream. The lilacs in the front yard challenged the plum trees as to who had the sweetest smell.

Then came the summer with the promise of spring fulfilled. And with it came the smells of wild blackberry jelly being made, and ripe peaches being canned. Cosmos pushed round faces with lavender petals through the paling fences inviting one to sniff their sweetness. The marigold made me sneeze and the golden grain of the wheat field that beckoned us to harvest had a dry, clean smell of its own.

It was a good year, the best I can remember. The radishes were larger, the cabbage was more firm, the roasting ears' kernels more round and juicy. The wheat fields, on which we had staked our all, lay lush and tossing in the breeze, like a land-locked ocean. Ah, the thrill of it all!

The giant threshing machine chugging up the lane, with smoke unfurled, excited the hearts of us young ones lined up on the rail fence to watch. The neighbor women gathered at our house to cook for the crew. Busy they were with fried chicken, potato salad, beet pickles, loaves of fresh bread, gooseberry cobbler, green apple pie with thick cream. The men folks ate first, of course, while the women fanned away the flies with peach tree limbs. Surprisingly this was the one time I can remember that there was plenty of food left over for the women and children. I ate so much; my back actually ached from holding my stomach up. It's a good thing to remember a full stomach once in a while. The hunger pains of most of those early years are forgotten, but this one time when I stuffed till my eyes seemed to pop out of my head, I shall never forget. What sweet misery it was!

But alas, we must not indulge often in this extravagant manner. We must tighten our belts and save and save for Annie's debut into the great big, wonderful world out yonder.

All the wheat must be sold so that she would have the money she needed. We could only eat cornbread, because it was cheaper than flour. The cream we skimmed from the milk, tablespoonful at a time. We did without butter and took cream to Toronto, gallon at a time, to sell along with all the eggs we could spare (a town at that time consisting of a mercantile store, post office, a feed store, and grave yard). We ate more squirrel, rabbit, possum and fish instead of chicken because the chickens we raised were salable. Annie did some sewing for the bottomlanders and helped with their canning, washing and ironing, thereby earning more money. Dollar after dollar went into Mother's sugar bowl for the biggest event of Annie's life.

Then came the day when Mother's steamer trunk, the one Grandfather Ingram had brought from Scotland, stood ready to pack in the middle of the girls' room upstairs. Annie's things were spread out on the bed. There were calico, voile, and gingham dresses trimmed in lace, cross-stitched and embroidered. One good dress of gray wool, a wool crepe skirt with a blouse made from Mother's beautiful wedding skirt, a plum colored velour coat from the mail order house, too beautiful to touch with grimy hands; fine, white muslin underthings trimmed with her own tatting and crocheting, hair ribbons, two pair of shoes, new and shiny with gray tops, patent leather bottoms, Cuban heels. There was a shaker knit sweater, red, I think; face powder, hair pens and a brush and comb all her own. We girls all stood around sighing over everything. Mother was as happy as a mother hen over a chick. Then Mother went too far. She offered Annie her bone-handled hand mirror that lay in a red velvet box, on the dresser. The mirror was something special to Ruth who snuck it out every chance she got and admired herself in it. Now when she saw it go into the trunk, she flew into a rage. She had been so helpful the past few months, skimming cream, carrying heavy loads of chicken on foot to town, but this was too much. None of us realized what bothered her; she flew at Annie like a whirling dervish and started pulling her hair. Mother parted them and scolded Ruth, saying she had ought to be ashamed of herself. But Ruth got madder and madder saying Annie always got everything and she got nothing and Mother didn't love her and she was going to kill herself. She would go jump in Dean's Creek and drown, and when we all saw her stretched out cold and stiff in her coffin, we would be sorry.

After long farewells to the cat (whose tail she had cut off in a fit of anger only a few days before), and to the hound dogs she loathed and kicked whenever the menfolk weren't around, she dramatically handed Mother her Last Will and Testament, written on tear-stained paper. This was nothing new to Mother. Ruth was a great one for writing wills. She had been impressed by an old melodrama that dwelt at great length on a Last Will and Testament. Trying to keep a solemn face, Mother read in a firm voice:

"To Whom It May Concern:

Being of sound mind, I hate everybody, so I am going to drown until I am dead. My collection of old bones I bequeath to Goldie, my amber beads to Francie, my mussel shells to Paul, my heart-shaped pincushion to Nellie, nothin' to Annie, and my appliqued dresser scarf to Jim. May I rest in Peace. Yours Truly, Ruth Wright

P. S. I died of a broken heart. I was a flower that faded too soon."

Mother looked up and in all seriousness said, "If you commit suicide, Ruth, you are the only one who won't get over it."

Ruth had stood very pleased through the reading, proud of her efforts, but at Mother"s words, burst out crying and dashed out of the house, slammed the screen door in our faces and tore down the path towards

Dean's Creek, determined to drown herself, we were certain. Mother noticed our concern. "Don't worry," she said, with a twinkle in her eye. "If she does jump in, she'll hold her nose. Let her go. She swims like a fish. There's no sense worrin' about her."

But I went after her, sick with fear, and sat on the bank and bawled while she swam around and cooled off. Finally, convinced I cared about her, she climbed out and kissed me and we bawled together. I remembered how good she had been not to yank out my hair after I had tattled on her when she and Goldie went in swimming naked. That had been an awful day and when I recalled it, I bawled louder, hating myself, thinking how I caused Ruth to get a whippin'. Mother had sent her and Goldie and me to Toronto with a load of chickens and cream and eggs. On the way home, they decided to go swimming in the creek. Not having bathing suits, and not daring to go home in wet clothes they decided to go in naked. They stripped, hung their clothing on a limb, and then Ruth stood on the bank, with her hands on her hips and did a hootchy-kootchy, singing in a shrill mocking voice:

Mother, Oh Mother, may I go swim?
Yes my darling daughter.
Hang your clothes on a hickory limb,
But don't go near the water.

Then she held her nose and leaped feet first into the water. They let me wade in the shallow part, cautioning me to hold my skirts high. Neither of them thought to warn me about tattling. So when we were all seated around the supper table and father had said grace, I announced triumphantly: "Ruth and Goldie went swimmin' naked today."

Shocked eyes focused on the culprits, for this was a sin and a disgrace. Ruth glared at me. "You little son-of-a bitch," she hissed. "I hope you get caught in a snowstorm and your goddam ass freezes solid."

Father rose to his full height, towering over us in the lamplight and roared at Mother, "Take your daughters out to the shed and chastise them." Mother promptly took both girls out to the shed behind the smokehouse, from which we heard the sound of gentle blows and loud bawling, even though all of us children knew the sounds we heard were just play acting to satisfy Father. Our meal was finished in miserable silence with Father cutting and chopping on his meat as if it were his daughters he could gladly carve up. I told Ruth now that I had expected her to yank me bald-headed the next day and now I wished she had 'cause I had deserved it.

"Oh, Ruth," I wailed, "I'm so sorry."

Ruth said she hated everybody in the world but me, and someday when she got together some eggs she'd bake me an angel cake 'cause I was an angel.

Before daylight the next morning, Annie stood in front of the dresser, crimping her hair by heating a big hair pin over the lamp chimney and wrapping wisps of hair around it until it kinked. Then she made dog-ears over her own shell pink ones, and donned a big sailor hat with a navy band. She slipped into Mother's velvet cape and lo: my sister was a lady!

Mother took her in her arms, "Goodbye my daughter, and remember, study hard, for knowledge is a treasure you can store away forever. It's a wonderful thing to have a treasure like that to share with other people. One wonderful thought, once shared with someone, could go on and on to the end of the world." She kissed Annie fondly, handed her a little purse with money in it, and told her goodbye again.

Father, looking handsome and debonair in duck trousers, white shirt and Panama hat, treated her like a lady as he helped her into the wagon. The boys lifted the trunk into the back and she waved a white-gloved hand coolly at us. The rest of us stood in our rags at the gate. As the wagon made a turn to go up the hill, Mother threw her apron over her face and wailed, "My baby, oh, my baby!"

Had we only known it, Linn Creek, twenty miles away, was a far cry from the big, big world Mother dreamed of. The school there was small and not an accredited school. Annie would have one year of training and then would receive a teacher's certificate which would entitle her to teach in the county, but would not qualify her to teach in the towns or cities of Missouri. Mother didn't realize that Annie would have to come back to the hills to engage in her profession. Alas for the lack of communication!

Unbeknownst to us, twenty-five miles in the other direction, there was a fine little college, where we could have attended, tuition free. I never heard of this college till thirty years later.

Three months later, Annie was due to come home on her first vacation. Mr. Traw, whose daughter Laura was attending the same school, had gone to fetch them home. There had been a lot of rain and there was fear that the Creek would be up. But Father was confident that Mr. Traw would get them home safely. It was Thanksgiving and Mother had sacrificed a turkey for dinner. Mother was busy in the kitchen making mincemeat pie. I was in the yard gathering wood chips for the fire in the cookstove, when I saw them coming down the hill. I dropped my chips and raced to the house to herald their coming. The family rushed out to the gate to greet them. At the sight of them, Mother screamed in horror and ran towards them while we all stood along the paling fence, aghast. Mr. Traw was lifting a pale and bedraggled girl from the bed of the wagon. Her clothes, dripping wet, were nearly torn from her body. Father held open the gate, and then the front door, and Mr. Traw laid Annie gently on the bed in the front room. Mother began to examine her with frantic hands while Father felt for her pulse. After what seemed an eternity, they said she was still alive and breathing. While they undressed and bathed the mud from her body, and wrapped her in warm quilts, Mr. Traw told us what had happened. They were half way across Linn creek, when a flash flood had caught them. A wall of water nine feet high had overturned the hack and swept them downstream. Mr. Traw had, of course, swum to the rescue of his own daughter and Annie had been left to save herself. After a long search he found her clinging, almost unconscious, to a willow limb leaning out over the water. He hauled her out and a neighbor on our side of the Creek had seen them and brought them home in his wagon.

The horses, tangled in their harnesses, were drowned. The hack, Laura's and Annie's clothes, and Annie's purse, with all her money, were all swept away.

Our sister would recover, but that night she tossed and cried feverishly in her sleep—she cried that she hated school; the other students made fun of her clothes and said they were old-fashioned. They mimicked the way she talked. They called her a hillbilly, and made her so bashful and scared all of the time that she could hardly swallow her food at mealtime. When she awoke she pleaded with Mother: "Mommy, please don't make me go back. I don't belong." Mother had no argument, for now there was no money to send her back anyway.

But Mother, still determined, did not give up. Perhaps next year, after we saved some more money, Annie and Nellie could go away together. And maybe with Nellie to keep her company, they would make it.

Of the older girls, Nellie was perhaps the most anxious to go away to school. She was eager to get her teacher's certificate so she could make her own way. Nellie was a serene, quiet girl. She had a face like an old-fashioned porcelain doll, with perfect brows and gentle brown eyes. Her hair was dark, and her body was slim, almost frail. But there was a hidden strength in Nellie, and something else that showed in the twinkle of her eyes and the smile that hovered around her mouth. I was very small when I learned to watch out for Nellie's pranks, lest I become a victim of her brand of humor.

One day we were gathering beans in the bottom field. I found a strange-looking melon. Now I know it was a citron, but at that time I had never seen one. The seed must have come with the bean seeds we had ordered from a catalog. I carried the melon to Nellie and asked what it was. The second she looked at it her hands flew up in horror. She said it was the kind of a melon that evil genies grew in, and for me not to drop it lest it burst and the genies fly out, swarm all over me and eat the meat right off my bones. I believed her and stood petrified with terror. Ruth went along with the gag and agreed that the only thing to do was to take it home and give it to Mother, since only mothers had the power to overcome evil genies. With this we started for home, me carrying the melon gingerly as though it were a time bomb set to explode any minute. Once I surprised a grin on their faces. Suspecting their duplicity I threatened to throw it away, but Nellie made as though she were about to climb a tree in case I did, with such a show of fear, that I held on to it for dear life.

When we got to the house, Ruth and Nellie rushed ahead. With great ceremony Ruth opened the door for me while I tiptoed carefully up to

Mother and handed her the lethal weapon. Mother was sitting, with the coffee mill between her knees, grinding coffee. She admired it, said it was pretty, and then tossed it onto the kitchen table. Still in fear of its potentialities, I rushed into the front room and hid under the bed while Nellie and Ruth giggled and laughed as they told mother the joke on their baby sister.

Late one evening in the Fall, Nellie, Ruth and Goldie plotted to make a visit to the Simpson's pear tree which was loaded with luscious pears, ripe and ready for eating. Nellie's idea was that Ruth and Goldie should go rob the pear tree after dark while she and I visited our cousins, the Simpsons. Ruth and Goldie made straight for the pear tree about a quarter of a mile from the Simpson's house. While they were committing this robbery, Nellie and I knocked on the Simpson's door pretending to be just making a neighborly call. Innocently we sat down in the front room and talked about the weather and the hen's laying eggs. Prim and polite we sat. I crossed my legs, pulled my dress down neatly as I had been taught by my mother, and asked sweetly if cousin Roscoe would play the organ for us. He sat down at the organ and began to pump with his feet and play "Home sweet home."

In about an hour, Nellie excused us and explained that we had to go home to wash the supper dishes. Off we started towards home. We came to the big gate at the end of the pasture and Nellie said, "Let's wait here for Ruth and Goldie." In minutes we could hear them coming, laughing and bragging about their apron tails full of pears. They hadn't seen us, and when they neared the gate Nellie, hiding, yelled in a gruff voice, "Where you girls goin' with my pears?" She frightened them out of their wits. They dropped the pears, sailed over the gate and took off running for home. My sister, "Naughty Nellie," gleefully helped me pick up the pears and put them in our apron tails and we sauntered on home. Needless to say, Ruth and Goldie were furious with us, but not too angry to enjoy the pears.

Nellie paid a dear price for her frequent mischief one night when she persuaded Annie, against her will, to go with her to a party where Nellie's boyfriend would be sure to be. On the way home in the dark, Nellie's horse, that Mother had told her not to ride because it was spooky, spooked at something in the shadows. She was thrown out of the saddle, one foot caught in the stirrup; hanging on for dear life, she was dragged over the rocks. She was saved only by her boyfriend, later to become her husband, who caught up with her and got the horse under control. She was brought home a badly bruised and scratched girl. Mother was very upset with her.

Another year passed. September came at last. Annie and Nellie with all their finery—not so grand as the year before—were packed into the wagon, and with Father driving, disappeared over the hill in a cloud of dust. Before they were hardly out of sight, Mother pushed back her hair, rolled up her sleeves, and started to make plans for Jim, who would be ready to go away to school next year.

Perhaps of all the family, Jim was the one who gave me the most attention as a child. Jim was the "hug around the neck" kind of fellow. I still can hear his "merry whistle tunes" and see his watermelon slice grin under his frayed straw hat, and long arms and legs extending from his clothes, whose patches wore patches. It was Jim I followed around the most. Mother condoned this, perhaps to get me from underfoot. Jim was ever amused by my astonishment at the expanding world. When I was with him I was very anxious to please, doing nothing to abuse his kindness in accepting me. I sat quietly when he put me on a stump while he cut down trees for cordwood or labored to clear the land. I would trudge for miles at his heels on fishing trips without complaining of mosquitoes, briars, or of the heat, or of thirst. I was clever enough to admire with enthusiasm the fish we caught, or the big fat possum, or the black skunk with hardly any white stripe (always a prize), or the few precious mink he and Paul trapped. I received with joy the pets he gave me—small wild rabbits that always died of fright; a land turtle, or a frog that I would tie up in our yard. Once he caught a crippled wild duck, which he gave to me for a pet. He even built a little coop for it in the chicken yard. It was a lovely thing to behold. Around its neck was a snow-white ring edged with black. The rest of its feathers gleamed with diaphanous colors that changed from blue-green to purple, to gray and white. The cunning thing slipped out of the coop one night and disappeared into the woods.

My brother would point out things for my interest—a whirlpool under the hanging rock along Dean's Creek; a cottonmouth swimming downstream; the glowworm in the creek bottoms at twilight; a tree toad that changed colors; a string of geese flying south; a bluebird's nest full of tiny turquoise blue eggs; the whippoorwill calling at twilight; or a rabbit sitting quietly in the bush, sure that we hadn't seen him. I stepped lightly and carefully when we were tracking game, and always volunteered to carry the catch.

Sometimes he made toys for me. Once he made me a little wagon. For wheels he sawed circles of wood from a tree trunk; he drilled, with brace and bit, holes for the axle to go through. Then he made a box for the wagon bed and for the tongue he used a broom handle. Packing me into the little chariot that was so small my knees would be rubbing my chin, he would send me sailing off down the hill with only buckbrush to keep me from ending up in the springhouse. Too often the wheels would split asunder and wreck my little vehicle and send me flying through the air. Laughing, he would gather me up, rub my bruised noggin, and swear the earth had shaken when I landed. Then with saw, brace and bit, he'd make another set of wheels and again risk my neck for me.

Jim and Paul had a trick that was great fun: they would bend a tall supple persimmon tree down to the ground and nestle me into the top branches; I would hold on tight, laughing, as they let go of the tree which shot back like a slingshot. Another trick they had, which my mother caught them at, I remember well. We always had a big ladder leaning against the kitchen roof. They loved to stand the ladder up straight between them and talk me into walking up it with my arms extended, not holding on, and then cross my legs over the top and walk down the other side. They convinced me that if I learned to do this successfully, I could join a circus. One day Mother came out the kitchen door during one of these practice sessions. She was furious at the boys and yelled, "What are you trying to do, kill your little sister?" She grabbed a broom; seeing this, my brothers quickly leaned the ladder, with me on it, back against the roof where I sat and laughed at the sight of Mother chasing two big boys taller than her, down the corn rows with the broom.

I was looking for Jim one day, when I came upon him vigorously sweeping the floor of the old log granary by the well. It still hadn't fallen down completely after all these years, and was used as a place to store walnuts and hickory nuts. On its walls Jim had tacked pictures of train engines, some of which he had drawn. I stood for a minute watching him make the dust fly. I said, "Hey, what's goin' on around here?"

He stopped and leaned on his broom, grinning from ear to ear. Then turning serious and seeming to want someone to confide in, he said, "Come and sit on the bench. Shut your eyes and don't peek."

I sat down, covered my eyes with my hands, but peeked out between two fingers when his back was turned. He went to an old board nailed carefully on the wall, reached in behind it, and took a book from a hollow place in the logs. Coming over to me, he placed the book in my lap.

"Open your eyes and see what I've got." There was a black leather-bound book full of diagrams and pictures of locomotives. "Lookee here. Ain't them the purtiest engines you ever saw?"

I'd never seen a train engine, but I agreed they were purty. Noticing my lack of enthusiasm, he picked the book up and read a passage about pistons, bearings, and shafts. Then he snapped the book shut, and forming his lips in a resolute line said, "Yup, I'm goin' to be a first-class engineer some day. The first thing I'm goin' to do is leave home and go work for a man who has a saw mill way back in the hills. As soon as I have enough money saved up, I'll come home and send away for a correspondence course on engineering. They send shiny precision tools to work with—the purtiest things ya ever saw."

Carried away with his plans, he strode to the stairs, pretended to glance at a pocket watch, climbed into an imaginary cab, made motions of pulling switches and levers—in the meantime emitting whistles and the sounds of a chugging locomotive. Then after a series of arm signals he shouted, "All aboard!" and waved farewell to me. I could have sworn he disappeared in a cloud of smoke. Then he began to sing:

A call called Casey at half past four.
Kissed his wife at the station door.
He mounted the cab with his orders in his hand.

And took a farewell trip to the Promised Land.

Exultant, he leaped over the banister, tossed me in the air, and sat me down hard on the bench. The rocks that held up one end of it collapsed and so did I, in a heap on the dusty floor. A bit remorseful, he helped me up, dusted of my dress and promised, "Honey, you're my partner. When I get rich, I'll buy you a motorcycle." I believed him and the thought of it frightened me a little. Then he became worried. "Don't tell a soul about my plans. Promise me now."

I didn't snitch on Jim, but my conscience pricked me at the thought of Mother going ahead with her plans to send him away to school and making the same sacrifices as she had for the others while he planned to run away. Then one morning he was gone. Mother wept her heart out.

A few years later it was Paul's turn to go away to school. Paul was a handsome lad and very serious about life. Mother, more tired, more worn, but nonetheless determined, was scrimping and saving her butter and egg money for Paul's big adventure.

Then one morning Paul arose at the breakfast table, cleared his throat, and said he had something to say. Tall and gawky he stood, first on one foot, and then on the other. Then in a voice that fluctuated from high to low, he began. "I'm not gonna be needin' any of the money you been puttin' away. I've been savin' my own money from cuttin' corn, haulin' hay and heppin' the neighbors. So you folks don't need to make no sacrifice to send me off to school. I got a job doin' janitor work at Tuscumbia High School, an' when Father comes to do some paintin' there, I'd like to hep out and earn a little more, I guess."

We were speechless. Before anyone broke the silence, he continued. "Iffen Ruth want to and will come with me next year an' go to high school, I think I'll have enough put by then fer her and my tuition an' books. I know where we can get a couple of little rooms that won't cost us a dime iffen Ruth will clean the folks' house on Saturdays. They teach four years of high school at Tuscumbia, and when a body gets through with high school he's got a purty good education. What you say, Ruth, and what do you'ns all think?"

Ruth blurted, "You crazy fool jackass. You'd kill yourself jist for me? Bless your durned old heart. 'Course I'll go." And she ran from the room bawling like a calf.

Father whispered, "My son," and choked up. Tears kept falling from Mother's eyes on to her cracked and chafed hands. She gazed around at my people with a heart full of rhapsody.

Ruth, the most beautiful of all us girls, with green eyes and auburn hair thick as a pony's mane, could memorize whole books and recite them like a famous actress on a haystack. Angry and rebellious, she was a difficult girl to manage. Yet at times so generous and out going, no one could be angry at her very long. She had a fine choice of salty phrases and would cuss like a seaman if crossed. She shocked Father and the boys who never swore; banged her brothers over the head at the least provocation with whatever was handy, including the broom. She boxed Goldie's ears when she thought Goldie outdid her, then they would go about their chores the best of pals. She yanked my curls almost out by the roots; talked me into climbing tall trees from which Jim had to rescue me; pinched pieces out of my rear just to see me jump; scrubbed me; pummeled me; kissed me; baked me sugar cookies, using my hand for a pattern; came to my defense if I was threatened by anyone or anything, including a fierce bull that chased me. She rescued me from quicksand once, and pulled me out of the rain barrel where I had fallen in headfirst and was nearly drowned. I wasn't the least shocked by her language or afraid of her in any way. Ruth was fun.

After Annie and Nellie went away to school someone had to take over the chore of milking the cows since this was a job that they had always done. Ruth being Mother's best helper around the house, garden and field, the task of milking fell to Goldie and me. Goldie was the bright one, the precocious one. The teachers almost feared her, so far ahead of them was she, with her glistening black eyes burning to show that she knew all the answers in the book. Her fine hands made the chalk on the blackboard squeak as she did sums too fast to follow with the eye. She out read and outdid everyone. I felt inferior to her always.

Twice a day we would gather up our pails and traipse off to the barn lot, push back the hip of a cow, and while it chewed contentedly we would squat and milk one side while the calves slurped and bumped their mother's bag on the other. Goldie, with her long slim hands, could milk twice as fast as I could with my small hands. So after every milking Goldie would march in proudly with her full pails, get bragged on by everyone, while Mother would look into my half empty ones and shake her head, frowning. Then Goldie, vexed at my nonperformance, would go back and finish stripping the cows I started, and bring in another bucketful.

As time went on, this show of importance on her part irked me more and more. Then I hatched a scheme to saddle her with the entire job. If she was so good at it, I figured she would like to have it all to herself. So began the execution of my scheme. I pinched the teats of the cows as I milked until they rolled their eyes and kicked. Then I was sorry and kissed them on their noses, whispering my apologies, since the cows were my favorite animals and I sensed they understood. Feigning helplessness, I begged Goldie to help me settle them down. She fell right into my trap, petted and soothed them and then finished milking them. She was certain that they behaved only because of her, and to this I heartily agreed.

One day, with look of mingled conceit and persecution, Goldie told Mother that she guessed she would have to take over the milking because the cows didn't like me and wouldn't stand still for me. Mother bragged on her. Then frowned on me and said to take after the boys who were about to go fishing. I was so happy I wanted to turn cartwheels and whistle through my teeth and shout out how I had outsmarted Goldie. But I kept my lips buttoned for fear of getting the milking job back.

Young sprouts—we were called—because we were young and green and tender, and full of promise.

8

The Sweet Smelling Boy

When I was eight, a wonderful, a beautiful, a miraculous thing happened. A thing that gave me a glow and set my head to spinning and whirling. But it did not addle me so completely as to not to start me to thinking, wondering, and watching. Oh, and even hoping.

I was sweeping the front room when I heard someone whistling, outside. Looking out the door I saw coming up the path between the lilac bushes the most handsome fellow I ever laid eyes on. He had on a white straw hat, the whitest shirt, the fanciest striped tie, the nicest blue serge suit, and the shiniest shoes I had ever seen.

I looked down at my bare feet and dirty dress threw the broom down and fled to the kitchen.

"Mommy, Mommy. There's a furriner comin'."

She hastily wiped her hands on her apron, smoothed back her hair, and went to the front room. I peeped through the crack in the green door that divided the two rooms. Mother held open the front door as she invited the young man into the house. He took off his hat and held out his arms to her.

"Aunt Lily!" he said with a warm smile.

"As I live and breathe," she gasped. "Orville Holdren. Orville, my boy. How are you?" And she went into his arms. My eyes popped.

"How good to see you!" they both said, and laughed.

"How are you, my boy? Where have you been? I never thought to lay eyes on you again. Bless my soul. How nice you look. You make me proud of you and ashamed that you caught me lookin' so tacky. Hope I didn't brush off on you. Do have a seat and tell me about yerself."

She fetched him a chair and beamed at him. Then she called, "Francie, go tell everybody that Orville Holdren is here to visit us. I believe the boys are in the barn."

But everybody had already heard the fuss and had made their way to the front room, the boys shaking his hand and clapping him on the shoulder. The girls held back, ogling. Mother remarked what a grown-up gentleman he was and handsome, too. She looked at him with tears in her eyes and glowed. "How long it's been. How time flies! Must be a hundred years since you left." I still hid behind the door with my eye glued to the crack in it. Suddenly he looked around, puzzled.

"There's someone missing…the baby," he said. "I want to see her. Where is she? She was such a beautiful baby. Yellow curls and a dimple."

"She's in the kitchen," Mother assured him. "Francie," she called. I fled out the back door and crawled under the smokehouse to hide, and lay in the dry dust. Mother caught me by the skirt tail. "Come and see Orville. He hasn't seen you since you was a baby. He wants to see how you've grown."

"But my dress is dirty and my hair ain't combed."

"Don't say ain't and come on. Its all right. He was born and raised here in the Ozarks."

She led me in like a calf at the halter, with me balking and hanging back. Proudly she presented me to Orville, saying, "Francie, dear, this is Orville Holdren, who used to hold you on his knee when you were little." He got up from his chair, smiled down at me and bowed from the hips.

"How you've grown!" he said. "I wouldn't have known her, Aunt Lilly. She looks just like you. She's beautiful." He took my hand, looked at it tenderly, and kissed it. My heart bumped and was lost to him. Then he sat down, pulled me to him, smoothed my hair, and said, "Can I marry you when you grow up? Will you wait, beautiful?"

Mother laughed and looked as pleased and proud as if I had just been born that day. And truly I had. I leaned against him and smelled the sweet, clean smell of shaving lotion and good tobacco. I had never seen such a white shirt and such a beautiful tie, or such clean hands on a man. While he talked of life in the city, I just leaned there between his knees and drank in the beauty and charm of his masculinity. I wanted him to kiss me again. I couldn't wait to grow up and be clean and lovely so I could marry him and smell like him. He said I was beautiful. No one had ever said that to me and I wanted to run to the mirror to see, but couldn't bear to leave him. Finally he rose, shook everyone's hand, gave me kiss on the top of my head, and said to me, "Don't forget to wait, now."

"Are you home to stay?" Mother asked.

"No, no," he laughed. "Catch me burying myself in these hills."

He held the door open while Mother went through first; her back straight and head high like a queen. He didn't put his hat on until he had passed through the front gate. There he tipped it at her and bowed and with long strides went down the hill.

My heart was singing! My feet were dancing; and I ran to the mirror. I saw a tall beautiful girl in flowing gown with red roses in her hair. Mother came back into the room.

"Oh, Mother," I said, "He wants to marry me."

She looked down understandingly from the height of her wisdom. "He was only joshing!" she said gently. And then I saw my own dirty face in the mirror and was crushed. I began to cry.

"He said I was purty and I'm goin to marry a city feller when I grow up," I declared. For right there and then my mind was made up.

"I'll marry a sweet smelling boy from the city some day. Just you wait and see."

She folded her hands as if in prayer and said, "I hope you'd do, God I hope you do."

Mother was everything: warm, compassionate, all knowing, all caring, and fun too.

Goldie, like my other sisters and brothers, liked to take her turn at teasing little sister.

It was a day in late July and it promised to be a hot one. Heat waves danced before our eyes as if one could reach out and grab them.

The garden, the meadow and the green fields of corn lay ripening under the golden sun. The cows lay in the shade at the edge of the meadow, contentedly chewing their cuds. The horses stood near, head to tail, each switching its tail to keep the flies away from the other's face. The sky was azure blue with not a cloud in sight.

Goldie and I skipped barefoot along the beaten path that led past the well and a rail fence that led to an orchard. We had stopped at the kitchen to put salt in our pockets in anticipation of dining on green apples once we reached the orchard, our favorite retreat. In the middle of the orchard was the largest apple tree, I'm sure, in the whole wide world. Its strong arms reached out and bowed to the ground in perfect symmetry.

The tree was old, as if it had always been there and never seemed to stop growing, "Surely planted by Johnny Appleseed on his way west at least a century before," Mother said.

Before we could climb its trunk, we had to crawl on our bellies beneath the outer limbs. The ground was carpeted with fallen fruit, bruised, worm-eaten and blown by the wind; the birds and the bees feasted on this fallen fruit and their buzzing and singing created a symphony in the air. Crawling along, we filled our pockets with green apples still wet with dew. Reaching the massive trunk we began to climb up and up; then high in the branches with still a great canopy of leaves overhead, we settled down comfortably on one large limb. It was cool and lovely here, the leaves barely moving in the gentle breeze, each leaf quivering as if it had a mind of its own.

A pair of bluebirds with red breasts were busy feeding their little family in a nest out of reach. The nest was full of little tiny birds with mouths larger than their bodies. I said to Goldie, "I don't see how their parents could love them, they're so ugly."

Goldie spoke out of her wisdom (she was now eleven years old and I was only eight), "Our parents would love us even if we were ugly." I thought Mother should start putting more cucumber cream on my freckles that I thought ugly, even though Mother called them sun kisses. Humbly I bowed to Goldie's wisdom. Wasn't she the smartest girl in school? Everybody said so. Settling down, we took some apples from our pockets, polished them on our sleeves, sprinkled them with salt, and took great juicy bites.

I suddenly realized I had bitten the head off a wiggly worm; I spit it out and started over.

Goldie said, "Let's play 'Let's Pretend'," our favorite game. Then I said, "What did you do last night? Did you go to the Queen's ball?"

Goldie said, "Yes, the Prince came for me on a great big horse with black mane and flashing black eyes."

"What did you wear?" She said, "I wore a golden lace dress trimmed in diamonds and pearls and it had a train about twelve feet long and I had a gold crown of jewels on my head and we danced the night away and the Queen said I was the most beautiful girl there."

Now it was my turn. I said, "My Prince came for me at sundown on a great white horse with mane and tail as white as snow and I wore a silver lace gown and had renamed myself 'Sylvia,' and I had violets and buttercups in my hair. The sleeves of my gown were large and flowing like butterfly wings and the skirt was so full I could hardly walk in it.

My Prince and I rode to the forest to a fairies' dance, and I danced to the music of harps." Then I paused thinking my story needed something more dramatic, so I said, "When my prince brought me home, he put his arms around me and kissed me tenderly on the lips."

With this remark, Goldie's eyes popped open wide, she gasped for breath and put her hand over her heart and whispered, "Francie, you don't know what you have done! Now you are in the 'family way' and you will have dozens of children!" Then I said, "Goldie, you've got to be funnin' me!" "No, it's the gospel truth," she said. "Goldie, who told you?" "Well, Ruth told me." "And who told Ruth?" "Nellie told Ruth." "And who told Nellie?" "Annie told Nellie, and I think it must be true because Annie is our oldest sister."

"My life is ruined," I thought; "No prince will want a girl that's been in the 'family way' and I'll die an old maid." The terrifying moment passed and then I laughed and remembered I was only eight years old and playing "Let's Pretend."

9

Drought but Christmas Anyway

Spring didn't seem to start off right this year. Like a wounded bird it fluttered, floundered, ran on for a hopeful spell and then, unbelievably expired.

It had been rather a mild winter, but when the 21st of March came along, spring roared in, dark-browed, with chilly fingers and frosty breath.

The wind blew day in, day out, for weeks. It howled around the corners of the house, screamed at the windows, clawed at every loose shingle and board. Then it rushed off, sweeping the tree-tops without purpose, angrily in all directions. With each gust we thought the roof would surely go, or else the entire house with us trapped in it would lift and soar away perhaps never to come to rest again on solid ground. The very sound of it pulled and stretched our nerves as bloody tight as a coonskin on a pointed board. Even our Ozark hills appeared to undulate as though rocked by inner conflict.

Father, Mother, and we eight children took turns feeding the hungry stoves in the kitchen and front room, stuffing them with wood as though we were stoking a locomotive on a cross country race. Yet their red-hot sides never seemed to warm the corners of our log house where the wind, coming through the chinking between the logs, fought and conquered it. We hovered close to the stoves, feet on the fenders, turning often to toast first one side then the other. We girls bashfully would lift our skirts in the back to warm cold cheeks, while the boys shamelessly massaged their icy posteriors.

The cattle stood shivering and bedraggled in the shelter of the barn, tails tucked in between bony hips. When they ventured forth to forage in the stubble of the dried cornfields the wind ruffled their winter coats, making them look even more ragged and gaunt.

I remember all of us going about our chores with our breaths billowing out like steam from a teakettle. Father had a heavy red mustache and the moisture from his breath would freeze on it and fringe it with dainty icicles. I recall him coming in with ice-coated logs and throwing them in the woodbox behind the stove. The melting ice formed puddles of water on the floor, offending our old tabby cat who slept there. I remember being amused when Father would kindle the fire so carefully, then when he got the flame going, how he would lift the lid from the stove, spit tobacco juice on the sad little flame and nearly extinguish it.

One or the other of us was always suffering from a cold: coughing, hacking, or wiping red noses. Mother would line us up at night, dose us with pine tar cough medicine, rub our chests with goose grease, and give us a stick of horehound candy to suck on when we went to bed. Sometimes she would hang a nugget of asafetida around our necks. To us it smelled like a mixture of garlic and sheep-dip. As she put this horrible stuff around our necks she would say, "Anything that smells that bad must be good for you."

We missed a lot of school that winter, not only because of sickness, but also for lack of warm clothing. Coats that were a close fit in the fall were now too small to be buttoned and were out at the elbows. Though we had started the school term each with a new pair of shoes, they were now worn through to their uppers. Mother mended every moment she had to spare; yet we always managed to keep ahead of her in wearing out our clothes.

The first day of April, our school closed for the year because the other children in the hills were having the same problems as we were.

The bitter weather continued unabated for several weeks. A warm sun finally came out but it was intermittently blacked out by high-flying clouds speeding across the sky, daring it to show its face. Finally, courageously and gloriously, things began to bloom. Almost all at once the lilac, plum, and peach trees in the orchard, and the dogwood, redbud and wild crabapple in the forest burst forth.

Then it began to rain. It rained for two weeks without ceasing. The earth drank its fill and when it could hold no more the water ran over in muddy streams down every gully and every little slope. Our shoes were sodden all the time and sloshed when we walked. They came apart at the seams, ran over at the heels, shrank and dried to half their size when we put them close to the fire. Dean's Creek, circling our farm, roared and tumbled over its boulders and gnawed away at its banks. At last the rain slowed down to a drizzle, quiet and steady. That night it turned freezing cold, encasing every bud, branch and blossom with a thick coat of crystal. The ground was a sheet of ice bristling with hoarfrost. I was too young to appreciate the disaster that would follow such a freeze—particularly to our orchard which was now nipped in the bud. I remember crawling on my hands and knees under the huge lilac bushes and sipping on the icicles that hung like tinsel from the lavender blossoms above. The forest was filled with the sound of popping and cracking of limbs as they broke from their tree trunks from the weight of the ice on them.

The next day the sun came out and tinted the ice-covered landscape pink and gold, and I wondered if it would be possible for Father to paint such a breathtaking scene. In a few hours the ice began to melt, exposing the new leaves and petals that were soon blackened as if a fire had swept over the land. As irrevocable as death, spring, like the Lord of Lords, had given and then taken away.

Then there was that long interval of waiting until the fields became dry and warm enough to plow and plant. Now we must work feverishly from morning until night sowing crops that were already late, too late we feared, for the usual spring showers to sprout the seed. The weather was simply contrary. Now there was no rain at all. Each day Father and Mother would worry a little more. The sun blazed down fiercely day after day, baking the earth hard, cracking and curling the clods in the plowed fields. When sprouts managed to burst through the dry crust above, they only came up in patches with bare spots in between. So the tedious job of replanting was begun. Every row had to be gone over and holes dug with pointed sticks so the seed could be planted carefully in the right place. We spent days at this task, and while performing it we would cast worried looks at the sky, mop damp foreheads, or lift hats or bonnets to scratch puzzled head, wondering if it was ever going to rain. Those last seeds we planted never came up at all. Since we had no more to plant we surrendered the fields to the sun and wind.

Father threw open the kitchen door one morning and called to Mother. "Mama! Old Maud's down in the barn. Come and see what you think is wrong with her."

We owned only two horses—Old Maud and Chester. Old Maud was a sorrel with a white star on her forehead. Although we called her Old Maud, she was in her prime, a fine worker and a good brood mare who was to bring us a colt this spring. It was not quite her time so there was evidently something else wrong with her. We loved the mare. Of the two she was the one we could ride. Chester was temperamental and mean, fast at kicking his heels, quick to bare his teeth, rear and paw at us. We younger ones could never get near him. If he had been the one who was sick it would not have been nearly the blow that this was. But here was gentle and patient Old Maud lying on her side on a bed of hay with her stomach now mountainous with bloat between her slender neck and flanks. Her soft eyes rolled back in an agony of pleading. Her breath came swiftly.

"It's colic, I think," Mother said. "If only we can get something warm down her she might be all right. let's do what we can."

The struggle for Old Maud's life began. Blankets were heated and spread over her. Raw eggs were beaten and warmed and forced down her throat. Father rubbed her with liniment, all the while talking to her soothingly. We children hovered anxiously around the barn door, exhorting her not to die.

By nightfall she seemed no better. Mother sent us off to bed leaving her and Father huddled by lantern light to watch over the mare. Sometime during the night she died. Tired and worn, Father and Mother told us about it at the breakfast table. This tragedy left us without a team to do the plowing, to pull the wagon to market, and all the other things needed for the farm, and it banished my dreams of a baby colt racing across the meadow to nuzzle my hand.

As we were dwelling on the magnitude of our loss, Mother, thinking as Robert Ruark observed, "When something of value is taken away there must be something else to replace it or else the spirit falters," began to make plans for the purchase of another horse.

Let's be very sparing with the cream, Annie and Nellie, when you skim it, and save every spoonful of it to sell. Then we'll sell that last large ham we have in the smokehouse. And John, if you can find a couple of house to paint, I think we'll make out all right. Ruth and Goldie, you know Mrs. Traw wants you to help her with the washing and ironing. Surely she'll give you at least fifty cents a day." Mother went on to say, "Jim, you and Paul can skin Old Maud and take her hide to town. We should get something for it."

Paul began to turn green and looked as if he was about to throw up. Before he could voice an objection Mother noticed and remembered how softhearted he was. She smiled.

"On second thought, Garsy, you and Jim can skin Old Maude."

Eager to help, I piped up, "What can I do?"

"You can do the churning, feed the chickens, set the table, make the beds, bring in chips for the fire, gather the eggs, slop the hogs, sweep the floors, and turn the grindstone for Father." At the age of seven I suddenly wished I was dead.

The two boys rose, took their caps from pegs behind the door, took out their pocket knives, found the whetstones on the window ledge, spit on them and began to sharpen their blades in a circular motion, so they could skin Old Maud. The girls began to gather up the dishes. I went and climbed up in the big apple tree and hid.

The summer wore on, and still no sign of rain. Since there was no work to be done in the fields, Father decided that he and the boys would clear the five-acre tract below the house along the branch leading to Dean's Creek. When cleared, this would give us a fertile new field for planting next year. For days Father and the boys grubbed out young oak sprouts, pulled out stumps, and piled the brush in huge heaps scattered about the five acres, while we girls gathered the rocks from the newly cleared land, which we carried in our aprons to the edge of the field.

One calm evening it was decided to set all the brush piles on fire to get them out of the way. Dry as the brush was, it exploded when the fires caught and flames shot roaring into the sky. Then from nowhere a stiff wind came up and began to toss the fiery branches about. In seconds it seemed that the whole woods below the house was on fire in several places. My sister, Goldie, and I, standing on the front porch overlooking the forest were wide-eyed in awe and fright at the burning spectacle below. Father, Garsy, Jim, and Paul came running up the hill shouting excitedly that the whole forest was on fire, as if we didn't know.

Mother and the older girls, Annie, Nellie, and Ruth, were in the kitchen finishing up the supper dishes. When they heard all the noise they rushed to the door. I had never seen Father so agitated.

"We may have to flee the farm and make for the creek to save our lives," he said. We were all in agreement, except Mother.

"Let's don't go until we have to, at least not give up without a fight. Let's gather up rakes, shovels, water, and towsacks and try to clean a path on the north side of the hill and backfire it. If it gets as far as the rail fence, it'll spread to the house. Then we'll have to run for it, and God help us."

So the nightmare struggle to control the fire began. Madly we raked leaves and cleared away dead brush to cut a wide swath across the hill. The flames continued to shoot skyward, leaping from treetop to treetop, coming ever nearer to where we were. We stood ready to use the water-soaked towsacks if the fire came any nearer. Then above the din someone shouted, "I think the wind's changing. Looks like the flames are blowing the other way." We paused and watched breathlessly. It was true. The wind had changed and was sweeping the flames back instead of towards us. The fire began to die out for lack of fuel in the charred forest behind it.

"Thank God," said Father. But we all stood mute, faces blackened, hair singed, too tired to comment on the narrow escape we had. Providence was surely on our side that night. Wearily we trudged home, too exhausted to bathe the smoke and grime from our bodies. We took pillow and quilts and made pallets on the lawn in the front yard. The house was too filled with smoke to allow for sleeping.

Summer crept onward and still no sign of rain. A dull enervation of body and spirit ruled our existence. A misery not only of our own, but of our animals as well. Their restless, glassy eyes, protruding ribs, and gaunt flanks make them a pitiful sight. Their plaintive cries for food and water haunted our every moment. The springs had all dried up and there was only one water hole left, almost a mile away. Sometimes we had to beat the weakened stock to make them stand up so that we could drive them to this water hole, to drink. Our chickens were no larger than quail. We managed to keep them alive by feeding them weeds cut up in buttermilk.

It was no comfort that most of our neighbors were facing the same problems and worse. Many of those to the north of us, deep in the hills, were on the verge of starvation. When we would visit with them, their first words would be, "When do you reckon it'll rain?" Mother would weep that we had nothing to share with them.

Finally came the time when our food was so scarce that it had to be portioned out a tablespoon at a time. At first Mother made a game of it but after awhile we tired of the game from the monotony of our limited and skimpy diet. What would normally be our harvest time, we spent in searching the woods for small game, rabbits, squirrel, and possum. But even they were scarce. As the cold weather set in we began to kill our domestic animals for food one by one.

The holiday seasons inexorably approached us. Halloween and Thanksgiving were not mentioned. The drought and the devastation left by the fire confronted us everywhere we turned. What had been a beautiful forest below the house on the east was a cemetery of charred limbs. Only the blackened trunks of trees rose above the ruins, grim monuments to the glory that was once theirs. To the west were the dusty fields we plowed so tediously with a one-horse plow for winter wheat, but where the seed was to come from, we didn't know. Even if we had seed there still was no sign of rain.

When Christmas drew near we had only a few chickens left, a turkey gobbler, several turkey hens, one brood sow, two milk cows, and the gelding, Chester. We never raised the $25.00 to purchase another horse so that we could have a team.

The day before Christmas we took stock of all the food there was in the house. There were some sweet potatoes, small and very shriveled, a peck of flour and some cornmeal, a few gallons of molasses in mason jars, some jars of blackberries and peaches left over from the year before. It was a poor outlook for Christmas dinner. We hadn't had any eggs for weeks, but that day two hens decided to lay, and Mother pounced on the eggs as if they were golden nuggets, meaning to make some cookies or a cake with them. She had been skimming the thin milk carefully hoping that we could churn the cream off it so that we all might have a pat of butter with our Christmas dinner.

To give the house a touch of Christmas spirit the girls gathered a basket full of persimmons and placed them in a bowl on the kitchen table. Goldie, who was, next to me, the youngest, made a wreath of cedar boughs and red berries from buck brush and tacked it on the front door.

Christmas Eve, after a scanty supper of potato soup, cornbread, and sorghum, Mother gathered up a few scraps to take out to feed our brood sow. I followed her out to the pigpen that joined the poultry yard. I stood close by and watched as she threw the scraps into the hog trough. Our turkey gobbler, in the poultry yards, starved and greedy, spotted the food in the trough, sailed over the fence, perched on the side of the trough and began to peck at the scraps. In a flash the sow pounced on the gobbler and began eating it alive. Frantically, Mother picked up a heavy stick and ran waving and shouting into the pigpen. Now with the taste of fresh blood, the vicious animal turned on Mother ready to charge and kill. In fear, Mother let fly the heavy stick and hit the sow squarely between the eyes. The animal stood rigid, then slowly collapsed and lay shuddering in death. I found my voice and began to scream. The family, attracted by the noise, came running from the house. When Father saw this dead animal he quickly pulled out his knife and slit its jugular vein so it would bleed properly and the meat could then be saved. Mother began to weep hysterically, appalled at what she had done. To have lost our only turkey gobbler and broodsow in a matter of seconds was heartbreaking. Father gathered her in his arms and comforted her, "There, there, now Mother, it's all right," until she ceased weeping. Drying her eyes on her apron she said, "Well, at least well have fresh pork for Christmas dinner."

After an interim of confusion the boys built a fire and brought water from the well to scald and dress out the animal. Hours later, it seemed, the meat was cut up and stored in the smokehouse, hung on wires from the ceiling out of reach of varmints.

We all sat around the fire, strangely quiet, watching the flames create patterns of light on the darkened ceiling. The lamp was turned too low for darning or reading or drawing on one's slate, as coal oil for the lamp was something we could hardly afford these days. The boys no longer seemed to derive any pleasure from their violins and banjos. So there the ten of us sat, talking in low voices about the loss of the gobbler and the sow. It was on these creatures that we placed such hope for increasing our stock in the spring.

An hour, perhaps, crawled by. It was Father's habit to stand on the front porch for awhile before going to bed, chew a cud of tobacco, look up at the sky for signs of rain, and perhaps to relieve himself. This evening, conforming to habit, he rose, put on his mackinaw and went outside. No sooner had the door closed behind him when he began to whoop and holler as though he had taken leave of his senses and gone completely mad. We fell over each other in our hurry to get to the porch to see what was wrong. When we saw what had affected him, we too whooped and hollered, for we found the landscape blanketed with what was at least a foot of snow. Large flakes were drifting softly on our hills. The fence posts wore white caps of fleece. The rooftops of the barn and outbuildings snuggled under ermine garments. The beautiful snow clung to the tree limbs, weighting them down. We, like Father, went wild with joy. We rolled in it, washed each others faces in it, hurled snowballs, stuffed snow down each others necks. Father, caught up in all the frolic, pelted Mother generously, she laughing all the while, and managing a few good shots of her own.

Moisture in any form would have been welcome, but snow on this Christmas Eve was truly a gift from Heaven. It was as if the very sky had said, "Renew your faith. This is your reward for your long suffering."

In the midst of the hilarity Mother cried, "Listen!" and her face glowed with a happy light we had not seen for many a day. "The bells," she said. "Do you hear them ringing? It's the church bells in the big cities tolling the midnight hour. You can hear them all over the world—ringing out the joy of Christmas."

We all heard them, although we knew there were no bells within miles of us, isolated as we were in these remote hills. A sense of awe seemed to grip us. The quiet of the snow drifting down and the peaceful landscape made our world look good to us. Good and dear, and best of all, ours. Without a word, we joined hands and began to sing. "Joy to the World, the Lord Has Come, and Heaven and Nature Sing, and Heaven and Nature Sing."

When we paused; Father, glancing at Mother's feet, shouted in amazement, "Mother, you're barefooted." Mother lifted her skirts and we all screamed with laughter at the sight of her pink bare toes sunk in the soft snow.

"Goodness, gracious. So I am," she said, and ran for the house.

We followed her in, brushing off the snow, pushing and shoving each other in our happiness. We were soon dry and warm again, but reluctant to go to bed, sorry to end the first happy time in oh, so many months.

Next morning we were awakened by the ring of a cowbell at the foot of the stairs.

"Rise and shine," called our parents, "It's a beautiful day. Merry Christmas, my children." They kissed us one by one as we came down the steps. We peeped out the windows at the sun shining on the snow where it sparkled like a million diamonds.

"Look," someone, said. "Our stockings are hanging on the foot of Mother's bed, and they have something in them!" I made a dive for mine, while everyone else exclaimed in wonder, "How come? We didn't hang up our stockings. We just knowed it was no use."

I emptied mine in my lap. Out rolled the largest orange I had ever seen and a peppermint stick as thick as my thumb. How had our parents managed it? There had been no money for weeks. We looked incredulously at each other. Even Father's face looked startled. Mother shot him a twinkly glance, then made an anxious confession.

"It was no miracle, just one of Father's paintings. I sold it to Mr. Thornton and got five dollars for it." We looked at Father, full of pride. How wonderful to think that without his fine talent we would have had no Christmas presents. Father laughed and said, "Mr. Thornton got skunked, I reckon, if you sold him the last one I did. I meant to burn it. I was out of the color green and had to make some by putting grease on the old brass kettle and letting it corrode. Hope it doesn't turn rancid and the flies don't blow it when warm weather sets in."

We all laughed now, sniffed our oranges and licked the peppermint sticks, while Mother, sighing with relief, made for the kitchen. Father's prayer was thankfully short when we were seated around the table. We had a huge breakfast of fresh pork, hot biscuits and natural gravy. But the best part of the meal came last.

Mother told Ruth to go outside to get our dessert. Ruth returned with a large bowl of rich, fragrant ice cream made from fresh snow, our two eggs, some cream, and flavored with vanilla and our last jar of peaches. "A treat straight from Heaven," Mother declared as she dished out heaping spoonfuls onto our plates. We ate until we couldn't eat another bite. Finished, Mother folded her hands under her chin and smiled confidently. "Things will grow now. I just know next year'll be a good year. I feel it in my bones."

We sat quietly, agreeing with her. We had almost as much confidence in Mother's bones as we had faith in God.

"You know," Mother began again. "People in the city have only one tree decorated for Christmas, while we have hundreds. And all they have are small winter scenes on Christmas cards, while everywhere we look there is a scene more beautiful than any artist could paint, including you, John. Yes, it's a wonderful place, the country at Christmas time."

Father nodded. "Things will grow now, I'll bet, now that the blamed drouth is broken. We don't have any money for seed for planting, but I hear tell some of the bottomlanders have enough seed left to spare, if we earn it. Now I'll tell you what let's do. let's help anyone who needs us to plow or to help put in gardens, or split rails for fences, and ask them to pay us in field and garden seed, and eggs and settin' hens. All that will give us a fresh start in the spring. Some have offered to help us, but if we earn it, that way we'll not be beholden to anyone. We must hold our heads up high. Pride is a mighty important thing to hold on to. A body hadn't ever ought to turn loose of his pride. It's worth more than a buck in your jeans any day. People with pride can weather almost any hardship."

While the older ones talked about plans I thought of how Father's fine talent for painting had enabled us to have our stockings filled on this Christmas day.

"Some day," I said to myself, "I'll be able to paint like Father. And perhaps if I'm as good an artist as he is, I, too, may sell a painting for $5.00, maybe more. With this money I can buy my friends back in the high hill country a peppermint stick and an orange just like I found in my stocking this morning."

And I thought how lucky I was to have so much; an artistic Father, a cheerful courageous Mother, nice big brothers and sisters who, I felt sure, could lick anything.

My eyes went to the window, still dreaming. I secretly wondered if any place I would ever go in the world outside could be more beautiful than the farm that day, all aglitter with snow—like a Christmas card, only prettier, as Mother said. Or if any world could be any more secure than the one right there with the faces of the ones I loved, around this table, all so near and dear to me.

10

Little Pearl

My world at first was very small, hardly more than a few miles in any direction. Except for a few times when we went to Brumley, which was eight miles away, or Richland, which was thirteen miles away, I never ventured beyond this perimeter but a couple of times. On these occasions, I learned that the higher one went back into the hills the worse the conditions were in which the people lived. On my second venture forth, I visited a little girlfriend named Pearl. The year after the drouth my world became a little larger.

Little Pearl was the closet neighbor child my age and she was one of my dearest playmates. She was one of ten children of a high ridge farmer and the only one who was "right bright," for it seemed her mother had married her uncle, and what this had to do with the fact the children were a little backward, I didn't know. All I knew was I loved little Pearl and that I thought she was the most beautiful child I had ever seen and that there was nothing wrong with her. I though she was rightly named. She had the pure iridescent quality of a pearl. Her hair was silky as milkweed floss, her eyes cerulean blue and her skin like the petals of a primrose. She had to tramp about four times the distance to school than we did, the last leg of her journey being by our house. Mother would go out and get her by the hand, bring her in, wash her face, comb her hair and give her gravy, fried potatoes and fried apples. She knew little Pearl had had no breakfast. Then hand in hand Pearl and I would traipse off to school laughing, talking, and enjoying each other as only two contemporaries can.

Little Pearl was very thin. Her tiny arms and legs were like cornstalks sticking out of her sleeveless sack of a dress. Her neck was so scrawny it seemed too frail even to hold up her small head with its mop of hair. We must have made quite a contrast, what with my sturdy body and bronzed skin that Mother kept trying to bleach by rubbing cucumber on my face, neck and arms.

In school little Pearl learned fast and even though she too, had to borrow her books, she seemed always to have her lessons ready when the teacher asked our class to rise and pass to the bench in front of her desk to recite.

Often Mother would gather up baskets of food which we could hardly spare and go visit little Pearl's family, but she would not allow me to go there. This neither Pearl nor I could understand.

Every day during the school year, little Pearl would come into our kitchen on the way home from school and while we sopped up a plate of cold cornbread and molasses she would beg Mother to let me go home with her and spend the night. Mother would either avoid the subject or insist on little Pearl spending the night with me, instead. This went on for two or three years as I remember. Then one day Mother gave me a long penetrating look, and to my surprise, said I could go. Little Pearl and I squealed and jumped up and down, hugged each other in ecstasy, and went running off over the hill.

It was a long four miles to her house, over rocky balds and through scrub oak, across rail fences, down deep washed gullies, and across clay fields, bare even of poorman's grass. Then we came in sight of their shack standing gray and forlorn in the midst of buck brush and pawpaw patches. When I first saw the house, I thought it must be the barn or granary, so small was the one room downstairs and the loft above. The house had been built of logs once, but as they decayed it had been patched with bark, boards, mud and rocks. There was no glass, no screens in the window, nor a single piece of furniture other than an old stove with one leg gone and replaced by a rock. Some boards across a stump served as a table. There was an old rag of a quilt over the doorframe. The door apparently had fallen to dust long ago.

Naked children played in the dust of the yard. Water and pus ran from their eyes, and there were sores around their mouths where the flies sat in black clusters and sipped. The stench of the house was so unbelievable I was tempted to bolt and run for home. On a pallet of corn husks in the corner lay a rag of a man, who, when little Pearl said, "Pa, I want you should meet my friend Francis Wright," looked at me through bleary eyes, took a long pull at a crockery jug and said in measured politeness, "Proud to meet'cha. Might proud to meet'cha."

I had never seen a man drunk before, but I knew what was wrong. He began to apologize for the house, for the condition of the children and for himself. Finally, he just threw up his hands, got slowly up off the pallet and staggered off into the brush and did not come back at all that night.

His wife sat on the doorstep, her hair stringing down over her face. She had on only a Mother Hubbard. She was filthy and bare footed, and continuously nursed a baby who pulled at her dry and shriveled looking breast.

The other children crept closer and closer to me, began to inspect my dress, and tilting their heads, looked up at me with watery eyes, seeming to examine every inch of me as though I were from another world. I had thought Grandma Abbots house was decrepit, but now I remembered how clean and cozy and homey it was compared to this.

I was ashamed of our log house whose logs were finally covered with weather boarding that never got painted because Father was so busy painting other people's homes, or because we couldn't afford the paint, but our walls were plastered and wallpapered now. Our roof leaked and the floorboards were worn thin and the windows were cracked, but it was a palace compared to this.

The weary mother mixed a pan of gravy made of possum grease, flour, water, and wild onions, cooked it, and we and the flies sat down to eat around the makeshift table and everyone dived into the gravy with their hands. I ate along with them for I was afraid I would offend little Pearl if I refused. At dark, little Pearl and I, and a couple of the girls who could not talk but only jibbered, crept up to the loft to sleep. Little Pearl tried to stir the cornhusk pallets into a more comfortable bed for me and we cuddled down together.

We lay there whispering and talking. "You know, Frances," little Pearl said, "Pa and Ma ain't rightly married. They just live together. Ain't that a fright? I love Pa, though. He's never anything but kind and sometimes he brings me a purty rock or a bluebird's aig, and sometimes he tells me stories about where he camed from, way back east. Pa's smart. He's the one who wants me to go to school. But he's got a weakness. He just can't get along 'thout corn squeezings. Poor Pa." And she sighed and went to sleep while I lay and looked at the Milky Way through the window and wondered if there was a God up there who looked after little children like these.

The next morning without any breakfast at all, little Pearl and I started off to school. When we stopped at our house, Mother had a platter of fried mush in the oven waiting for us. She had that, "I told you so," look on her face so when she asked me how I had enjoyed my visit, I said, "Fine, fine," both of us knowing that I lied, and me now having more respect for Mother's judgment.

Little Pearl didn't come to school for quite some time. There was a knocking on our door one cold wintry day. I had just gotten home from school and was hanging up my wraps. I was huffing and puffing and laughing over a race I had had with Goldie. In fact, I had left her somewhere in the cornfield above Dean's Creek. Before I could turn around, Mother had answered the door. I saw Pearl's father, with matted hair, hands blue from the cold, and elbows sticking out of a coat much too small. Old, worn-out shoes covered his stockingless feet. Tears streamed down his pinched face as he shifted from foot to foot to keep warm.

"Please, Mrs. Wright," he begged, "Can you and Frances come home with me. My old woman thinks Pearl is dying, and she keeps calling for Francie."

"I'll come," said Mother, "But Frances just got home from school and it's too far for her to walk after being at school all day."

The thought of my little friend dying frightened me so. I sat down weakly on the stairs and began to tremble. I couldn't think of a thing to say to the poor man to comfort him.

Mother was swiftly gathering up her wraps and putting half of our supper into a market basket. She scooped a pan of cornbread into the basket, collected some eggs from the cupboard, added a fruit jar of milk and another jar of canned peaches. In the skillet back of the stove was some fried squirrel. Half of this she also put into the basket. She said, "Come on. let's hurry."

They were almost to the top of the hill before I came to my senses. I grabbed my coat and ran to the smokehouse where I gathered up two of the best apples I could find, even though they were quite withered and frostbitten. Clutching them I ran wildly after Mother and the man.

"Wait for me. Wait for me," I called. They stopped and waited until I caught up with them. "If Pearl asked for me, I must go to her," I announced.

Mother shook her head gently. "No, Francie. Mind me now. Go home and help with supper and the dishes. I'll take care of Pearl tonight. If she's all right tomorrow, you can stay home from school and go see her."

I handed the apples to Pearl's father. "Here," I said, "One for you and one for little Pearl, and tell her I'll see her tomorrow."

Sometime in the night, Mother came in quietly, I raised up and whispered, "Can I go see Pearl tomorrow?"

"No," Mother said, "Tomorrow will never come for little Pearl."

I turned and wept bitterly into my pillow.

Father made her a beautiful coffin and put a white ribbon in her hair. Then he preached my little friend's funeral with great tenderness. I loved him for the way he said, "How sweet and fair she must seem to the Heavenly Father. How lovely she would be dwelling among the angels forever." When she was lowered into her grave, I slipped my hand into her Pa's in an effort to comfort him, for had little Pearl not said that she loved him? Tears fell on both our hands.

The next time I ventured further from the farm, it was with Father. We had another disastrous experience together, but this time Father couldn't blame me for what happened. In fact, he longed to apologize, I think, but was too proud and too embarrassed to say a word.

It all started with the incident of the blacksnake getting into bed with Nellie and a wasp stinging me on the arm in the middle of the night. I was asleep in my trundle bed under the stairs, when I was awakened by a stinging pain on my arm. Something stabbed me again and again. I began to scream at the top of my voice. I thought Mother would never get the lamp lit to come to my rescue. It was a big black wasp that she knocked off my arm and killed with the heel of her shoe while I sobbed in pain. The children were all tumbling down the stairs and someone got cold water and baking soda and applied cold packs to my arm while Jim held me and tried to divert my mind with a story. Finally, though my arm began to swell, the pain eased and everyone went back to bed.

In the quiet I heard a screech owl, out in the big cedar and a mockingbird full of rapture trilling his repertoire over and over again. I thought he'd better shut up or the screech owl would get him. Those things always frightened me with their weird screams. I shivered and pulled the covers over my head. As I started to doze off, another piercing scream shattered the night. This time it came from the girls' room upstairs. Mother's feet hit the floor with a bang while Father grumbled, "What in tarnation is the matter now?"

Mother hurried upstairs carrying the lamp, with Father following close behind in his long underwear, in too big a hurry to don his britches. I followed on bare feet. When we went into the girls' room we all began to yell. A huge blacksnake was wrapped around Nellie's leg. It was clasped so tight her foot was turning purple. Father rose to the occasion. He forced the snake from Nellie's leg with one hand while holding it with the other to keep it from biting him or Nellie. A blacksnake isn't deadly poisonous, but can cause a leg or arm to swell double its size if it strikes. Father flung the slimy, ugly thing out the screenless window while Nellie went into hysterics, Annie fainted, and somebody fell down the stairs hurrying to get water. Ruth cussed. Paul prayed quietly, and I began to cry again. Goldie had climbed to the top of Father's big trunk and stood cowering against the wall, her eyes as large as saucers.

Mother, who rarely spoke up to Father, lit into him for fair this time. She turned to him with flashing eyes.

"John!" she yelled. "It's all your fault. I told you we have simply got to have screens on the windows and door. I'm sick and tired of the varmints wanderin' in and out of the house."

"Now, now, Lily. You know we ain't got no money for screen wire."

"Then paint a picture and sell it so's we can do something to protect ourselves. Next thing you know a copperhead will crawl in bed with somebody and kill them!"

"All right. All right," said Father trying to calm her along with the rest. "Tomorrow I start a picture. A doctor in Richland said he wanted one of a waterfall. Just settle down now, everybody. Were gonna do somethin' about this. Just don't worry!"

I don't know how long it took for the rest to settle down, but I couldn't go to sleep for thinking that if Father started a picture, would I be allowed to go along.

At the breakfast table the next morning I made a big show of passing Father everything first and fought Goldie to get to sit beside him. I reached over and pinched her hard on the arm and when she dodged, I scooted in quick next to Father. As Father served himself, his cheeks bunching up in a grin, he said, "Yes, Frances, you can go with me today." This rated a hug around the neck and I squeezed him 'till his face was purple.

Off we went down the hill towards the creek, Father walking free and easy carrying a fresh new canvas made by stretching oil cloth over a frame (he could not afford real canvas), and me carrying the paint box, following in his tracks on bare feet with soles as tough as hooves.

"Tell you what let's do. The doctor wants a picture of a waterfall. Let's follow Dean's Creek upstream and see if we can find a nice falls to sketch. I never followed it too far, but I betcha there's some pretty ones up at the head of it."

While the sun climbed high in the sky, we followed the ever narrowing stream up and up towards its estuary. We went through tall patches of reeds, scrambled over the boulders, slid down deep banks, and skirted pools of still water where willows leaned over to admire their reflection. We climbed over fallen trees and up steeper hills. Mourning doves cooed their mournful call. Robins ran swift spurts along the ground, thrusting out rosy breasts and bobbing black heads. A covey of quail, disturbed by our footsteps, rose on whirring wings in rapid flight. We saw an owl, round eyed, staring out of a hollow place in a tree. Redbirds and bluejays flashed their vivid colors in and out among the thickets. Woodpeckers hammered frantic heads in search of borers. Cottontails leaped over logs and squirrels chattered and scolded. It was a radiant day and I was in Heaven. Ever we followed the glistening stream upward.

The sun was straight overhead and our shadows pointed north, indicating it was noon, when we heard a roar and saw through the trees a tumbling waterfall, pounding mossy rocks and sending up misty sprays in rainbow colors. We stood enthralled. Father began to look for the best view to sketch it.

"Let's climb to the top first and see how high it is, and then come back," Father said.

That was our big mistake. We climbed almost hand over hand up the steep hill to one side of the falls. As we came over the top out of the jungle of wild fern, bleeding heart and bluebells, the sky opened up. We found ourselves looking down the barrel of a shotgun and behind it two of the meanest and beadiest eyes I have ever seen with a voice to match.

"Watch it, he said. Whatcha doin' around chere? Lookin' fer moonshine?"

"Why, no," said Father politely. "My daughter and I just wanted to paint the pretty waterfall down there. I hope you don't mind."

The face, with tobacco-stained beard, opened up and yelled, "Grandpappy, here a feller says he want to see our waterfall!" and he spit, still holding the gun steadily on us, and chuckling in an evil sort of way.

We looked around at the clearing. Buildings like a buzzard's nest nearly covered it. It was a wretched jumble of barns, granaries, pens, broken wagon wheels, and the like, and one couldn't tell the house from the outbuildings so scrambled and tumbled together were they all. They were made of rough-hewn weather-beaten logs and curled shingled roofs with crooked stovepipes. It was a picture right out of a Halloween nightmare. One felt like a flock of bats and witches might take off any minute for the moon on broomsticks. I held tight to Father's hand. Suddenly we were surrounded by dozens of hound dogs, mean, mangy and growling low. Also surrounding us was a herd of vagrant men, mean and mangy-looking as the hound dogs; bearded, with ragged overalls, pointed black hats, and barefooted. At first they just stood and looked. The dogs, tired of barking and baying, slunk back to their holes under the house. Then a tiny little twig of a man, bent almost double from age, with a bushy pillow of a beard, eyes mere swollen slits, and a head as bald as an onion, pointed a crooked stick at us and said, "You furriners?"

"Why, no," said Father. "We live down the creek a ways and we just wanted to find a pretty waterfall."

Then one young lean giant of a fellow slapped his thigh and said, "Oh, I know him. He's the preacher feller in that thar church down the holler. I seed him through the winders. I axed to see one of his daughters home onc't."

"Lower your gun, Seth," the old one ordered, "and invite the preacher in an' let's see how Godly he is after we fill his gut full o' corn squeezin's. Come on in neighbor, and share some grub with us. You catched us 'bout ready to settle down to dinner." Father refused politely and said, "You people had ought to come to school and church."

"Well now," said the old one. "Iffen you buy 'nough white mule fer us to afford shoes, we might consider it. Anyhow, ain't none of us seed a book since my pappy fit in the Civil War. We don't hanker much fer book larnin'. 'Sides, we'uns got nearly everything chere we need; wimmin, corn squeezin's, huntin', an fishin'."

Father, sparring for time, and still hoping to win them over, took out a square of Beeswax Tobacco and passed it around. They all cut off a chaw and soon the men were jawing 'bout tanning hides, trappin', huntin', and fishin'; and wimmin an' licker. Then the young man who bragged about trying to date Nellie, I believe, said, "I think I'll keep that thar purty tin box you got there. Hit'd be good fer to carry worms."

"I wouldn't do that," said Father quietly, hands in pocket.

My heart began to pound, as I looked around at the bushy faces now surrounding us, belligerent and threatening. Father stood tall and straight, the muscles of his good painting arm bunched. He was fifty-eight, but every inch a man.

Daring Father, the young clumsy giant reached out for the paint box. Father's fist flew out so fast and hard that the young man must have thought he was struck by a bolt of lightning when he found himself laying face downward in the dirt. Father wiped his hands on his hips and said, "I suggest you stay there unless you want to be knocked down again." Outwardly calm, he took me by the hand and turned on his heel. Then he called over his shoulder, "Don't try to spark my daughter either, young feller, or I'll fill your britches full of lead. And you other folk better behave or I'll come an' clean out this hell's nest."

It then occurred to me what a frightening man Father was when angry. I was never so proud, and yet never so absolutely scared in all my life. I fully expected a bullet in our backs as we walked away. But, it was strangely quiet in the clearing, and I thought, "Can it be that they're afraid of Father?" We walked on matter-of-factly until we reached the first low bushes. Then we began to run in earnest. We scrambled down the hill like frightened mice, not even stopping to look at the beautiful waterfall as we took off for home. Father, wiping the sweat from a pale and beaded brow, cautioned me not to say a thing to my brothers and sisters, or even to Mother, saying, "It'd worry your Ma to know such people lived so nearby. If you won't tell," he promised, "well go sketching down the creek tomorrow and maybe well have more luck." My lips were sealed.

Father explained to Mother he hadn't found anything nice to paint. The next day we set off again, but this time we followed the creek downhill towards the wide bottomland farms. Father painted all morning, and I sat on a low stump in the sun-flecked shade, chin in cupped hands, and held my breath at his every stroke. He talked low about why he did this or that, or whistled under his breath, but not once did he mention our harrowing experience of the day before.

This day at noontime, a young neighbor working a binder in a wheat field hollered at us, asking if we would come and have dinner with his folks. Father thanked him, and we followed him to a large neat frame house Father had painted the year before. We had a bounteous feast. Two kinds of potatoes were served, three vegetables, canned pickles, fried chicken, fried pork, and slabs of rhubarb pie. Although the men ate first, I remember there was plenty left for the women and us children.

Generally, before any of us children visited anyone for dinner, Mother always took us aside and gave us a lesson in etiquette. We were sure to pass the food politely, and to hold back and eat slowly, with lips closed, and not to reach all the way across the table. We must wait until everybody was finished before excusing ourselves to leave the table.

She needn't have worried about my good manners. I was so bashful, I could not eat at all, and could only sit quietly with my hands in my lap. Once I got up enough nerve to put a bite of food in my mouth, I found I was unable to swallow. It simply wouldn't go past my throat. So I sat with jaws locked and eyes popping out at all the beautiful food, and could have wept. Never had I had my fill of fried chicken but once, the time I had swum the flood behind Mr. Willoughby, and now when my chance came, I found I could not eat a bite.

After the meal was over, I helped dry the dishes, another thing Mother had always instructed me to do. Then the two little girls and I went out to play, while Father and the men sat for an hour in the cool shade of the porch, and chewed tobacco and talked. The little girls and I slid down the haystack, sucked on long sweet stalks of cane, rode bareback on a fat mare, and petted some white-faced baby calves.

I envied these well-fed girls with sateen bloomers (ashamed of my flour sack ones), and their outdoor privies. We only went behind the hen house or out in the woods. I was jealous of their parent's fat cows and sleek horses and round silos full of green fragrant ensilage. I noticed their white bed spreads, kitchen safes with glass fronts, sugar bowls with lids, their gramophones and their cold, musty parlors.

These children accepted me as an equal, I believe, but I could not accept myself as theirs and because of this, I became a fantastic liar. My tongue loosened and I talked about what wonderful food we had to eat at our house, about my sisters' beautiful clothes, of how much money my father made when he went away on painting trips, of how much grain we got from our nine acres of bottomland (three times more that it could possibly have produced). Of how rich we would be when Father sold his next painting, upping the five dollars he would get for it to two hundred dollars. Sometimes they giggled and whispered behind their hands, so I am quite sure they were not fooled one bit. But the fibs made me feel better.

I might have envied the bottomland children more, but when I saw their men eat first, I thought, "Their women are held in no higher esteem than the ridge woman. What I want for myself is not to be found in either the hill peoples' or the bottomlanders' homes!"

Remembering the sweet-smelling boy and how gallantly he had held the door open for Mother I mused, "Someday, somewhere, someone will hold the door open for me."

Father painted a beautiful picture that day. He and Mother went to Richland in the wagon, sold the painting, and came home with some precious screen wire. So, for the first time we had screen doors and windows to protect us from flies, hornets, bees, and snakes, and rats and mice.

"Someday when I am a famous artist, I will build a house of my own, with screen doors and fine carpets and tall windows like Twelve Corners."

11

I Help Father Make A Coffin

The skies had been cloudy for a week. Although it hadn't rained, everything was damp and soggy from the heavy moisture in the air. The mood of the family matched the sullenness of the weather. I leaned on my elbow, staring out the kitchen window. I hated cloudy days. I wished it would either rain or clear up. I was bored and depressed. I was tired of the family's activities of quilting and shelling corn, making ax handles, playing the violin, reading and all the things the others were doing. I longed for something new and different to do for entertainment. The thought of moving to set the table for supper, or having to listen to the grinding of the cream separator, or the noisy clatter of dishes, irritated me. My nerves were on edge from being confined to the house with a cold, and the damp weather. How I wished something exciting would happen. Mother poked nervously at the fire as she slammed the lids off and on the stove.

"The wood is so damp it won't burn," she complained. "I'll never get supper ready this evening. I promised Cousin Laura I'd be up before dark and bring her something for her cold, and I won't make it if the stove doesn't get hot. It'll be black as pitch out soon." And she glanced anxiously out the window.

The boys shuffled in, not bothering to clean the mud off their feet and slopped milk on to the floor as they lifted the foaming pails on to the workstand. They were sulking because somehow they got roped into the milking chore which they considered to be the girls job.

"Ain't supper ready yet?" they grumbled as they lined up around the table.

Ruth stormed in from where she had been primping by the mirror in the front room. "Can't you wait until the table is set?" With that, she started slamming dishes on the table.

Father came in just before dinner and threw an armload of wood into the woodbox behind the cookstove where it fell with a dull wet plot. He cleared his throat and in a weak attempt to be cheerful, remarked, "Lily, it looks like it's goin' to be clear by morning."

"You've said that every day for a week," Mother snapped as she pulled the cornbread out of the oven and set it down with a bang on the back of the stove.

The meal was finally over. I had sat without an appetite, watching in disgust as the boys stuffed cornbread into their glasses of milk and sopped up molasses and butter with the crusts. The stack of fried rabbit in the middle of the table sickened me. I could still see their raw bloody bodies, and I thought it a sin to kill the dear little helpless creatures. I heartily wished that I never would have to look at fried rabbit again.

Mother rose from the table, put on her overshoes and Father's slicker, and began gathering up her favorite remedies for Cousin Laura's cold.

"Wish you wouldn't go out in such bad night air," Father scolded.

"Oh, pshaw," scoffed Mother. With a toss of her head, she slammed the door and was gone.

The boys slouched upstairs as if their backs were too tired to hold up their galluses.

Goldie got out her slate, spit on it, wiped it clean with her sleeve, and cast a scheming look at me.

"I'll beat you at tic-tac-toe if you'll play with me.

I knew she would beat me, so I refused to play. She started to draw on her slate and while no one was looking, I slipped quietly under the table, one of my favorite retreats. Old Tiger, our cat, was curled up underneath, purring like a well-oiled motor. I stroked his back and he stretched out to receive the full benefit of my petting. Sparks flew from his fur in the semi-darkness and crackled under my hand. I hoped if I sat real still I might escape having to help with the dishes. It was Ruth's turn anyway, I reasoned. For once, however, Nellie and Ruth went about the dishes without quarreling while I enjoyed my privacy.

Soon the kitchen was empty and still. The girls left the lamp lit for Mother and went off to their room to read. I was alone at last. I crawled out from under the table where I had hidden from the task of dishwashing and peered with one eye through the crack in the green door into the front room. The room was empty except for Father, who sat reading the Bible by the light of the lamp on the dresser. A pencil was poised in his hand for jotting down notations on the margin.

Glowing with the satisfaction of having everyone out of the way, a rare treat in our crowded household, I was interrupted in making plans for entertaining myself by a loud knock at the front door. My eyes still glued to the crack in the door, I saw Father rise stiffly from his chair and calmly lay his book on the dresser and proceed to the door. When he opened it, although I couldn't see anyone, I heard a hushed voice say something about a coffin.

Then I head the voice, "Imagine, a little baby. And she's been dead for two days. Nobody knows where her husband is. In the caves, I reckon, gambling away his last nickel. It's a sad thing, and her little baby was dead at her breast."

Father kept exclaiming in an awed voice. "You don't say? What do you know? Sure I'll make the coffin. Give me the measurements. Put the cloth and lumber in the shed." In a moment Father had his coat and cap on and went out the door

Now I was really alone. That was just fine with me, but that one terrifying word, coffin, had taken a little of the joy out of it. I looked about the dimly lit room for some source of entertainment. Finding nothing of immediate interest, I decided I was hungry and wouldn't some popcorn be just the thing to enjoy on a dreary night. What a pleasant outlook. By this time the wood in the stove had dried out and was crackling merrily. I shelled enough corn just for me. Soon it was popping and banging against the lid, but not loud enough to keep the word coffin and mother and baby from ringing in my ears. I wondered where Father had gone.

The kitchen door suddenly opened and Father's head popped in. He scared me so badly that I threw the pan of corn in the air. It landed in the middle of the floor where it continued to pop and bounce around as if suffering from the fits.

"Come and help me," he said. "I got a little sewing job for you to do. Bring your needle and some white thread."

With that brief command he turned back into the night. I threw a longing look at my scattered plans on the floor, then went to the sewing machine for the needle and thread, and out the back door where Father was waiting for me.

The blackness of the night engulfed us. There was but a dim strip of light from the kitchen window to light our path. Against Father's predictions, it had again started to rain. It fell so softly that only the dripping of the eaves disturbed the stillness. Cautiously feeling our way with our feet, we made our way to the toolshed that adjoined the chicken house. There a lantern hung over the workbench where Father's tools were scattered about. As we entered the shed a breeze sprang up and the door slammed shut behind me with a bang. I jumped as if I'd been shot. It was then I saw the long narrow crude box mounted on two sawhorses in the shadows by the wall. I gasped.

"What's the matter with you?" scolded Father.

"Nothin'," I quavered. "What do you want me to do?"

"Here's some lace," he replied. "Just gather it and we'll tack it around the edge of the coffin inside. I'm goin' to pad the coffin with cotton and cover it with white muslin, and with the lace it'll look mighty pretty."

It was my private opinion that it would take more than that to make a coffin look pretty. And, I was scared. My hands shook so, I could hardly thread the needle. I crept closer to the lamp and Father. The shadows seemed to creep up with me. I dared not glance towards the coffin for fear I would lose all self control and begin to scream.

A hen fell off the roost in the next room and mice rustled the shavings under the workbench while I sat rigid with terror. A chill, not from the cold, penetrated my bones. I had a thousand questions to ask about who was to occupy this coffin, but they couldn't get past my throat. Father whistled and sawed and hummed until I thought the very night would shout at us for disturbing its peace. Time held it's breath and so did I.

"Just hold the lace here," ordered father. "We'll tack it on. Then we'll plan the lid and put screws on it and it will be done. A pretty good job if you ask me."

I couldn't have asked him anything at the moment. Then I noticed that there was no pillow for the head, that the nails showed on the white muslin, that there were no handles to carry it by and that the lid would look better padded. I pointed these things out to Father who said, "By cracky, you are right. There's room for improvement." All at once my fears were forgotten and I was carried away with new ideas. We would fill a pillow with saw dust and put lace around it, cover the nails with padded buttons, make a pleat on the lid in the form of a cross at the apex and Father would turn out some handles on his foot-peddled lathe and we would paint them gold, from his precious paint kit. We went to work again. It was no longer a coffin to me but a thing of beauty and a thing of beauty is a joy forever, albeit a coffin.

Father was proud of me; we were pals; this was a night to remember. "Ah gosh," Frances, "you are a smart girl, I swear."

The next morning everyone was at the breakfast table when I awoke. I slid into my place on the bench between Jim and Ruth in time to hear Father finish giving "Thanks" and the rest of the family rushing with the "Amens."

The events of the previous evening came back to me in a flash. With the entire family around me it seemed very romantic and exciting, now that it was over. And with my usual knack for the sensational, I piped up. "Father and I made a coffin last night, and hit's the purtiest thing you ever saw, didn't we, Father?"

Hoping he would brag on my efforts, I looked to him for approval. His brows lowered and he seemed disinclined to discuss the subject. But the rest of the family responded beautifully and they all started asking questions.

"Who was it?"

"Mrs. Woolery."

"Starved to death, I betcha. Them people never got nothin' to eat at their house."

Mother said, "We won't have anything to eat either if we don't finish our breakfast and get to work."

"So that was what all the hammerin' was about in the middle of the night."

"It's a mighty pretty coffin and she looks awful fine laid out in it," Jim added—trying to look honest and succeeding as far as I was concerned.

"Gee, dead for two whole days afore they found her. Must be kinda stinkin' by now," Ruth commented.

"That's enough," shouted Father, as he banged his fist on the table. "Quiet, every one of you, or I'll whale the tar out of you. Such talk at the table."

Silence reigned for a few moments. But I had to get my say-so in, and blurted out, "It's a wonder all her cats didn't get in and eat her eyes out. I heard cats like dead people."

"Frances," said Father, in an obvious effort to control himself. "Go eat your breakfast on the stair steps. Maybe that'll teach you to be quiet when you're told."

To be expelled to the stair steps was a disgrace in our family. I obediently rose, picked up my empty plate, but was too chagrined to fill it. I wanted to bawl. Besides I was hungry, what with having no dinner the previous night. Before I took a step, Jim tugged at my skirt, and with a sly wink, put a rabbit leg and a slab of fried mush on my plate. Ruth added some flour gravy. I started to round the corner of the table; Goldie held a bowl of fried apples in her hand. She motioned to me, and when I held out my plate, she emptied half the bowl into it. Nellie giggled as she handed me a glass of milk, and remarked, "Looks like Frances is going off to starve."

"Have some molasses," Paul offered politely.

To this I smirkingly replied, "How can I have mo'lasses when I ain't had any lasses?" No one dared laugh at this old, old chestnut.

Content with my well-filled plate, I seated myself comfortably on the stairway. Halfway through with my meal, though, it suddenly occurred to me that perhaps Jim wasn't fooling, that there really might be a body in the coffin. Burning with curiosity, I decided to go and see how they looked in our beautiful handiwork. Since I sensed that the rest of the family wouldn't approve of my being so nosy, the only thing to do was to sneak out without them knowing it. And now was the opportune time, while they were all at breakfast. Our coats hung on nails behind the door at the foot of the steps. I took the first one I saw, threw it over my head and cautiously opened the front door. It was now pouring down rain and a strong wind was tossing the cedars about. The wind snatched the door from my hand and filled the room with a cold blast of air. I shivered. The grayness of early morning was barely penetrating the sheets of heavy rain. Father and his predictions. The tremendous roaring of the wind almost made me turn back, but I was firmly resolved to see the body in the coffin, so proud of my work was I. Bracing myself against the wind, I pushed my way around the corner of the house.

The chicken yard was like a lake. Hens, bedraggled and soaked, stood around with water pouring off their tails. Surely they were the stupidest creatures on earth not to have enough sense to come in out of the rain. I knew I was pretty stupid myself to be out in such weather, but I had a motive. My feet sank in the mire and the water ran over the tops of my shoes. I began to wish I hadn't ventured forth. Hanging on to the paling fence, I waded towards the tool shed. The violence of the storm was beginning to dim my curiosity.

A thought struck me. Suppose there really were some bodies in the coffin. Did I really want to see them? By this time I had reached the window to the tool shed. I reached the sill and hung on for dear life. Shuddering and shaking and dreading to see what might be there, I slowly raised myself above the sill and peered inside. For a minute I could barely see the dim interior. Then, well, I could hardly believe my eyes. The coffin was gone.

Even though this incident definitely brought an end to boredom, the humor of the situation soon passed. What with all the hushed and horrified whispering about it later, the full significance of the fact that a woman and her child that we all knew had actually died of starvation finally dawned on us and filled us with shock that such a thing could happen to folks who lived in our hills.

The neighbors later told us that when the dead woman's husband finally came home and was accused of neglecting her and the baby, his only remark was, "I didn't reckon as how she could have starved, 'cause when I left there was a peck o' cornmeal and a gallon of 'lasses in the house."

12

Meeting In A Brush Arbor

It was when Father built "Twelve Corners" that I learned that when a true artist touches anything, it becomes artistic. I tried hard to remember this myself in the many things I have done since.

At the age of ten, I saw this tiny church as a thing of perfection and beauty. A chapel built by fantasy in a misty glen, its carved columns and cornices shone like the inside of a seashell. Its doors were like portals swung back to invite one in. It surely could only be inhabited by angels. As it turned out only wasps and the little creatures of the forests were to know its paneled walls and slim arched windows. I couldn't imagine where all the money came from to erect this church but now I imagine it was sent from other churches, perhaps in Kansas City or Salt Lake City, hoping to convert us natives to Christianity.

I do not mean to cast reflections about any religion, believing that any faith is as good as the man that practices in it, but what happened at the brush arbor meeting, outside of that little church, when our hill folks tried to settle the serious business of the after-life in such a rough and tumble way, was so hilarious, that looking back and trying to write about it, I can't keep from getting carried away by the humor of it all.

When the world points a finger and laughs at the hillbilly in song and play and dance, it makes me mad, for I don't think being born and raised in the hills is a thing to be snickered at. But I feel free to joke about some of it, for after all, I was a hillbilly myself. It's like, "I can talk about my relatives, but I don't want you to."

Our community believed in hell-fire and brimstone. We were taught that the straight and narrow path was very narrow indeed, whereas the road to iniquity was wide. This I still think good, for we were not confused children. There were no shadings, no in-betweens; only right and wrong, good and evil, heaven and hell. A child needs to believe in something and simplicity in faith for the very young is an excellent foundation to begin building on.

The way of the transgressor was easy and the serpent his constant companion. The casting out of the Devil was quite an operation. It took a lot of praying, not to mention threats and persuasion on the part of the saved to bring this about. I gazed round-eyed and open-mouthed as the sinners came to grace.

I can see now that they had the best of it, although everyone enjoyed these revivals. The sinners were cleansed inside by weeping and wailing and confession; cleansed outside by immersion in the creek; and then accepted and ever-welcomed by the people who had never bothered to speak to them before.

It did not matter that the saving did not usually last very long. There would be another time, and one day the reformation might stick. Or maybe the sinner had tried the wrong church. It was confusing to me that the Baptists said you would go to Hell if you didn't join their church and the Holy Rollers and Mormons preached the same thing, with our church, the Church of Christ, equally positive about the question.

It came close to being settled once and for all in our community and perhaps it would have, except for the cussedness of human nature. Folks never seem to learn until it's too late that no religious question was ever settled through argument or debate. It happened this way:

Outside of the Holy Rollers, who came and went like gypsies, there were three sects in our area. We belonged to Glovers Chapel, which was the Church of Christ—we and the Simpsons and the Traws and everyone who amounted to anything so we thought. It was a closely-knit little congregation and quite smug in its sanctity. It was pretty much of a closed shop, so naturally there wasn't room enough for the Mormons and Baptists. They, we thought, looked upon our sect with envy.

Being fellow outcasts, they got together and decided to do something about it. Obviously the first thing they had to have was a church. There were too few of them to afford a house of worship for each faction, so they combined their efforts and resources and finally acquired enough to build a chapel.

Father was asked to do the job. He accepted much against his better judgment, since it was enemy territory.

Of course, friction followed. The Mormons would tell him to put the door here and the Baptists would come along and tell him to move it. At the same time they were both impatient to get the job done. Father finally threw his tools down and threatened to quit. Not until then did they agree to let him do it his way.

That was a mistake, too. They told him how much floor space they wanted, but no one mentioned how high the ceiling should be. So with him, the sky was the limit. People kept asking, "When are you going to put the roof on?" And Father would say, "It'll be a little while yet." Mother remarked, "He must have gotten up on his ladder and can't get down." It was the tallest little building I have ever seen. He put his heart and soul into it, however, and called upon all his skills to make it the talk of the countryside. It was. There were hand carved cornices, fancy columns, and a dream of a pulpit, with a little niche for the organ which turned out to be so small they couldn't get the organ in. Now everyone was exasperated.

Ultimately Father got the roof on. The good brethren took one look at the high ceiling and said, "Well never be able to heat it." Ruth observed, "Shucks, Hell ain't below. "It's right here in this cold place."

If they had only known it, the heating situation was to be the least of their worries. Father had so much fun decorating little corners; he couldn't seem to stop, so the building ended up with twelve corners. So this house of worship became known as "Twelve Corners."

It was situated in a grove of large black oak trees at a crossroads about two miles north of our house. After months of anxiety and impatience on the part of the mixed brethren, the edifice was completed and it was a beauty. "A little tall, perhaps, but none the less a beauty," everyone admitted. Once more, I thought my Father the most wonderful man in the world. The Baptists and the Mormons were elated over it. They were so proud of it, in fact, that when a Mormon spoke of it, he called it a Mormon Temple; the Baptists referred to it as "our Baptist Church."

This was what started it all. They began to wrangle about which Church it should be dedicated to. The tension rose pretty high. Finally someone suggested settling the thing by debate. Whichever side won the debate would be the sect to which the church would be dedicated and the creed they all would embrace.

This idea seemed to suit everybody. It was decided that until the church was dedicated properly, it would not be used and the debate would be held in a brush arbor on the church grounds. The brush arbor was made of saplings braced erect with trunks of larger trees which were also used for rafters, and on the beams was placed a thick thatch of oak boughs with their leaves still on. It was a crude shelter, but it served to keep out the sun and the rain. Under it, benches were set up for the congregation and a platform was made to serve as a pulpit.

Each side tried to outdo the other in hiring the best representation. The Mormons sent to Salt Lake City for the highest-powered preacher available, while the Baptists ordered their strength from Kansas City. Tension mounted. Four men of God finally arrived all done up in spotless white shirts with celluloid collars, black ties, long coats, and trousers with razor sharp creases. They looked mighty out of place when they got 'round to preaching under the brush arbor to our poorly clad hill people.

The meetings were to last from ten in the morning until nine at night for six days. Everyone from far and wide, regardless of belief, was invited to attend. And everyone came who lived within a radius of forty miles. The women had planned for days what they would fix for basket dinners. Chickens and turkeys, usually considered a delicacy only for Sunday, were fried everyday. And, of course, jars of hoarded preserves, pickles, and fruit were sacrificed for the affair. Yeast bread was put to rise at night and baked early in the morning.

Our household was up at the crack of dawn, hurrying to get the chores done, the house cleaned, molasses cakes and vinegar pies baked, and real light bread, and our baskets packed. The horses had to be hitched and the wagon filled with clean straw. By nine o'clock we all stood scrubbed, starched, and ready to pile in and start off over the hill. It was a lot of work but nobody in the family would have missed the show for anything.

The debate was rough from the very start. The opening speaker threatened to skin his opponents and hang their hides on the fence. He was the belligerent type, calling names, threatening, cajoling, and extolling the benefits of his faith in a steady blast. His voice would boom till the leaves trembled in the rafters. Then it would descend until it was hardly above a whisper and everybody had to lean forward in their seats to catch his words. He had a large bay window and a forelock of straight hair that fell over one eye, covering it completely whenever he brought his fist down at each point. Then he would toss his head, throwing the forelock back as if it were a mantle over his shoulder. He would glare long and hard at all of us as if daring us to contradict him. Then he would hitch up his belt and start over. He always began his sermon neat and immaculate, but by the end, his hair, collar, necktie, and clothes generally would be so disarrayed that he looked as if he'd been on a drunk.

The next preacher was suave and profound. He was tall and slim with a blond mustache and a weak chin, and big, soft, expressive calf eyes. He was calm, patient, and persuasive. He folded his hands, leaned on his elbows, and reasoned with you. I gathered the only thing to do was to join up with him, quit this helling around and be assured of a nice private cloud of your own beyond the pearly gates. Smoothly he described what his opponents were offering as the fires of Hell, and it seemed to me it would be pretty risky not to do it his way. His voice had a soft purr, even though his tongue was as sharp as a salamanders. I thought he had the other fellow pretty well licked. I liked his salesmanship.

The next speaker was short and squat and blurted out such potent deadlines that when he gulped a glass of water at the end of each searing statement, I thought he was washing his mouth out to rid it of the poison. He stood straight and stiff folded his three double chins neatly and pursed his lips; then quotation, chapter, verse, and interpretation rolled out without a pause.

The last preacher to mount the platform was tall, dark, and handsome. No one gave a hoot what he said. He was so wonderful to watch. The women fell head over heels in love with him, even the married ones. Some husbands were going to have a pretty hard time living up to him. His only weakness was a pronounced twitch of one cheek. It seemed to twitch just so many times before he could get it latched down and express his thoughts. For my money he was way out in front. My past convictions were swept away, and so was my heart.

The preachers were only a part of the show. The singing was nothing short of a race, with the Baptists and Mormons still trying to outdo each other. But it was the sidelights which kept me entertained. Being unable to always fathom what the preacher was saying, I kept a sharp lookout to see what was going on around me. Here are a few of the things I remember:

There was one mother so rapt in the sermon, while her child nursed at intervals, that she never bothered to put its dinner away. A little girl kept begging, "Mommy, I wanna go pee!" She was ignored until she stood still and let go. Then she cried because she was wet. This aroused her mother, who felt her pants, discovered the indiscretion, and spanked her soundly then and there. This sort of performance was not unusual. The old folks chewed tobacco, keeping time with the singing, and when the preacher had them spellbound, they would quit chewing while the drool ran down their chins. They always put spit under the seats. Corn liquor was passed around regardless of creed, and discreetly swallowed behind psalm books.

What provoked Mother but amused me was the sparking. It was a wonderful time for the boys and girls to get caught up on their lovemaking. There was one couple that must have been awfully far behind. It seemed that every time we turned a corner or went behind a wagon or tree for private purposes, there they were in a tight clinch simply eating off each other's faces. This went on for six full days, apparently without their getting tired.

The testimonials amused me, too. Each preacher would call on a person in the audience of that particular faith to get up and tell what God and their church had done for them. I remember one old man, particularly, who was unshaven, had a large Adam's apple, and wore a battered straw hat and baggy trousers. He rose, hesitatingly. The preacher encouraged him:

"Speak right up, brother, and let the Mormons know what the Lord and the Baptist Church 'as done for you."

"Wall," the old man declared, "My old woman was half etten up with sores. She had scabs all over her. But bless pat, we jined the Baptist Church and started prayin'. She got plumb well." He sat down shyly, while the preacher gazed about triumphantly. Mother began to laugh quietly. I could see she was trying to control herself, but the tears rolled and she shook all over. I kept tugging at her elbow pleading for her to tell me what was so funny. Wiping her eyes, she finally managed to explain, "Her sores got well, but the old lady died."

They finally began to use what I considered unfair tactics. Volunteers from each side would pass up and down the aisles and pounce on certain victims whom they believed need converting, trapping them so they couldn't get away. The opening speech might be, "Are you saved?" If you said no, you were really in for it. Then they would say, "Now is the time to meet your Maker. Kneel with me and let us pray." Rather than disclose to the world that you weren't willing to be saved, you knelt in embarrassed silence while they prayed fervently for the Lord to forgive your many sins. We quickly learned to say "Yes," when asked if we were saved.

I was always happy when noontime arrived, when religion was put aside for an hour and our feasts were spread under the trees. Then we could gorge ourselves. The youngfolks would pair off, slip away to the springhouse about a quarter-mile off, pretending to be very thirsty. There was much lingering along the path. Lovers were so thick you couldn't get past them. Watching the lovers with wide eyes and a sly grin was Hank, hidden behind a tree or lying flat on the ground behind a log.

This went on for six days. Surely such fiery preaching was never heard before. The testimonials, the sparking, and eating continued. The sectarian tension rose further. People started forming into groups, calling each other names and making threats. No matter which side you were on, you were a dirty so-and-so. Father didn't want to go the last day. "There is something rotten in the woodpile," he said, "and I don't want to see it dragged out." But not for anything would the rest of us have missed the showdown. We all went anyway.

The last preacher to speak was the handsome one. It was plain to see, he stormed, red in the face with his twitch uncontrolled, that what had been shown and proven by his able assistant and himself could leave no doubt in the minds as to the proper course to take. Then he began to pray for his opponents. He felt it his duty to ask the Lord to forgive these sinners.

The audience became restless and began to mutter. Mother gathered us children together, herding us to the outside of the crowd. Suddenly a man picked up a heavy stick and threw it at the preacher, striking him directly across the middle. With a startled look on his face, he grasped his stomach and folded up like a jackknife, rolling off the rostrum

For a minute there was dead silence. Then all the pent-up emotions broke loose. The crowd became a howling, writhing mess. By this time Mother had us on the outer edge of the mob, where she commanded us to stay. Father and the boys were raring to get into the fight, but Mother held onto their arms and sternly forbade them. It was a bedlam of grunting, swearing, screaming, and mixed with loud groans as seats were banged down on people's heads. Women scratched faces, pulled hair, and kicked and pounded each other. One old man threw away his cud of tobacco, rolled up his sleeves with deliberation, spit on his hands, and then literally dived into the melee. Dust rose like a cloud. Onlookers screamed, prayed, or encouraged the mob. Through all of this, the organist kept playing!

I saw four men separate themselves from the scene. They were the preachers, but I hardly recognized them. One had a black eye, another a bloody nose and they were all limping. They tore out through the brush as fast as their legs could carry them, and sailed neatly over the wire fence. One slit his trousers down his leg on a barb. He didn't even pause to examine the damage, but raced with the others as if the devil himself were pursuing him. His flight was so fast that a body could have skated on his coattail. None of the four was ever seen there again. It was thirteen miles to a railroad, and they must have made it in record time.

The mob fought on until exhaustion overcame them. One by one they dropped out, nursing their wounds. A lot of people had been hurt, but no one was killed. Then each family gathered up its wounded and left for home. The debate was over. No one had won. Both Mormons and Baptists avoided looking at the church while driving away. It was plain to see that they loathed the cause of their loss of dignity and prestige in the community. They would never be able to live this down.

The church was never dedicated. It stood deserted for years and finally tumbled down.

We rode home a very sober and quiet family. Mother remarked, more to herself than anybody else, "Who can say who was right and who was wrong? Surely there must be a better way of settling opposite views than by bitter words and blows."

"Well," said Father, "These people around here ain't got much to live for so their kind of heaven is mighty important to them and worth fighting and dying for I reckon, and they all got a different notion as to how to git there."

My comment was, "Why didn't they jist take turns about using the church?"

Mother patted my curls and said, "Sometimes I think that's a head you have on your shoulders, Francie."

Father sat silent and angry, unable to talk about it at all. His beautiful church that he had worked so long and hard on; all his labors wasted.

Finally he burst out, "They didn't need a church anyway. If a man wants to worship God and has faith in his heart he can worship just as well under a temple of trees or the heavenly bodies above. His voice can be heard if he lifts it in prayer no matter where he is."

13

The Years of the War

While the Allies waged war with the Germans (World War One) and before that conflict touched us, my folks continued their endless war against the hills. For a while it seemed that some of Mother's and Father's ambitions for their older children were to be realized. Annie and Nellie had gone away to school to Linn Creek, studied a year, and came home, each with a teacher's certificate. The following year Annie taught at our own George School. My, we were proud of her. She made forty-five whole dollars a month, stayed at home, saved her money, and bought nice things like a steamer trunk, ready-made middy blouses from the mail order catalog, a sewing machine all her own and even a gold watch to pin on her lapel.

Nellie got a better paying job, sixty-five dollars a month, but her school was several miles from home. It being too inconvenient for her to ride horseback to and from the farm, she found a place to board in a home near her school. She'd get home on weekends, weather permitting.

Jim had run away and gone to work for a sawmill operator who paid him two dollars a day. Mother hadn't given up on his going to school and often reminded him that money wasn't everything; that the correspondence course he was taking was a poor substitute for classroom study. Jim was happy though. Unbeknownst to us at the time, he had other ideas.

For a couple of years Mother and Father were in heaven. Their children were doing as well as could be expected. There was no doubt in their minds that as soon as the older ones had saved a little money they would be off on their own to seek broader horizons.

The only thing wrong with the picture was that their chicks had made the mistake of coming back. That and the War, dashed their dreams for them in the dust. As isolated as we were in our landlocked island, still we were not so far removed from world affairs that the conflict that shook the rest of the world could leave us untouched.

When the United States declared war on Germany, the cry of War was heard even in our hills. Garsy, along with dozens of other young men in our area, joined up so fast, families barely had time to be appalled at the idea of loss till they were gone. But most of these young patriots failed to pass the physical tests, mainly because of tuberculosis and glaucoma, or were later sent home because of illiteracy, inability to adjust, or a combination of both.

Mother went ahead with whatever she had to do, drying her tears as she worked, for farm women have not time to sit and wail.

The boys came home on their first furloughs looking so handsome in their uniforms, all spit and polish, stalwart and straight, that there was no telling a ridge boy from a bottomlander and our girls were a twitter over them. Young people began to get married in a hurry before the furloughs were over.

Annie and Nellie married two ridge farm boys right away. Annie's husband had been accepted in the service, but Nellie's husband was not accepted. Jim, not old enough to be drafted, troubled and somehow feeling he should do something, ran off and married a girl barely fifteen years old from another ridge farm above us. I was the only one in the family who knew that Jim was planning to get married. I swore not to tattle, to keep quiet, and not even hint that he was about to take the most important step of his life. I came upon his secret as I was pressing his pants one Sunday morning before going to church. In his pocket he had left a marriage license and wedding ring. From then on, when we were alone together, I would torment him with a ditty that went something like this:

Now young man, take my advice,
And don't be in a hurry to wed.
You'll think you're in clover,
Till the honeymoon's over,
And then you'll wish you were dead.
With a cross-eyed baby on each knee,

And a wife with a plaster on her nose,
You'll find true love don't run so smooth,
When you have to wear second hand clothes.

The following Sunday, noticing him dressing with unusual care, and combing his hair over and over again, I knew this was to be the day. His girl was pretty and I liked her, and I adored Jim. I was sure she would make him happy and so felt that Jim was doing the right thing.

He had a horse of his own now and often let me ride part of the way with him when he went to visit his sweetheart. Today, when he started to leave, I climbed up behind him, wrapped my arms around his waist, and leaned my head against his back. He patted my hand gently, saying, "You can't go with me today, honey."

It was then I knew for sure we were losing him. All I said as I climbed down was, "I'm going to miss you very much."

Mother and Father could not resign themselves to their children's marriages. They both all of a sudden seemed to age beyond their years. They tramped around the house, and wailed, "Why, why." They beat their brows, wept, stormed, made dire predictions, threatened, tried to think of ways out—but there was nothing they could do about it. Three of their children were gone, trapped by their hearts and their youth, and although they did not seem to care, trapped forever by the hills, encasing them in a culture that had let civilization bypass its inhabitants and fencing them in with poverty. What was in store for them in their marriages to poor ridge farmers, Mother and Father could only guess. It was not good or promising.

Mother could be heard pounding her pillow at night and weeping: "The children will never have anything now. They'll never know anything but hard work. No fun, no pleasure, no nice homes, or clothes or furniture. Just work, work, work, and have more and more babies, and never get ahead. And if their husbands are like the rest of the men around here, they'll never dress up again. They'll put away their wedding clothes never having them on again until the day they are laid in their coffins. It's not that the ones they married ain't good enough. They're every bit as good as ours—sweet and honest and kind. It's just that I wanted our children to get out into the world; to see the difference."

Father would try to comfort her. "Now, now, Lily. Don't take on so. They ain't dead." Then he, too, would begin to cry and wipe away tears. Although Father's life here in the hills was not too unhappy, still it was not the kind of life he wanted for his children. For them, he had hoped, as Mother had, that they would find a better way for themselves.

While all this went on, I wondered why marriage seemed to be an end to love and romance. Why, I puzzled, was marriage an end to living and not the beginning? Why should it tie one down so, keep one from doing the things they wanted to do? Why couldn't Nellie and Annie keep right on teaching and working? Why couldn't two work and save and do even better than one alone? These things puzzled me, but not for long, for they were soon "in the family way" and even I knew that a mother-to-be could not ride a horse over the hills in pursuit of a career.

One day I remember shortly after Nellie's marriage, Nellie and Ruth sat on the steps of the henhouse plucking duck feathers and putting them into gunnysacks for a featherbed for Nellie. I helped by running and catching the ducks and bringing them to the girls. Ruth was in a nasty mood and took it out on the poor ducks, who quacked in pain and struggled as she furiously plucked her victims. The feathers flew around her and Ruth's hair was full of them. One clung to the end of her nose, which she blew at angrily. She was unhappy about Nellie's marriage and addressed her unhappiness to the duck.

"Quit struggling, you! You and me have got to make Nellie's feather bed nice and soft and bouncy."

Nellie blushed and picked gently as her duck lay quietly in her lap. She was a young girl in love, and softly sang a then popular song.

There's a song in the land of the lilies,
Each sweetheart has heard with a sigh.
O'er high garden walls a sweet echo falls,
As the soldier boy whispers goodbye.
Smile awhile as you kiss me sad adieu.
When the clouds roll by, I'll come home to you.

So wait and pray each day for me,
Till we meet again.

Ruth threw down her duck and said, "Bring on another one, Frances." I handed her a struggling bird. On the side, she said to Nellie, "Did you know Annie's in the family way. She'll be swelled up like a melon in another six months. And don't tell me you ain't got one on the way by now, either."

"Hush, Ruth! Shame on you for talking like that in front of Frances."

"Well, ain't you?" demanded Ruth.

"Yes," was the reply, almost too low for me to hear.

Then Ruth got up and threw down the duck. It went waddling off, shaking itself and grumbling indignantly. Glancing at it, she added hatefully. "You don't need to look so damn mad and sassy at just losing your feathers for a bed. Look what Nellie's lost."

Father and Mother turned their minds to the Great War, and for a while put aside their own frustrations. We subscribed for our first newspaper, "The Kansas City Star." Its headlines screamed, "Chateau-Thierry Battle Rages," "Pershing visits LaFayette's Tomb," "Germans Use Poison Gas," and there were pictures of terrible men in spiked helmets, and people sang, Over There, and

Kaiser Bill went up the hill
To take a look at France;
Kaiser Bill came down the hill
With bullets in his pants.

Everybody we knew was busy knitting sweaters, gloves, and socks, and mailing them to the Red Cross. The school children were asked to gather walnut hulls by the barrel full, for gas masks, I think. The war was so far away it did not seem real, but the vacant chairs and tears and the anxiety at food scarcity, disease, and would the Allies win, and would our help be too late, were real enough.

Being too young to appreciate what was going on in the world conflict, my principal impressions can be gathered from the fact that we had a hound puppy named Woodrow Wilson and a cute colt, with a white blaze, we called Verdun, after the battle of that name.

Mother's patriotic gesture was to make a game of our meager fare. We should say, "Now let's pretend we are all soldiers on the battlefront. That the rolling kitchens just came up, but that there wasn't enough for everybody. I'll ration out the portions, and remember, there are no second helpings. Good soldiers don't complain!" Then she would give each of us a spoonful of whatever there was. She tried to make us feel better about it all, by reminding us that there were others who were much worse off than we were. This didn't make us any less hungry, but it did make us ashamed to complain.

Besides the regular chores, there were other things we younger children did to help out. One of our jobs was to trap rabbits for the table. We had traps which we visited every morning. To me, rabbits were such darling, timid creatures that I hated to catch and kill them. But like everyone else, I had a certain number of traps to visit daily. I would trudge to the traps, across the snow, over crisp dead grass and frozen leaves that crackled like broken glass when I walked. As I approached the traps, I dreaded to see tracks around them, for fear I had caught something.

If the rabbit in the trap was unhurt, and no one was with me, I would peep into the long box affair, and watch the timid, trembling creature. Then, I'd open the door and let him out, laughing with joy when he went bouncing off into the brush, kicking up little puffs of snow with his hind feet.

The family often wondered why everyone's traps caught rabbits but mine. My excuses were not very good. The crows had eaten all the corn, or the string was broken on the trapdoor, or a fox had gotten in and eaten the rabbit, or simply, I hadn't caught anything. I think my acts of mercy were suspected, for it seemed that I was the one who was always made to help skin what the others had caught. I had to hold the poor creatures' legs while its insides were being pulled out and the soft fur peeled like skin from an onion, from its bloody body.

Annie came home to have her first baby, a boy. It's a wonder the little fellow survived from being handled so much by all the affectionate uncles and aunts and Grandma and Grandpa. I loved to hold him and would sit motionless as a Buddha for hours, just watching him sleep. He was such a wonder to me. He was the first baby I had ever been around. If I'd only known it, this was just the beginning. I now have fifty-one nieces and nephews and the novelty of watching them sleep has worn off, to say the least. I am quite sure that my family started the population explosion. Jim had seventeen children, Annie nine, Nellie eight, Goldie nine, and Ruth six.

Then smallpox began to break out across the country and to fill us with fear, more frightening than the war itself, for it was striking close to home.

The schools closed down as the epidemic neared and Mother would not allow us to even go to the little country store for staples. Visiting the neighbors was out of the question.

Paul had been working and helping out a bottomland farmer about six miles away. He could come home on weekends, bring news and give Mother his money; sometimes he'd bring flour and sugar, and leave before daylight on Monday. He was the only one allowed to come and go. Not even Father dared to leave in search for work. Then one weekend, Paul didn't come home. Mother and Father walked the floor fearing the worst, that he had been stricken and was perhaps dying. Yet it would be unthinkable to go to him and bring the disease home to us all.

But Mother wanted to go, saying if he was ill, she should be at his side to care for him. Father held her back, pleading with her to be sensible. How could she help if she became ill too, he argued. Then Father decided to go, and it was Mother who talked him out of it. So for six weeks, we waited and prayed and watched every path for Paul, and waited and prayed some more.

Then one day we saw him coming down the hill, reeling and staggering, barely able to drag himself along. We all rushed out to greet him. He was skin and bones and his eyes were sunken so deep in their sockets they looked like burned-out coals of fire. Father took his frail form in his arms and carried him into the house and laid him gently on the bed in the front room. Paul kept saying in a voice so weak he could hardly be heard, but with a note of triumph in it, "I made it. I stuck it out! I ain't contagious no more! I said I'd stay away till I got well, and I did. I made it!"

It was days before he was well enough to tell us the whole story. The couple he was working for were stricken first. He was tempted to come home, but he refused to expose us all. Besides, it was his duty to help, he said. Paul came down with it the next week. Although burning with fever, he crawled from his bed to the pump on the back porch to bring water to first one and then the other. He said that it seemed to take hours to drag his body across the floor the twenty feet to the pump and back to the folks in bed. He had saved their lives and his. Of that we were thankful and proud.

We wept over him and praised him, and I'm sure no soldier on the battlefront performed a more heroic feat than our Paul. His body was covered with bedsores, but as he said, he had made it.

Then while the battles raged on foreign soil, we fought some fierce ones of our own on the homefront. (Fortunately, the war ended before any of my brothers had to be sent overseas.)

All in one year, we were invaded by some terrible enemies, enemies that tried our patience, our ingenuity, and our strength. We seemed to suddenly have more insects than the Congo.

One morning at breakfast, I sat scratching my head while shooing flies away from my biscuits and molasses. Mother watched me for a minute and with suspicion in her eyes got up and walked around the table and began to part my hair with her fingers and examine my scalp. Taking me by the collar, she pulled me over to the window where the light was brighter and she could see better. Suddenly she let out a blood-curdling scream that nearly frightened me out of my flour sack drawers.

"Lice!" she yelled, "Lice! Francie has got lice!"

Everyone's eyes focused on me in terror. Then they all began to scratch their own heads. Father completely lost his composure and began to shout orders as if he were the colonel at the head of a regiment.

"Get some wood! Build a fire! Get some water! Get the coal oil! Get the big medical book!"

"Lordy," I thought, "are they going to delouse me or boil me?" I began to feel like a missionary among cannibals. Then it was discovered that Ruth, too, was crawling with lice. With each of us by the nape of the neck, like two kittens that have misbehaved, they hustled us out to the smokehouse. We were plopped in tubs of scalding water, doused with coal oil, and scrubbed with lye soap. Then Father sprinkled us with strange smelling weeds he had gathered years ago and dried—to prepare for what he must have anticipated would happen some day. After the lice were drowned or asphyxiated, we had shed at least two layers of our epidermis. Like two boiled lobsters, we sat on the steps wrapped in an old quilt, while Mother combed the nits out of our hair with a fine-tooth-comb. Father burned our clothes in a bonfire in the yard. Mother hadn't noticed what he was doing, but when the rags began to smolder, she smelled them and began to yell again.

"John! John! You are burning their only school clothes! I could of boiled them just as well!"

Father, red in the face, hollered back, "Better to be safe than sorry," while I thought, "How sorry can a body be?" Here were Ruth and I, wet, scalded, stinking and lousy, and naked as jaybirds. Ruth began to swear. Father stopped tending the fire long enough to ask the Lord to forgive her. Mother saw that I had had enough and was about to pucker up and bawl.

"Never mind, my little Paw-Paw. You can wear your Sunday go-to-meetin' clothes to school tomorrow."

Ruth and I went off to school the next day all spruced up in our Sunday best, and proud too, for this was the cleanest we had ever been on a Friday. I don't know who brought home bed bugs. I swear it wasn't me, for I had been so careful not to let Hank touch me when we sat side by side in school. But one night we all started slapping ourselves and looking at sticky, bloody spots on our clothes and smelling the raw biting smell we all recognized, and we knew we were in for it.

It was the same show, the same performers, the same lines as the lice episode, only this time the whole family was attacked.

Father shouted, "Get some wood! Build a fire! Get some water! Get the coal oil! Get the big medicine book!" Soon we were burning our straw mattresses, boiling the bedclothes and going over the springs and bedsteads with rags soaked in coal oil. Ruth slapped the wall with laughter and killed dozens with that one blow that were hidden behind some loose plaster. To fumigate the rooms, Father brought in a boiling pot in which he had mixed some strange concoction that smelled so terrible that we and the bed bugs left en masse. The horrible odor was so pungent it permeated the walls and we had to sleep in the yard for nights. Since we had no mattresses, we would have had to anyway, for bare bedsprings with only quilts over them are not too comfortable. Mother and the girls did some fast peddling on the sewing machine the next day and whipped up some muslin straw ticks. The boys took them to the straw stacks, filled them with fresh golden straw and it was mighty fine to sleep in their fragrance without slapping at bugs all night.

Then we all got the seven-year itch. When mother screamed when she noticed us scratching and examined our bodies and found sores, and Father began to shout the same lines, I thought I would go crazy. Out came the medical book and out came the same wild remedies, only this time a new innovation was introduced. To the herbs and scalding water and coal oil was added skunk oil, clay mud, and sulfur. Father made a paste out of this and plastered our bodies all over. I didn't know whether we would suffocate or blow up.

Don't get near the fire, shouted Mother, or you'll ignite. Personally I didn't think we needed a fire. My skin was hot enough.

After we were all plastered and looked like a bunch of mummies who had been disinterred, Father said, "Now all we can do is pray." He then got out the Bible, and with his specs on the end of his nose, read us a chapter about Job and his sores, and as we bowed our heads, he asked the Lord to deliver us from our afflictions. Something worked: whether it was the mudpacks or the prayers, we were cured and the itch went away. Ruth's comment was, "Wouldn't you!"

The flies were so much a part of our lives we hardly noticed them, but just shooed them off our food, off our noses as we slept, and let them be for the most part. Like the "Man who Came to Dinner," they never went away.

Mother and I white-washed the roosts and the walls of the chicken house to get rid of the mites and carried out tubs of chicken manure spreading it on the garden to rot the winter through. Mites gave us a bad time, too. It was while trying to rid the hen house of them that I nearly lost my life: Shortly afterward, I fell deathly ill. The doctor was called. My temperature was 106 degrees and stayed that way for days, I was told. He said there was nothing he could do for me; that the disease was typical of that area and mostly affected children and was always fatal. Never had he known anyone to recover from it. This was a fungus of the bloodstream, he said, and affected the lungs like tuberculosis. Fortunately for me, perhaps, he didn't come back, and fortunately for me, Father wasn't home or he would have doctored me to death. For six weeks, only faces swam before me. Then when my eyes began to focus again I was better. What Mother did to save me, I will never know. But I lived through it, "Because I was pretty tough," she said.

Many years later I learned about the disease that had nearly killed me. It was called histoplasmosis, a fungus infection caused from being around bird droppings, and nearly always fatal. All the geologists that explored King Tut's tomb had died of it, I understand, and it was said to be a curse on them, because it was written that, "All who violate this tomb will die." The disease destroyed two thirds of my lung tissue, and I have lived with this condition ever since.

When I started to get better, I enjoyed being the center of attention and getting out of school. Soon the long days began to pall on me, even though Mother did everything she could think of to entertain me. She let me cut out paper dolls from the mail order catalogs, made me dozens of cornstalk fiddles and cornstalk horses, and clothes for my celluloid doll, and at bedtime, she would curl up for awhile beside me and tell stories of King Arthur, Alice in Wonderland, and Goldilocks. I wasn't long before mother tired of entertaining me, and I then started to do the thing I have returned to all my life when under stress. I began to draw. I am sure the pictures were as simple as any child's, but when Mother saw them her face lit up and her eyes shone. She was sure I would be an artist someday.

Towards the end of the war, folks in our countryside were anxiously waiting for the end to come. Our cousins, Crate and Lucy, Uncle Oliver's son and daughter, were visiting us during this time. One night we heard a cannon roar from the little town of Richland, twelve miles away. It was November 11th, 1918. With this loud boom we knew that peace had come.

Although the war was over, our family suffered from the epidemic of German measles that was spreading across the country. Father returned from a painting trip with red blotches on his back and told us he had been exposed to the measles. Mother said, "Oh my. We're all in for it." And so we were! At one time she was the only one in the family still on her feet; the rest of us were all very ill. Her strength and courage got all of us through, but Father and Goldie developed pneumonia. Their condition lingered. Father was finally up and around, but Goldie was doubled over with fluid in her lungs. A cousin, Dr. Preston Thomas, came from Brumley every day on horseback to tend us. He finally came to the decision that Goldie would have to have her lungs drained by removing two ribs and inserting drainage tubes.

The kitchen table was moved into the front room and padded with ironed sheets. Father and the doctor sterilized the instruments in boiling water. Mother rendered the anesthesia—which was ether—to her daughter while the surgery was performed. I sat at the top of the stairs and watched the scene below. I was amazed that my parents could assist in this frightening and dangerous procedure. I'm still amazed. Fortunately, the surgery was a success.

After sickness and health, joys and sorrows, work and play, worship and war, love and anger, and birth and death filled our lives, they were accepted as part of God's plan.

14

Day is Done

The next few years after the First World War, our farm and family struggled through a healing process. Nellie and Annie with their own little families had moved into cabins in bottomland farms a few miles away, their husbands working as sharecroppers. Garsy was still tending our farm while Jim and his pregnant wife were also sharecropping on a nearby farm. My brother, Paul, was waiting to go to school in Warrensburg, Missouri to get his teaching certificate. He had already helped Ruth through one year of school in Tuscumbia and was planning on helping Goldie the next year. Time and nature and good weather were greening our valley that had been so damaged by the fire.

I was growing up and spent a great deal of time looking at the wishbook: the Sears and Roebuck catalogue. I talked Mother into ordering a pair of black patent leather shoes with white high-tops. They were far too impractical and fell apart the first time I wore them to school in the rain. Broken hearted, I went back to the catalogue, and although I knew I was getting too old to play with dolls, I saw in the catalogue some beautiful ones which opened and closed their eyes. I had always been a little jealous of the keepsake doll that Dr. Preston had brought to Goldie when she was ill. I had never had a really pretty doll.

The month before Christmas, Mother asked me what I wanted Santa to bring. I said I wanted a pretty doll like I had seen in the catalogue. The week before Christmas Mother said we were out of staples: we needed flour and sugar and lard and coal-oil for the lamps. Mother and Father decided to go to Crocker, a little town about fourteen miles away, to take a few turkeys to sell so as to purchase what was needed for the household. The night before, preparing to go the next morning early, they loaded the turkey crates into the wagon. They went to bed early, planning on starting out at daybreak. When we all woke next morning, there was a raging blizzard. Blowing snow was piling drifts everywhere. Father said the weather was too fierce to venture forth, but Mother was not willing to change her plans. She was on a mission—there was no persuading her to stay home. She climbed up on the wagon seat by herself and said, "I should be back by dark."

All day the snow was getting deeper and deeper. As we went about our chores, we would worriedly glance at the top of the hill above the house looking for Mother. Then just as she had promised, she appeared at dark so covered with snow she looked like a white ghost.

The next few days I went off to school as usual, but each day when I came home I noticed a box of sawdust in the front room and fabric on the floor, which was most unusual.

Finally, Christmas morning arrived. I awoke and saw a box at the foot of my bed. Everyone gathered around while I opened my present. Goldie helped me take the tissue paper off of the box, and inside was the most beautiful doll I had ever seen. Mother had made its body out of sawdust and sateen and dressed it in a blue calico pinafore and bonnet. The china bisque head with blue eyes that opened and closed had real hair, and had been the real reason for the journey to Crocker through that horrible blizzard. This beautiful, beautiful doll has been my most precious treasure throughout my life.

I was eleven years old and growing up when it became apparent that I might have to live out my life there in the hills if Mother did not find a way out for me.

One day I came upon her kneading light bread dough on the kitchen table. She had flour up to her elbows as she worked the dough with patient and experienced hands. I leaned on the table and drew pictures in the flours. Having been told that Goldie was going to Tuscumbia to high school in another year, I asked Mother if I could go away, too, after I graduated from the eight grade. It was my wish that there was some place where I could go to school and learn to be an artist like Father. Times being what they were, I sensed that when it came my time to go off to school there wouldn't be enough money to send me.

Wistfully, I said: "Ain't I entitled to get an education like the others?"

Mother's face suddenly looked drawn and pinched and old. Tears filled her eyes. She covered her face with her hands and the tears trickled down her arms. "'Course you're entitled to your chances. Everybody had ought to get all the learnin' they can. But I don't know where the money's comin' from. It seems a shame to raise children in these barren hills and never let them go no place, and where there's nothin to do for pleasure or to better their lives. Just work, work, and more work, and not a thing a body can do about it.

"I ain't never had no chance, myself, and I never will," she continued. "Why I've never been nowhere. Sometimes I see no use fightin', no use at all. I'll never escape these hills. I'm trapped, and you may be too. Like rats, we're trapped." And she looked around as if she were searching for an opening to escape. I sat numb and aching with pity, and for the first time really hurting for someone else. She paced back and to, across the floor, picking up one thing after another and looking at it in disgust, and then discarding it to go on to something else. "Not enough of nothin'. Not a decent pot or pan to cook in. The stove door fallin' off its hinges. Broken down furniture not fittin' to clean. Flies and dirt, rats and mice. Look at my hands!" They were cracked from lye soap. "Not even a tiny little ole cake of sweet smelling soap to wash our bodies with." She brushed at her dress. "Not even a dress fittin' to be seen in decent company. The house and everything is wearin' out, and I'm wearin' out too. I wish I'd never seen this god-awful country where nobody can get ahead. I wish I was dead before I ever come to these hills."

And then she saw my stricken face and was suddenly compassionate for me. She came to me and knelt down and took my hands in hers. "Never mind what I say, honey," she said, "I just got carried away with self-pity." She patted my cheeks and smoothed my hair, seemingly unaware that her tears and the flour were making dough all over us. Then she added with deep passion in her voice, "You get out, my child. Go somewhere, anywhere. Do something and make something of yourself. Don't matter what direction you go. Just go where other people can teach you things you can't learn here, and then come back and tell me all about it. I want to know what happens in other places. I want to hear about where people don't live like hogs, and where women is women, and treated like human bein's. Promise me you will go? Go marry a city boy like you said, become an artist, you can do it. I know you can."

"I promise, Mommy," I whispered. "I promise."

"It don't matter about me no more. I don't care. But you get out and go somewhere. Do you hear! Then come back and tell me all about it. Ahh," she murmured, "By that time I'll be dead and gone. Dead and buried in these awful hills, and I don't suppose nobody'll care."

She went to the window and laid her head on her arms and wept long and bitterly. I went to her and touched her gently on the arm.

"I care," I said softly. She raised her head and looked at me and then went to the washstand, dipped some water from granite pail into the washpan, and bathed her face and hands. Squeezing out the washrag, she came to me and started to wash my face. I took it from her hand, saying, "I can do it. I'm big enough to wash my own face."

"Oh, yes, I keep forgettin' you're grownin' up and life's just not standin' still."

She saw that my tears were flowing as fast as I wiped them off. "Don't cry, honey," she said. "I got no business makin' you cry and talkin' to you like this. I got you and the other children and the sun is shinin' and my dough is raisin' all over the table."

She began to shape the dough into loaves and put them into the greased pans. "We mustn't forget to count our blessings." Then because she was what she was, a woman who had a sunny disposition and a heart that couldn't stay unhappy long, she flashed me a radiant smile as fresh as a spring morning washed with dew. I dried my tears and smiled back at her when she said, "A woman needs a good cry now and then." Inside of me there was a good new feeling. The feeling a woman has for another woman who understands and shares her problems. For the moment this sufficed, and I was sure Mother would see to it that I had my chance when the time came.

Spring came. Mother had been ailing off and on all winter, her feet and hands were swollen twice their size, and it was easy to see she was in constant pain. She complained very little, however, and went about her work as best she could, even tramping four miles one day in a driving rain to help a neighbor whose child had pneumonia. This spring Father had been away quite a lot on painting trips. Mother, with Garsy, Paul, Ruth, Goldie and me to help her, had done all of the planting. Paul's and Ruth's school term was over and they had come to help; Annie, Nellie, and Jim were married now, all with children of their own.

When Father was away I always slept with Mother and felt this to be a special treat. Many of those nights I can remember awakening to find Mother sitting on the edge of the bed and rubbing her arms and legs. I worried about her but was not aware that she was seriously ill. Years later I would come to understand that Mother's symptoms were the consequence of kidney failure.

On the fifth of April my Mother turned fifty-one and on the fourteenth of April, my twelfth birthday, I celebrated by coming down with a sore throat and a throbbing headache. I crept upstairs into the girls room and crawled into bed hoping to sleep it off. By night I was burning with fever and my brain seemed to be spinning around like a wheel. Ruth discovered me and brought me some water. I seemed to be dying of thirst and drank a great deal of water. After that I went to sleep and sometime in the night I began to have a horrible nightmare. Although it was vivid and real, I knew it was only a dream. Still, no matter how hard I tried to waken to reality, I simply could not get rid of it. I seemed to see my Mother's casket being carried out to the graveyard, lowered slowing into the ground, and I could hear clods of earth fall as the grave was being filled up. Then the dream would start all over again. Sometimes I roused enough to look about the room and recognized familiar objects, but still I kept on dreaming. This kept up all night. Finally I could bear the torment no longer and I began to scream, "Mommy! Mommy! Mommy!" In a moment she was beside me and with my arms clutching her wildly, I sobbed, "Mommy, I dreamed you were dead and buried."

"There, there," she soothed, wiping the perspiration from my forehead. "I'm right here and all right. You've got a fever and have been having nightmares."

She lay down beside me, stroking my hair and patting me until I fell into a peaceful sleep. I can remember, as my head lay against her bosom, hearing her heart beat very fast and loud in my ear. I was able to be up and about in a week, but I felt exhausted as I went about the work that never ends from dawn till dark on a farm.

Right after this, Mother seemed to become worse. Finally she took to her bed, getting up only to come to the table to eat. Then came the time when she was unable to do that. I often caught her looking at me as if she wanted to say something then seeming to change her mind. Then, for a time, she seemed better.

The warm weather came on very suddenly that year and things began to grow rapidly. The farm was a symphony of color. The green crinoline skirts of spring were tucked and gathered with the usual bouquets of color everywhere you looked. The woods and forest wore their dogwood, white haw, pink crabapple, and redbud gracefully. Sweet William, lavender and pinks, paraded along the gullies. Cowslips and wood daisies peeped from around rocks or old stumps. Bluebells threw a scarf of their lace down the north slopes. Around the house the plum blossoms filled the air with their fragrance. Next, the peach trees bloomed in all their pink delicate glory. Then the apple trees burst forth in splendor, and lastly, the cherry trees. The scent of the lilacs in the front yard penetrated the house. In the latter part of May, the peonies and roses burst into bloom as if they couldn't hold back any longer.

With the spring came the inevitable urge to go swimming. Ruth and I kept making trips to the creek, sticking our bare toes in, to test the water to see if it was warm enough. Even though the water was still cold to the touch, we kept telling Mother it was plenty warm enough.

On the twenty-ninth of May, we just couldn't wait any longer. We begged until Mother consented to let us go. She had seemed unusually well that day. She had gotten out of bed and was sitting on the front porch in the sun. She sniffled the lilacs and remarked, "It's good to be alive in spring. Ruth, you and Francie go ahead and go swimming. I wish I could go with you. Just don't stay in the water too long. Goldie will stay with me, so run along."

Grabbing some old dresses to swim in, Ruth and I blew Mother a kiss and raced towards Dean's Creek. We splashed and paddled until almost sundown. Suddenly Ruth looked up and said in surprise, "Here comes Paul."

He was racing at breakneck speed down the hill and in a moment stood on the bank above us. I saw his face. Tears were streaming down it, and then he said in an agonized voice, "Mama is dead."

All three of us climbed the bank and ran towards home. In a few seconds the others had disappeared over the hill; I seemed to be running on a treadmill and getting nowhere. My ears were bursting with sound. My breath came with great effort and a terrible weakness held me. Still I ran on. Finally I realized that the sound I heard was my own voice screaming, "No! No! No!" I was so bereft of reason that I though if I could only get there in time I might save Mother. The limbs of the brush lashed at my face. I stumbled over the stubble in the cornfield and fell time and again.

At last I reached the well and the sight of the log house brought me up short. It looked so still and quiet standing there in the late sunshine. Something unbelievably frightening had happened there, and there was nothing I could do. Then I knew I couldn't bear to enter the house. Where could I turn to hide from this terrible reality? I sought shelter under the old apple tree where I had whiled away so many happy hours, but there was no comfort here because death seemed to be here, too. So I fled from there and skirted the house to the barn and climbed up into the hayloft. It was getting dark here and I was haunted by the same spectre. So I climbed down and started around the house, going I don't know where, when I ran straight into the arms of Cousin Laura. I had always thought of her as an unemotional old maid, but she soothed me with great compassion and tenderness.

Stroking my hair and weeping herself, she said, "Don't try to run away, Francie, dear. Try to be brave and face it. My mother died, too, when I was a little girl like you."

She led me into the house. We walked past the still form on the bed in the front room. We hesitated a moment, then went upstairs to the girls' room where I undressed and climbed into bed. Fixing my pillow, she said, "Now weep your heart out. That is the only way you will be able to bear it."

Sometime, an eternity later, Nellie crept into bed beside me and put her arms about me. I touched her face and found it wet with tears.

The next day neighbors came in. Meals were prepared and eaten, and dishes washed. A long gray casket was brought and carried into the front room and the door closed. I went outside and wandered about the farm for hours. Whether I walked in the meadow, the hills, or the woods, I do not recall. At dark I crept upstairs again to go to bed, and found Ruth kneeling alongside the bed. She was whispering over and over, desperately, "God help us all."

During that evening we lay and listened to the clatter of the sewing machine in the room below. I knew Mother's shroud was being made, and the sound of the machine nearly drove me to distraction.

In the morning Jim came to the door, saying, "Francie, honey, get dressed and come down and see Mommy." For a flash I though it had all been a bad dream, that Mother was alive and waiting for me downstairs, but when I saw Jim's face, I knew that the past hours were a reality.

Mother's casket stood on two chairs. I walked to it and looked at her. I examined her serenely folded hands, smoothed her hair and touched the familiar curl in front of her ear. I felt of the lace of her gown. Then I touched her hands, half expecting them to return my pressure.

Jim said, "Don't we have a beautiful Mother?" and I though my heart would break.

The funeral was held that afternoon. The day became ugly and hot. A storm began to threaten with white thunderheads mounting along the horizon and thunder rumbling in the distance. My throat and chest ached so, I could hardly breathe. Hysteria kept mounting in me, but I kept fighting it down as I sat in church and gazed at the casket with flowers banked around it. Even the poorest had brought sprays of cedar and wild flowers. Someone slid into the seat beside me and took my hand. It was dear Uncle

Oliver, Mother's only brother. I looked around for Father and found him sitting with bowed head, still and remote. A choir had been brought from Tuscumbia, most of its members being our cousins.

The minister was a young man who had known Mother all his life, and conducting the service was obviously an ordeal for him. His voice would fail him and he would take out his handkerchief every little bit to dry his eyes. When he was through with the service, the choir sang, "God Be With You Till We Meet Again." Then everyone filed past the casket. The family lingered as though trying to memorize every feature of her beloved face.

"Goodbye, Mommy," I said, as the lid was fastened down.

At the graveside, the minister read this poem Father had written:

Just as the sun swung low in the west,
And its rays fell gently on the crest of the hills,
Just as nature seemed so gay,
And whispered hopes of a summer day,
Our hearts were wrung at her passing away—Mama.
The silent pitcher at the well,
The splash, the spray at the water-mill,
As the dewdrops on the window sill, of the hills,
Calm, serene she reached the tide,
And passed away to the other side—Where Jesus Is.

As she was lowered into her grave and I heard the sod being shoveled into it, I remembered my dream. This I knew was not a dream; that this time Mother could not come and comfort me in her arms.

There on a hillside beside the little church that Father had helped build, lay all that meant love and security for me. Gone was the champion of all my hopes and dreams. Gone, too, were the dreams she had of seeing her eight children in a world far from these hills. Her dreams were no more, now that the earth embraced her still form.

I had made Mother a promise to leave the farm—to make something of myself other than remain a hill woman. Now I wondered. Just how does a twelve-year-old child of the Ozarks, who had never been more than a few miles in any direction from home, go about fulfilling such a promise?

15

How Strange It Seems

After the funeral was over, we all came home to mourn, each in his own way.

The Blithe Spirit that had steered our ship of state was gone and with her went the very soul of the house and the farm. Nothing seemed the same. The house seemed older and forlorn, the rooms empty and quiet. The very trees in the wild wood seemed to grieve and hang their heads in sorrow. The cry of the dove was lonelier; the caw of the crow more distant; the wind in the orchard softer in reverence; the murmur of the spring below the house seemed no louder than the fall of a tear.

The neighbors came after the funeral, patted me on the head, took my hand, and told me what a wonderful woman my mother had been; all said if there was anything they could do for me, I was to be sure and call on them. They left and never came to the house again in the four remaining years I lived on the farm.

I was to know the vacant heart of the farm, far and beyond any reasonable period of mourning. Mother had passed away on May 29th. By the middle of August, everyone of the family had left but me and had taken their grief with them, and for most of the next four years, except for rare occasions when they came home for a few days, or a week, I was entirely alone. For a child of twelve, used to companionships, this very aloneness was indescribable.

Garsy took his grief to the dark caves where drink and cards and unsavory characters could deaden the pain in his heart, coming home only occasionally to sell a hog or corn for money to gamble away.

Annie and Nellie helped clean the house and put it in order, and, clutching their wee ones to their breasts for comfort, left, and I cannot remember them ever coming home again.

Jim stole away quietly, walking with aching heart back to his child bride, and they both soon left, for Jim to take a job that was to spell disaster for him.

Paul was planning on going back to school in the fall and Goldie was to go with him, so they both had to get work for the summer and save all the money they could to help them along.

Ruth stayed home the longest of any of the brothers and sisters and was most reluctant to leave me. But, she kept getting offers to go to work as a housekeeper, so finally she took a job for $2.50 a week on a neighboring farm where she could at least come home on Sunday, check up on me, help me clean the house, wash and iron, and give me instructions on how to do the chores and care for the garden.

On the fifteenth of August, Father left. So many of my childhood recollections are as clear as cut glass, but this time of my anguish I remember not at all. It is as lost as a foot print in dust after a swift breeze has swept over it.

At this time, Mother Nature protected me as gently as a hen who gathers her brood under her wing. There is no other explanation for my lack of memory of those first days after Father left and I realized I would be alone indefinitely. I was used to Father leaving home ever so often, so when I told him goodbye at the gate and watched him disappear over the hill, I was not disturbed. But when I turned back toward the house, saw how it loomed, old and gray and lonely, I realized all that had made it a home and livable had fled. Abruptly a reaction set in and I thought, "I can't bear to enter it and to live alone in its empty rooms." I thought, "I must run after Father and explain this to him, to tell him that he mustn't leave me there all by myself." If I took a short cut across the west field and through the woods to the lane, perhaps I could catch up with him, stop him and ask him to return or to take me along with him. To think was to act. I was through the gate in an instant. I raced through the plowed field where the corn was sending up new green shoots. I leaped the gullies and on entering the woods, dodged the trees that blocked my path. I came out at the gap at the far end of the lane only to see Father disappear over the next hills. I knew that I could not catch up with him now. I called, "Father! Father!" again and again at the top of my voice. He could not have heard me. He was so far away. I climbed the gate and continued to call, "Father! Father!" Then the curtain fell, gently darkening the stage. He was gone and I can remember no more. Of what happened then I cannot recall a single thing. How I got back to the house, what I did or did not do, I have no idea. Whether this oblivion, this state of shock, lasted a day or a week I do not know. I can't remember where I was when I started to recover. I do remember extreme thirst and that the cows were bawling plaintively as if their bags were bursting from not having been milked.

It was as if I had been rolling down a steep hill and had been halted by an outcropping rock. Then the rock had loosened after a time from my weight, and I had started to roll again. But even then I don't know what I did first. If I went to the well for water or took up a pail to milk the cows, I cannot say. I do not even remember if it was morning or evening. All I know is that by the time I had awakened to full reality that I was alone; irrevocably alone now, and that I must face up to it.

As far as I was concerned, I think that each of the family thought that I was more or less the responsibility of the other, or that someone or the other would be home every day or so, or that Father would come home more often. Annie and Nellie were both expecting again so could not ride horseback the five and six miles over the roads caring a baby in arms to see me. I went to visit them but not often, tramping barefoot over the hills through weeds and woods and cow pastures, where I was still terrified of mean bulls, and across creeks to spend the day or sometimes the nights. They fed me and I played with the precious little ones, but they always seemed concerned about the farm, that I should be there to see to it, and that the house not be empty when Father did come home, for they knew how lonely it must be for him to come and not find Mother there as he had always done.

I wanted to beg them not to send me home to the vacant house, to sit at an empty table and eat my meals alone or to climb the dark stairs in terror to bed, but my pride would not let me say how I felt. They would brag on me and tell me how brave I was and how proud they were of me to keep the house so well while Father was away, so that I said not a word.

If I visited the neighbors, they were kind and asked me to partake of their meals at mealtime and made me welcome, but hinted that I must get home in time to milk, lest the cows dry up, or feed the chickens lest they fly to roost hungry.

The neighborhood girls had always been allowed to come and visit me, spend the night or weekend when their parents could spare them, so naturally I felt that there would be no change now, that they would be allowed to come and stay the night and relieve the loneliness of the long days. This was not to be. The first time I asked a girl to come and visit me, her mother asked if Father would be there, and when I said no, she flatly refused. All the mothers naturally had the same attitude, for they did not want their girls to spend the night unchaperoned in a house alone with another young girl. They asked me to spend the night with them, which I sometimes did, but then I began to feel like a star boarder who forever took something and never paid anyone back, so fewer and fewer times would I spend the night away from the farm. At home, I lingered over everything so as to fill my days. Still, milking three cows, slopping four pigs, and feeding a few dozen chickens and turkeys can take only so long, and washing dishes for one isn't a very time consuming job. The house didn't seem to get dirty in the times between Ruth leaving and coming home, so for the most part I just wandered about the farm, or stood at the window looking out or buried my head under the quilts.

At first, I cried day and night, then it seemed all my tears were shed, that their source was all dried up and there were no more. In a daze, not quite being able to believe what had happened to me, I wandered the fields where the weeds were taking over, or I saddled a horse and rode for miles, often till long after dark; or I climbed the old apple tree and just sat there. I was not particularly afraid of the dark or of the stillness around me. Sometimes a hen cackling, or a cow bawling far away would make me break out in a cold sweat. Other times I would run along the cowpath as if I were running away from something. Then I would stop short and breathless, and with pounding heart realize there was no place for me to run.

The latter part of August, Father, Paul, Ruth, and Goldie came home for a week; Paul and Goldie to prepare for the coming school year, and Ruth to help them.

A week later, Ruth and I sat on the posts on either side of the gate and waved goodbye to Father, Paul, and Goldie as they drove over the hill in our wagon on the way to Tuscumbia where Paul and Goldie were to attend high school. Even though we did not know it then, it was Goldie's farewell to the farm. She was never to return, except for two short visits, for she too would marry a country boy the following year. It was a hot day and the maple leaves had turned bottom side up, as they were supposed to do before a rain, but there was not a cloud in the sky, I noticed.

The horizon, as I saw it then, is so clearly etched in my memory that even now I can draw the outline with its every dip and rise and swirl. It drew closer where the maples and cedars around the house rose to a clear blue sky. Then it receded to blend with the soft haze of far distances.

Mine was a small world, I though. I felt that I could almost reach out and touch the sides of it in all directions. The hills, though, appeared very high, and for a second I knew a vague fear that for me they might prove unscalable. So, anxiously, I searched for the familiar three small cuts in the horizon made by paths that our feet so often trod, and weighed their ultimate destinations. As I stepped them off backward and forward in my mind, they seemed to hold little promise. Two of the paths came to an abrupt end at Glovers Chapel and George School. The third held more promise as it was the only path that led to the "outside." With questioning eyes and troubled heart, I faced this one that day. This was not a tiny path as the others, but a real road though marred by ruts and washed by the rains. It cut a wide swath at the horizon, a cut that at one moment was filled with the silhouette of a well-loaded wagon, and the next moment was as empty as if the wagon had disappeared into a vacuum on the other side.

Goldie had worked hard and saved her earnings of the entire summer in preparation for this day, this beginning of her great adventure. Ah, but she would have help. Father and Paul, convinced of her unusual abilities, had pledge their every effort to see that she had the opportunity to round out her education. Their hopes were high for her, and they were proud. And, she, secure in the dignity of their approval, was filled with happy anticipation of the future. But for Ruth and me, left sitting on the fence, the future looked very dim indeed. Ruth, sensitive, temperamental, and emotional had not been able to adjust to housework and had come home. Long we sat, leaning on cupped hands, meditating.

    I cannot imagine Ruth's thoughts or even guess at her mood, but mine took on a dream-like quality. I felt like I was standing and gazing up at a large picture. I tilted my head and examined it from different perspectives. Suddenly, I felt as if I had stood there gazing for years. The picture had changed very little. Only the people in it had increased in number, but they were all waving goodbye in much the same manner, and all leaving me with various degrees of loss. The background, of course, was the rocky hill and the blue sky, but filling the foreground were hosts of people facing the other way and marching towards the cut in the horizon. I felt that I was no part of this scene, but was left outside as if the frame were too small to include me.

    Sister Ethel was at the head of the procession and far in the distance. I had grown so large and she had become so small in my memory, I could hardly see her. Only when she turned and blew a kiss, did I remember her smile; so vague, as if she couldn't fathom what life had done to her. Then marched Uncle Oliver, so broad of shoulder, so solid and jolly. He waved both his hands high in joyous farewell. Below them marched the boys in uniform, Garsy and Carl, not looking back to show tears, which were no part of being brave. Then two brides went away, Annie and Nellie, so shy and lovely, with so much love and faith as their gifts to give. Jim rode close behind, not even looking back, so filled was he with thoughts of his Sybil. Next followed Creighton and Lucy our cousins on Mother's side of the family shouting and laughing. Then at the bottom of the picture went Mother, never to return. Now just this minute, Goldie had waved a farewell. Her going made me sad and lonely already, but mingled with it was a real joy at her adventure. However, deep inside of me was the question,

"When shall I go forth?" Would there ever be a time for me? Doubts filled me. Perhaps I'd never leave the farm, but be condemned to grub in our poor soil until my strength failed, and I became too old to care. From the depth of my being, I cried, "NO! NO!"

Ruth looked up surprised. "What did you say?"

"Nothing," I said, and guiltily wiped away a hot tear.

A couple of days later, a neighbor from the valley came and asked Ruth if she would come and help his wife out. She hated to leave me, but she needed the money and I assured her that I could manage very nicely alone. This time she was working too far away to even come home on weekends. So began my nightmare struggle to run a house and farm entirely alone. I had a lot of talent for never doing anything right the first time. I never made the same mistake twice, but went on to bigger and better ones.

Canning time came and I had to tackle that stupendous job for the first time. My hands were not strong enough to tighten the lids of the jars. I canned gallons of lovely peaches, blackberries, apples and tomatoes, only to have them spew out around the lids, or crack like a rifle shot when the jars burst, usually in the middle of the night, scaring me half to death.

Before school started, I would have to have some clothes. That meant I would have to get money for material and make them myself. Father had never had to bother about clothes for his children. Mother had taken care of that task. So the only way I had of obtaining the money for them was through the sale of chickens, so I decided to market enough for my purpose. I singled out the ones I thought weighed the most and caught them by the simple method of chasing them until, exhausted, they ran for cover under a gooseberry bush, where I crawled on my stomach under the thorny branches and drug them out by their feet and wings. They must have lost pounds that way. Tying their feet together with twine, I turned a washtub over them to keep them from flopping away. By the time I had caught six in this manner, which was all I could carry in both hands, I was so exhausted I could hardly bear the thought of trudging the four miles over hill and hollow to the market at Toronto carrying my heavy and squawking load.

Arriving barefoot, dirty and tired, I stood eagerly over the clerk as my chickens were being weighed. I was chagrined to hear the market price was only eighteen cents a pound, but that was not to be helped. There wasn't any material in the store that suited my taste, only drab, colorless prints, and I loved bright colors. So, I splurged on a stick of Long Tom chewing gum, clutched my chicken money in my pocket, and set out for home arriving long after dark.

I had no trouble making up my mind from the lovely pictures in the mail order catalog, and carefully I wrote out my order, addressed the envelope, and waited patiently at our mailbox two miles from home to purchase a money order from the mailman.

After weeks of waiting, my package arrived, and eagerly I went about the task of making dresses from the material. From the start everything I did was wrong. After I cut out the sleeves, I found I had cut them wrong side out and left the print on the inside. Then I made the neck too big for the collar. And them, because I was too impatient to take time to baste the side seams, I ended up with one side of the material longer than the other and had to pucker and gather to make the ends meet. In vexation, I spent hours picking out the tiny stitches I had sewn wrong. For me the sewing machine became a contrary monster. It sewed forward for other people, but for me it seemed to want to sew backwards. It maliciously broke the thread, causing me to spend half my time rethreading the needle. I shed tears of frustration over those dresses in the making, and more bitter ones when I finally tried them on and saw how the beautiful garments I had planned, looked as if I had donned them upside down. Nevertheless, I had to wear them since I couldn't possibly afford any more material. These dresses were a source of amusement to the other children in school. But I had an answer for them. I would toss my head and say, "At least I can make my own clothes and don't have to have someone sew for me like a baby."

One rare evening, Father was home and sat on the porch with shoulders slumped and head in his hands. I had prepared a most horrible meal—lumpy gravy, lumpy potatoes, and cornbread with the soda forgotten. I knew he was furious. I sat down by him, took his arm and snuggled my head against his shoulder and began to cry.

"Father!" I said, in a plaintive voice. "Don't expect too much out of me! I'm only twelve years old and don't know nuthin'. I'm trying to learn. I'll do even better if you will treat me as an equal, Father. Don't treat me like a slave!" At this he drew his arm away as if he didn't want to touch me. My hurt turned to anger and I began to say what was in my heart.

"I ain't sweet and meek like my sisters, Father. I want things for myself. I want more than grub to eat and a roof over my head. I want to go away and learn to be an artist. I don't want to live out my life here on the farm while the great, big world passes me by. Annie and Nellie and Jim are trapped, but I ain't yet and I promised Mama I would go away and amount to something. Carl and Arley are nice and sweet, but they don't think! Imagine them ever selling a cow or a pig or a load of hay to buy their wimmin a pretty. I don't aim to be treated that way! I know no matter how hard I work here on the farm, it won't do no good, and it won't get me nowhere, and I'll be looked down on as a woman!"

Father looked at me coldly. "You are stayin' right here and take care of me and the farm like your Mother did! Better to quit trying to get above your raisin', youngun," and he got up, went into the house, and slammed the door.

I leaned against the porch post and looked at the moon for hours, and thought of my problems.

Father left the next day, and I did not see him again for several months.

Once that winter Ruth and Father came home again for a few days, and then a terrible thing happened, and I realized the only way to leave the farm would be to run away.

Death struck all around us that year taking the young and the old. Of course, we attended all funerals, as country people were obliged to do. These sad occasions made us feel the need of our friends more than at any other time. We attended so many funerals that year; I got to where the passage of comfort, "Be not afraid. Ye believe in God, believe also in Me, for in my Father's house are many mansions. If it were not so, I would have told you. I go to prepare a place for you and when I go I will come again and receive you unto Myself, that where I am there Ye may be also," neither sustained nor soothed me. People seemed to be forever bringing us the news of someone's parting. The time came that whenever I saw anyone coming, I began to shake and tremble with fear. Some of these deaths touched me lightly, such as Uncle Joe's in March, and Uncle Jim's in June. They were Father's brothers and both lived at Tuscumbia. Uncle Joe, who had visited us once, I remember as being a fat jolly person even though he had been a cripple from a stroke, I gathered. Uncle Jim, I had never seen at all. But I felt sorry for Father when he came home from his brothers funerals looking drawn and gray. He seemed only to resent any effort to comfort him, so I stayed as far away as possible. Annie had a girl friend, Laura Traw, who had always been her playmate when they were children, and they were still very close friends. In this year they shared equal sorrows. Laura's came first in winter. She lost two beautiful baby boys and I felt so so sad to see such a young mother grieving over their sweet still forms. Jim lost his first baby around the beginning of October. He was so very fond of children and had looked forward to this one with such anticipation. It lived only four, happy days, and then it was gone. I remember how he insisted on carrying the tiny casket alone to the graveyard. Five days later, Annie's little baby girl, Geneva, died very suddenly. This went very hard with all of us. Such a sweet, happy, cooing darling. We were all crazy about her. I remember I was milking the cows, when cousin Roscoe came down the hill to tell me Geneva was very sick. It was almost dark. I stopped milking, looked up to the sky to pray, and saw the first star of the evening. I could think of no words to say, so I leaned against the barn lot gate, folded my hands and prayed a poem I knew. "Star Light, Star Bright, first star I've seen tonight, I wish I may, I wish I might, have the wish I wish tonight. I wish you would let little Geneva live and be all right."

My prayer wasn't granted. That evening, her little soul slipped away from us forever.

In the winter death struck twice again in the same family. The Scotts lived about four miles from us. Gilbert was about twenty. Silvia died first. She was my age. When I saw her lying so still with folded hands, I then realized life was very short and I knew that this could happen to me. What happened at Gilbert's funeral, her brother's, was one of the tragedies of my childhood. It brought on an emotion that, before this, I had never felt and was the actual cause of Ruth and me trying to run away. For the first time, I resolved, at no matter what the cost, I would not stay on the farm and from then on directed all my thoughts and efforts towards escape. For the first time, I looked with open eyes at my Father and saw a man so wounded and hurt by his own tragedy that he wanted to deal out vengeance on the whole world, and I was struck with a terrible shame that he was my Father, and with the fear of a mind so troubled.

It was indeed unfortunate that he was asked to preach Gilbert's funeral. With Mother's and his brothers' deaths still a stone in his heart, with most of his children gone, old and tired, full of pain and wrath, his inner agony expelled with every word. Gilbert was a young man who was reported to drink a great deal, and spend a lot of time in the caves gambling. With that as the text of his sermon, Father stood over his coffin, used him as an example of sinfulness, and with chapter and verse, told how such wickedness as his would find its reward in the fire and brimstone of Hell. He chose this opportunity to bring out other things that happened in the community and threatened, pointing at the corpse, that if some people did not change their ways this would happen to them too. As I remember, Ruth and I were the only other members of our family there. We looked at each other and stared, stunned with mortification and shame. Whatever possessed him to stand in sight of God and pronounce such judgment over a corpse? I remember it was a bitter cold day with a thin, dirty crust of ice and frozen snow upon the ground. Ruth and I fled from the church as soon as he had finished his long harangue and the congregation had been asked to pass and view the body for the last time. We ran swiftly away from the church, over the frozen ground for home, and fled to our room, slamming the door as if the devil were pursuing us. Ruth turned to me with horror in her eyes.

"He's mad, Frances! I know he is! Stark, staring mad! He's out of his mind!"

I burned with humiliation and my heart ached with fear and anger. My idol had fallen from his pedestal completely and the fall left me bruised and hurt. Suddenly, I felt unloved, unwanted and miserable. The one person, above everyone else, who I wanted to be proud of me, had humiliated me. I was bereft. What had become of the kind man who used to talk to me by the hour and had conducted such a gentle service for little Pearl? Where was the fine and patient artist I had tramped the hills with?

"Father is hateful! He's mean! He ain't thinking of nobody but hisself no more. He doesn't love me. He doesn't care what happens to us or what people think, or he wouldn't embarrass us this way to where we can't hold our heads up no more! I never want to see him again and I ain't gonna let him keep me here like a prisoner all my life! I'm gonna clear out of these hill! I'm goin' to go somewhere where I can do somethin, to be an artist, be somebody. Mommy tolt me to! Mommy tolt me to!" I wailed and pounded my forehead against the door, feeling no pain but the pain in my heart.

I told Ruth and the room and the heavens above, "I can never face those people again!"

Ruth and I came to the same conclusion in almost the same breath.

"We have got to run away! We have simply got to get out of the hills and away from Father and the things that could happen to us here." Actually, Ruth was free to go anytime she wanted to, but we both realized I was too young to strike out on my own. Who would hire a twelve-year-old child? What would I do?

It was strange that Father had wanted the other children to get away from the farm, but for me, the last, things were to be different. I recalled the conversation I overheard that night when he and Mother had talked about our future and I remembered how he had said the youngest should be the one to stay home and care for the old folks until their deaths. Ruth and I both knew I was elected. I was the one link Father had with the life he had loved there. I was the one to take Mother's place, and keep his home for him as she had, safe and comfortable for his return. If he had been selfish in letting Mother live out her life there, he could have less reason to spare me, I reasoned.

I knew that the rest of the family were on his side: that they, too, wanted me there to care for him and the home place. Ruth alone seemed to understand my position. So she and I must run away together. Run so far away that we could never be brought back. Make a clean break. Take the train at Crocker, the furthest railroad station we knew of. Then we would go to St. Louis where Ruth would find work and care for me till I was old enough to be on my own.

But we had no money, so Ruth must now go back to work and save every nickel she earned. I must, for the time being, stay on the farm, raise chickens, save eggs, raise turkeys and sell what little cream I could, so that I too could add to the funds. That we must hurry with our plans seemed a matter of life and death that bitter day. I had been a child asleep in the womb of Mother's tender care. Now I was awakening to the web I was caught up in. Father and the hill men were suddenly my enemies. I had been brought up in the tradition of being wife, mother and drudge to some man, but every cell in my body rebelled against it. Still, I wanted their approval and I wanted Father's approval to go on with my life. But I knew if he kept me there, I would eventually marry a country boy. Already awakening in me was the hunger that lies at the soul of all creation. I knew without knowing that to marry a farm boy would be the death of me as an individual; that the thought of death to this inner self was more fearful than death to the body. I knew now that Mother had fought against this happening to all of us. Father had gone along with her when she was alive. Now with her gone, he had reverted to the hill type and was prepared to see that I took the place of the woman of the hills in his life. I was to work and wait for his return as Mother had done.

I must now do something no hill girl I knew had ever done. I must defy my Father and run away.

16

Try, Try Again

Ruth went back to her job full of resolutions to carry out our plans. I saw very little of her now. Father and Garsy seldom came home at all any more. The winter passed slowly. The reluctant spring finally came.

There was very little left to eat on the farm in these early months of spring. Apples, onions, potatoes and pork hardly ever lasted the winter out, and since my effort to preserve the fruit had been so unsuccessful, our cupboard was bare indeed. So for the next several months I had very little to eat.

Loneliness and lack of proper food began to tear down my resistance and wear on my nerves. I recall that the neighbors remarked how puny I looked and about the dark circles under my eyes. But not for the world would I have disgraced the family by asking them for help. Too, I had terrible pangs of conscience. I knew that it was wrong to feel the way I did about my Father, and I wondered if I were being punished for these sins. All this preyed upon my mind day and night, making me ill with its conflicts.

One night I just started to fall asleep when I heard someone stealthily open the door and enter my room. I heard the floorboards creak next to the bed and knew that someone was standing over me. My heart rose in my throat and seemed to pound so hard the bed shook. I was certain that this stealthy visitor was intent on doing me harm and for a while I was so frightened that no sound would come from my throat. The room was pitch-dark and I could not see a thing. Suddenly I had an intuition that whoever it was would not carry out his plan if I remained calm and let him know that I knew that he was there but suspected nothing wrong. Reasoning thus, I was able to say in a fairly calm voice, "Ruth is that you?" knowing that Ruth wasn't within miles. My intuition must have been correct, for I heard the footsteps retreat and the door close, and I knew I was alone again. I lay there bathed in sweat and in an agony of trembling, not daring to get up and search the dark house. When daylight came, still the terror would not leave me. I was sure now that there was some great evil in the house. What it was I didn't know. Maybe it was the spirit of hatred, or maybe it was the awareness of sin and the secret lusts of our countryside which had taken body in the night. Or was it that I was losing my mind and that this was but the product of my imagination?

So now, in addition to hunger and mental stress, I suffered long nights of terror behind the barred door of my little room upstairs, fearful of every noise around the house. I went to bed at dark, and under no circumstances would I leave the room until broad daylight.

One fine day Father returned looking well-fed, well-dressed, and obviously comforted by his visits with old friends and relatives in Tuscumbia, and jingling a little money in his pocket. He brought home a good stock of groceries, sugar, flour, lard, and smoked jowl, and coffee and I prepared a meal for us. When we sat down to the table he started to offer thanks as he always had. Before he got a word out of his mouth, I looked him squarely in the eye and said, "While you're conversing with the Lord and thanking Him for all this fine food, you better ask Him what I had to eat while you were gone. And you'd better ask Him to forgive you for leaving me alone in this God-awful house. And maybe you'd better pray that you'll never be as hungry and scared as I've been lately. On second thought, I don't think you'd better ask Him for anything because I don't think He'll listen to anybody as selfish and thoughtless as you are."

He was stunned and speechless, and without eating a bite he rose from the table and left the kitchen. I too, was unable to eat. But I kept saying over and over again to myself, "I don't care. A body's got to stand up for their rights."

Ruth happened to come home the next day and I told her my story between hysterical sobs. She took me in her arms and assured me that no one would harm a sweet little girl like me and promised faithfully she would never let me out of her sight again.

"I'll quit my job," she said, "And I'll stay home, and we'll starve together."

Ruth was virtually a goddess of wrath when she was angry, and she was angry now, and I realized how beautiful she was with her green eyes flashing, her fine teeth and firm chin, and her chestnut hair. Her tall figure made her the personification of strength and grace. Her attitude towards me was a miracle of loyalty and love.

For a couple of weeks while she and I cleaned and scrubbed and set the house in order, we mulled over our problem and by and by we began to evolve a plan. It was essential that no hint of our plan get out to anyone. We knew that with our most careful scheming it would be at least a year before we would be able to carry it out. Our hope and prayer was not only to escape the farm, but to sever ourselves forever from country existence. We hadn't the faintest idea how much money we'd need to establish ourselves in the city or how to go about finding work there, but we were determined to put so many miles between us and the farm that there could be no possibility of ever having to come back.

And then one day, Garsy came home, and that was bad.

What he did to spite and irritate us was not my biggest worry. It was Ruth's anger after any one of these incidents that troubled me the most. I lived in mortal fear that she would finish him off some day in an uncontrollable fit of temper. There were times when I would listen for hours to her threats of vengeance while I tried to soothe and placate her.

One evening Garsy brought home one of his gambling cronies, who had a reputation for stealing watermelons, pelts or anything he could get his hands on. They sat in the front room, which Ruth had just scrubbed, and shed the mud from their shoes while they laughed and Garsy played the violin—waiting, we knew, for us to put supper on the table. We held back as long as we could, hoping they would leave. At last Ruth boiled over.

"It's bad enough to cook for Garsy, who won't do a thing to earn a living since Mama died," she said, "but I'll be damned if I'll cook for that other skunk."

She tore out the kitchen door and went around the house to the front porch and picked up an armload of firewood that was stacked by the door. Dashing into the front room, she started hurling sticks of wood at Garsy's guest. To say that he grasped the situation at once is an understatement. He ducked through the door like a scared rabbit. Down the path to the front gate he sprinted and cleared it in one long, clean leap, and continued off down the hill in a dead run. Ruth followed him and hurled stove sticks until she ran out of ammunition. After hurling the last stick, she turned around and tripped over Paul's old hound dog, who had rushed after her in the excitement. This made her madder than ever and she began to swear at the dog.

"Some day I'm gonna kill that hound for always being under foot. I mean it. All it does is take the food out of our mouths to feed it. I wish Paul had killed it the time he threatened to for eating everything it catches."

I was so relieved that it was only the hound dog she wanted to murder that I said impulsively, "I'll tell you what let's do. Let's hang him tomorrow and get him out of our sight." I had been reading Treasure Island and had been impressed by, "Fifteen men on a Dead Man's chest." I was only joking, but to my horror, she agreed.

"You've got a good idea. Tomorrow, you sonofagun," she said, pointing at the dog, "You'll hang at sunrise."

I went along with this murderous plan in the hope of keeping her mind off Garsy and half expecting that she would have cooled off by morning. I was wrong, for evidently she had seethed all night. In the early morning hours she woke me with the words, "Don't forget the execution." The hounddog saw us coming and got the picture. He took off like a streak of lighting into the woods; we were never to see him again. Ruth and I looked at each other and rolled in the grass and began to laugh. She was over her temper.

I wrote to Paul and told him that poor old Brownie, his hound dog had disappeared; that he had crawled off and died pining for his absent master. Paul was properly touched.

It seemed that there was no limit to what Garsy would do to hurt us.

In the spring, a calf, a scrawny runt, had run under a scythe that was hanging on the fence and cut a gash about ten inches long on his shoulder. Father said if I'd run and get Mr. Willoughby, who was the neighborhood veterinarian, and had been my friend since we swam the flood together, to come and sew up the cut, I could have the animal if it lived. I ran as fast as my legs would carry me to the Willoughby house and entreated him to come to my aid. He willingly obliged, carefully sewing up the wound. For weeks I treated the wound with a salve he gave me made of lard and carbolic acid, to keep the wound soft and the flies away. Slowly I nursed the calf back to health. Twice a day I tended him, making sure he had plenty of milk before I took him away from his mother to milk her. His wound healed and he thrived.

I dreamed of adding a good sum to our shrunken fund—perhaps even buying a dress and shoes. I had no idea how much the calf would bring, but as the summer progressed and I saw how he grew, I became more and more optimistic.

One early morning I awoke to a loud hello at the front gate. I heard Garsy get out of bed and greet our visitor. I peeped out the window and saw them cut off and exchange chews of tobacco, the usual courtesy when two men got together. I recognized the man as Joe Holdren, one of Garsy's friends. They talked and chewed and spat, and I noted that they were nodding their heads toward my beautiful calf. Finally, they appeared to come to an agreement. Joe put a halter around my calf's neck, counted out some bills and handed them to Garsy, and before my very eyes led the calf away.

I was outraged. I ran crying to Father who was home for once, and fast asleep. He listened to my tale of woe and then turned over, "There ain't nuthin' I can do about it. I thought, "When Garsy goes to the caves to gamble, as he is bound to do, I will follow him and march in and take the money away while it is lying on the table and I hope he will be too embarrassed to try and stop me."

I was terrified of the caves, remembering my mother's story, but I reckoned that my brother being there would prevent anyone from harming me. Besides I was so furious I didn't think about what might happen to me anyway.

I watched him out of the corner of my eye all day. Sure enough, about an hour before sundown, he took off and I took off after him. I didn't try to keep in sight of him for I knew where he was going.

I crossed Dean's Creek following the same paths I had traversed when I went looking for wild onions and mushrooms and finally came to the Glaze. I swung my arms to balance myself as I clung with bare toes to the foot log that lay across the swift waterfall. Then I began to go slowly as I climbed along the dangerous precipice to the mouth of the caves. I was terrified now at what I was going to do and wanted to turn back but made myself keep right on going. I heard voices and laughter as I rounded the big rock. Cautiously I peered around it and into the darkened cave. Sure enough there was Garsy sitting with a dozen other men playing cards and on the table was a pile of money. I took a deep breath and marched in, straight up to the table and before anyone could stop me, grabbed up a handful of money. I'll never forget the startled look on their faces as they sat there holding onto their cards, mouths open and eyes staring. "This is my money," I said and glared at Garsy who couldn't seem to say a word. "You sold my calf and took the money that should have been mine," and I started to turn and run. A big brute of a man, dirty and bewhiskered, leaped up, grabbed me by the wrist and twisted my arm till my hand unclasped and the money fell to the floor. He pulled back a clenched fist and I thought he would surely kill me. Then someone shouted, "Don't hurt her. That's Mrs. Wright's girl." He then lowered his fist but flung me from him so hard that I staggered out the mouth of the cave and fell within inches of the precipice where the water boiled a hundred feet below.

I crawled back from the edge of the cliff, went back to the mouth of the cave seething with anger. I gathered up a mouthful of spit and spit it at them. I saw that Garsy sat with lowered head. "I hate you, you dirty scum, I yelled. I hate you all!" Then I went staggering along the cliff towards home trembling with rage and rubbing my bruised wrist.

Now I knew that we had to escape. My feelings were becoming as violent as Ruth's. Our one asset had been taken from us. In angry council, we decided that the only thing to do would be to sell everything on the farm that we could turn into cash, and keep the money.

Such an action on the part of hill women was unheard of. It amounted to revolution. But our minds were made up. We would wait our chance.

There came a day in the fall when Father and Garsy were both away, and Ruth was home. Here was the chance we had prayed for. We went into action. The first step was to sell the livestock. I lit out on a dead run for Joe Holdren's, hoping to persuade him to buy the pigs since he had seemed so willing to purchase my calf. The result was typical of how hill countrymen regarded women.

"Nope," he said, "Can't do it. Don't think your pa'd like it."

"You men make me sick," I answered spiritedly. "You had the nerve to buy my calf from Garsy, and maybe Pa didn't mind. But I did." With that I sprinted for home.

Ruth and I went hurriedly about crating up the chickens and pigs and loading them into the wagon, a task inspiring a great deal of swearing on Ruth's part.

First we had trouble hitching up the horses, as one of the hooks was off the singletree. Then we had difficulty loading two cans of cream that we had saved. They were so heavy we could scarcely lift them into the wagon. The chickens proved hard to catch because they were always wary in the middle of the day. They had been fed in the morning, so they were not hungry enough to be enticed with corn now. However, we finally got some of them crated and loaded. The pigs came next and presented new problems. We backed the wagon up to the pigpen gate and then made a ramp out of a couple of planks. Then with Ruth holding an ear of corn to lure them and me behind to shoo them along, we finally managed to get one of them into the wagon.

We worked in an agony of haste for fear Father or Garsy might suddenly return. At last we were ready. Neither one of us had ever driven a wagon, so we decided to take turns. I was first; I seized the reins the way I had seen others do and cracked them across their backs quite forgetting that Old Verdun was skittish. He took off at a run dragging the wagon and the other horse along with him. The cream can bounced, and chickens squawked and the pig squealed in fright, while Ruth and I hung on helplessly. Up over our hill and down the lane we sped; down another hill into the creek where we came to a halt in the soft gravel of the creek bed. We hit the stream with such sudden force that the water rose in a wave and drenched us and everything in the wagon. The horses stood panting for breath while Ruth and I looked in back to see what damage had been done. When she saw the bedraggled chickens and pig, Ruth began to laugh. She said, "I reckon they'll weigh more wet." We decided it was her turn now, so she gathered up the reins and spoke to the horse. "Now let's don't rush this thing."

The rest of the trip was uneventful. The horses trotted along serenely while Ruth and I discussed our next move.

We had already worked out a way to get to a railroad station to catch a train to St. Louis. Ruth's best friend knew our plans and had told Ruth that her Father took a truckload of cream every Friday to the railroad station at Crocker and would be glad to take us. We planned to go to her house, spend the night, and leave with him in the morning. We had no idea what we would do when we got to St. Louis, but Ruth's friend had assured us that her sister who lived there would be glad to take us in and help us find work.

In Brumley, we were able to dispose of our pig, chickens, and cream in a hurry, and with the huge sum of thirty-six dollars to start us in a new life, we raced home to pack our clothes and clean ourselves up. We were in a fever of anxiety. One suitcase held everything we both owned. But then we began to worry because we felt we ought to have one apiece; it would look more respectable, and besides Ruth might get a job and have to live apart from me. We decided to carry the empty one for show.

Although we were tired from such a full day, we were happy and thrilled as we trudged along in the dark to the Pemberton's. Ruth's friend welcomed us and told her Father of our plans. He agreed willingly to let us ride in the back of his truck to Crocker.

That night I slept lightly, sick with nervous anticipation, perhaps a little sick at leaving everything of my life with Mother. We were roused long before daylight and were obliged to sit at a table loaded with food. I'll never forget how strange that breakfast by lamplight seemed. I could hardly force down a bit of the gravy, sowbelly, fried potatoes, biscuits, and preserves. I was deeply excited. The truck had been loaded the night before, so Ruth and I scrambled into the back with the cream cans. Rain was pouring down and we crawled under some tarpaulins, covering ourselves completely. The truck pulled out and we bumped over rutted roads for a long spell. Suddenly, the truck stopped, and Mr. Pemberton called, "End of the line. Jump out."

We crawled out, then gazed in amazement. The truck stood at our own front gate. Father stood by the gate glaring at us.

"Where is the money for the chickens and hog?"

Ruth fished it out of her stocking, threw it on the dirt and ground it with her heel.

"There's the filthy money. Pick it up out of the dirt," she cried. "You're welcome to it."

We ran to our room and wept from our souls.

17

Hands Along The Way

Ruth and I were forced to the realization that her promise never to leave me again could not be fulfilled if we both were ever to leave the farm. Sometime back, she had located a job through an advertisement in the Autogram. A doctor in Iberia, Missouri, a small town about fifty miles north of the farm, had advertised for a girl for housework. Ruth had written him and he had replied that she could come when she was ready. Now she decided to go, save her money, and come back for me, hoping in the meantime that she could eventually find a way for me to join her.

So in a few days she left again amidst many tears and misgivings on the part of both of us. She was to walk the six miles to Brumley, catch a mail truck that took passengers to Tuscumbia, and then take another mail truck to Iberia.

Life for me had to go on somehow. Father being gone again, I resumed fastening the latch on my door at night, and pushing the washstand in from of it for added protection. Father had said not a word to us about our escapade, only stomping around in silence, slamming doors, and glaring.

For a while it looked as if I might not even be able to finish the eighth grade, but when my cause appeared most hopeless a hand reached out to help me. The result was one of the most important factors in guiding my life into new channels of confidence and ambition.

I suspect that most of us can look back and remember crucial times when some kind, understanding person has reached out to guide us into the light that we did not see ourselves. We sometimes forget the faces and names of these people, but their influence remains with us for the rest of our lives. Such a person for me was my teacher, Ida Shipman, who came to teach at our school when I reached the eighth grade. From the very first we were drawn to each other. Whatever the basis for this mutual attraction, she became an outstanding force in my life. I was a shy and retiring child, overshadowed by my more aggressive sisters whose self-confidence I envied and who in the past, unfortunately, made the situation worse by worrying with me in their eagerness to help. They had practically convinced me that I couldn't stand on my own two feet. This defeatist attitude had been readily recognized by my previous teachers and classmates to the point where I was regarded as being inferior generally. By the time I reached the eighth grade, I was a sad and lonely girl indeed. It wasn't that I was disliked, but nobody sought me out as they did the popular girls. Like an angel from heaven, Ida Shipman became my champion and helped me develop along the lines of my own personality.

She was not from our immediate part of the country. The first day of school was the first time I had ever seen her. She was a tall blonde, with dark skin, and serious brown eyes that had a direct way of looking into your face, appraising you calmly, so that when her gaze left, you felt that you no longer had any secrets from her. She had a way with children. She would take troublemakers and bullies, of which there were several in our school, and talk to them so convincingly that they fell into line. She had a system of segregating the little children and not letting them be run over by the stronger ones. In class, when she asked a question, she never seemed to hurry you, but would glance around the room patiently to see that all was well, giving you the impression that there was plenty of time to think the answer out. And when the answer was given correctly, she had neither praise or comment, but a look that said she had expected you to come through with the right answer all along. In the past I had never had courage to speak the answer out loud, but only to whisper it for someone else to shout out and receive the credit. Her keen eye caught this, and she would point to me as the first person to have the right answer. This gave me confidence almost immediately.

I felt her impact the first day of school. When I rose in my turn and said my name was Frances, she gave me her long look, while I stood straight and looked back at her, trying to fathom her expressionless face. At last she said, "You may be seated." I sat down, uncertain as to whether we were to be friends or not. But something deep within me had responded to her steady scrutiny. It was a strange experience to me to be looked directly in the eye, as we hill people were essentially bashful and secretive and seldom talked directly at each other. Our eyes would play about objects all around us rather than focus on the face of the other person. It is strange, but this mannerism was common even within families.

I cannot think of a good reason for this inability to be frank and open either in speech or gaze. I do believe that is was this one bashful trait, more than any other, which kept the hill folk from adjusting themselves when they were transplanted to strange environments.

The first day of school, to my consternation, Miss Shipman informed the children that all our textbooks were obsolete and every child would have to have new books. This was an order from the Superintendent of schools. Now, although books for required reading were furnished by the county, the textbooks had to be purchased by the students themselves. As long as I could remember, there had never been any new editions of these textbooks in our school. They had always been handed down from the oldest to the youngest, and to tear or mutilate a book was considered quite a crime. Nevertheless, with the passage of time the pages became torn and were sometimes missing. I had never owned a book and never expected to own one. The fact that parents were required to purchase the textbooks was one of the reasons why so many children did not attend school. The parents couldn't or wouldn't spare the few dollars necessary. We who did attend just borrowed from each other. I had no books, so I had to wait to get my lessons done after someone else was through with his. This had always caused me embarrassment and humiliation.

Now I was confronted with the problem of purchasing all new books. It was a very real problem since the ones I had to have—a geography, arithmetic, history, hygiene, and agriculture, were going to cost around $14.00. I broke this news to Father as bravely as I could. He received this information grimly.

"Don't see why you can't borrow like the rest. younguns don't learn nothin' in school nowadays, anyway, except how to paint their lips and bob their hair." With that he dismissed the subject. So, as this was not an absolute refusal, I took my courage in hand and told the teacher to order the books.

In the meantime, while washing Father's shirt, I found a checkbook in his pocket and discovered he had a couple of hundred dollars in the bank. I tore out a blank check and hid it under the dresser scarf, eagerly awaiting the arrival of my new books. When they came about six weeks later, I filled out the check, signed Father's name to it, and gave it to my teacher, and the precious beautiful books were mine. I held them carefully in my arms and hurried home, hardly able to wait till I got there to examine them. I never walked so carefully. I was so afraid I might drop them in the Pemberton's barn lot—in the thick, slimy, manure—the first obstacle on my way home; or that I might slip on the footlog crossing Dean's Creek, the second obstacle; or tear them on the wire fences as I slipped through them on the final stretch.

Once home, I spread them out on the kitchen table. I loved the clean new covers, the interesting odor, the shiny pages, and crisp print. My geography was the largest book and cost the fabulous price of three dollars and fifty cents. It was the most beautifully illustrated and the most interesting book I had ever seen. It had colorful maps, which I meant to copy, pictures of foreign countries, of mosques, temples, shrines, and pagodas, Roman and Gothic architecture, strange animals and stranger people. I wanted to draw every picture in it. The descriptions of different climates and odd vegetation and vast forests and mighty rivers filled me with wonder. I hurried through it, and then went back to go through it, more slowly. I was vaguely aware that it was time to start supper and to feed the chickens and get the milking done, but I couldn't tear myself away from those fascinating pages.

I heard the front door open, and looked up to find Father staring at my treasures.

"Come and see my new books," I invited. "They're the prettiest things you ever saw."

"Take them back. We can't afford to pay for them."

But I've already paid for them with a check I found in your pocket. I just signed your name to it and gave it to Miss Shipman.

His face became livid with rage. He pointed a shaking finger at me.

"That's forgery. And that's a crime. And you cain't get by with it. And don't ever do a thing like that again or I'll take a limb to you. You'll jist have to return the books tomorrow."

My pleading that without books I couldn't go to school only brought on his raging that, "A bunch of tom-fool ideas, this newfangled stuff. It's jist works of the devil, that's what it is. No sense in you goin' to school, anyway. Better stay home and learn how to cook. You got enough to do right here at home."

He had never seemed more furious in his life and I realized it stemmed from a fear of losing me, not so much because he loved me, but only because I was to be the one to wash and cook and mend and keep his home for him till he died. My heart nearly failed me now. But the fear of the empty years stretching ahead, with my life lived out here alone on the farm, day after monotonous day, and all my dreams of painting beautiful pictures slipping away, gave me the courage to speak out.

"I have a right to these books as much as anybody," I cried. "The other children's parents paid for theirs. I've jist got to go to school, or I will always be ignorant and dumb. The teacher says everybody ought to go to school. High school as well as grade school if they're goin to amount to anything, and Mommy said so, too. I can't just stay here and never learn nothin'." I wanted to cry, but was too angry. "It ain't fair. If other people can go to school, why can't I? You got enough money to pay for the books. I seen your bank-book!"

For a minute I thought he was going to explode. And again he pointed his finger.

"Now listen here, young woman. You are the last of the younguns. It's your bounden duty to stay here on the farm and care for me in my old age. 'Children are the crown of old men,' he quoted, 'and the glory of children are their fathers'."

He put his hand to his brow and moaned. "Nine children have I begat, and they have all deserted me in my declining years. Now you, the youngest, would backbite and leave me all alone. You are foolish to think you could get an education and become anything but a farm woman. Women never amount to nothin' anyway."

On he raved, "He that begotteth a fool doeth it to his sorrow and the Father of a fool has not joy, and you Frances, are a fool if you become too ambitious. Children must obey the parents in the Lord, for this is right, and I command you to obey me. Stay home and learn to care for the farm until I enter into rest which will be soon enough." And he beat his breast and looked as persecuted as Job.

He went on, "Surely you are as a daughter of Canaan, evil and wicked to steal my money and plot against me. Your teacher is a worker of iniquity and a tool of the devil to put into your head such notions that women are anything but 'tenders of sheep' as Rachel in the Bible was willing to be. Why, the men in the time of Christ did not talk to women, for was it not written in St. John, 4th Chapter, 27th Verse, 'And upon this came his disciples and marveled that He talked with the woman'. And in the 42nd Verse, 'They said unto the woman: Now we believe, not because of them saying, for we have heard Him ourselves and know that this is indeed the Savior of the world'. So you see, women weren't even listened to. So why should they be listened to now? They are as chaff before the wind; they are as beasts of burden. You must accept this lot in meekness and forbearance and face up to it. I am head of the household and I order you to do as I say. 'Until the mountains falling cometh to naught, and the rock is removed out of His place'. When I am gone, then you can go your way, live in sin, and perhaps become 'a jewel of gold in a swine's mouth'. But if you have any devotion to me, you remain here and comfort me 'until I am cut down like a flower and flee as a shadow and continue not'."

On and on he preached until I became deaf to it all, I was used to his preaching and quoting the Bible, but never had he used the Bible in such desperation, and never had he indulged in such histrionics.

He continued, "Now you take them books back first thing in the morning and tell that no-good teacher of yours that I said to return 'em. He went out and slammed the door, and then stuck his head back in. You'd better be getting supper ready and the milking done."

Apple Butter Days brings back old fashioned food

By Jeff Thompson

LINN CREEK - An apple a day may keep the doctor away, but a copper pot full of boiling apples keeps the visitors coming back every year to the Apple Butter Days fall festival.

Held at the Camden County Museum (CCM) and hosted by the Camden County Historical Society (CCHS), the event harkens back to when food was more hands-on, when milk came fresh every morning and butter was churned by hand.

The spirit of Apple Butter Days is a far cry from fast food breakfasts with jelly and jam in hermetically sealed foil packets.

The apple butter that comes from long hours of peeling, coring and boiling fresh apples in a huge metal pot over an open flame just naturally tastes better than anything mass produced by machines and conveyor belts.

It's a simple recipe - apples, a little spice, a little sugar, and lots of elbow grease.

Dale Jeffries was out back behind the museum, applying a liberal amount of that elbow grease.

The smell of burning hardwood mixed with the aroma of apples, spices and a little bit of

Continued in this week's Reporter

Dale Jeffries stirs a copper pot full of sliced and diced apples; just one step in making apple butter at the Apple Butter Days fall festival held Friday and Saturday at the Camden County Museum in Linn Creek. (Reporter photo by Jeff Thompson)

FOR SALE - 19" ViewSonic" CRT computer monitor, excellent condition, $25. Sunrise Beach. 374-6534.

fb47-50

FOR SALE - RCA 32" theatre TV

wards wire welder Minnkota 27lb. ist, trolling motor $50. anon 417-664-6341.

fb47-50

FOR SALE - Open bow 21' Concord with trailer, cover, 350 Mercruiser out-drive, white and yellow, asking $4000 OBO. 913-980-0612.

fb47-50

WANTED - Looking for 14' to 16' Jon Boat, wide hull, front drive trolling motor. 913-636-4086.

fb47-50

FOR SALE - '97 Ford Taurus SHO, black, 149000 miles, runs good, leather, power everything. Asking $220 OBO. 573-552-5053.

fb47-50

FOR SALE - 1977 Thunderbird Signa Tri-Hull, need to sell, $2000. 573-347-2560.

fb47-50

Bear Market

Now Over 30,000 Sq. Ft. of Fun Shopping for the Entire Family

"Socket's a big town with small town frien

I had stood up to him, but I knew now that my cause was lost. My world seemed to have ended.

The next morning I walked to the teachers desk and laid my precious books upon it.

"Father says I can't keep them. We can't afford to pay for them and you'll jist have to return them."

I tried to keep from crying, but one tear found its way to the end of my nose. I blotted it with the back of my hand. Miss Shipman looked at me keenly and without a word opened the books and wrote my name on the flyleaf of each of them. Then she penned a short note and slipped it into my geography. Handing the books back to me she said, "Please return to your seat and get to work. You're late."

Without hesitating, I turned around. No one disobeyed Miss Shipman. In amazement I hurried back to my seat, found the note she had written and read:

"Don't worry. I knew the check was in your writing, so I tore it up and paid for the books myself. Don't bother to thank me. You're worth it. Just be a good student and I will be well paid."

I looked up and met her eyes and then and there she became my idol. She winked at me without another sign of expression on her face, and turned towards the blackboard.

This wasn't all she did to win my undying gratitude. Little by little and day by day she began to bolster my ego. One day, on the playground, when everyone was playing ball but me, and I leaned against the schoolhouse and watched, she suddenly yelled, "Catch, Frances," and the ball came flying at me. I caught it and hesitated.

"Well, throw it back to me," she commanded. The next time they were choosing up sides, I noticed that she was one of the choosers. As they called out the names of those they wanted on their side, she said, "I'll take Frances." I walked up uncertainly and lined up beside her while they continued. I was not used to being wanted for a game.

When it came my turn at bat I thought I would die of fright. And I stood there shyly with all the kids yelling and shouting, "Come on, come on. If you can't bat, get out of the way so somebody else can." Miss Shipman fixed the bat in my hands, while I pleaded, "I jist can't bat, I cant."

She said, "Just watch the ball. That's all there is to it."

I raised the bat and the ball came spinning at me. I swung. There was a loud crack and the ball was flying high across the field. I stood and stared in astonishment.

"Run, Frances, run," Miss Shipman shouted. And I took off on two very fast legs. It was a home run and I had made it. Coming up to the home plate, panting, I looked at her for approval while the rest of the kids screamed and gathered around to compliment me. Everybody loves a winner. From the serene look on her face she apparently though it was nothing, giving the impression that she had known all along I would do it and would expect me to repeat the performance next time. When it was her turn to bat, she struck out. Without seeming perturbed about her failure, which would have left me without courage to try again, she glanced sideways at me and said, "There, see, I'm not as good a batter as you are." At this, I nearly burst with pride.

One day, when everyone was studying quietly in the schoolroom, I finished my lessons and was doodling on a piece of paper. Without really thinking of what I was doing, I drew a caricature of Miss Shipman and her beau, a young man who came often to school on horseback to ride home with her. She slipped up behind me and saw the picture. Taking possession of it without a word, she walked to her desk and slipped it into her drawer. When school was dismissed at the end of the day, she announced, "Frances, I want you to stay after school."

The rest of the children filed out, while I followed her to the desk with a sinking heart. I thought, "Suppose I've made her angry. If I have, I'll never forgive myself."

Sit down, she said, pointing to a bench close to her desk. Then she sat down herself and she pulled my sketch out of the drawer.

"It's about this picture. It's wonderful you know." With a broad smile she continued, "It looks just like us. Do you know that people get paid lots of money for doing things like this? You've got a lot of talent and I wish, as a big favor to me, that you would work hard at it. It's worth developing, and it's something nobody can ever take away from you."

As I sat gaping, she caught a glimpse of her boyfriend riding up to the door. Hurriedly she dabbed a powderpuff across her nose. The she reached up and untied the ribbon that held back her shiny blonde hair. Suddenly she looked so young and sweet and vulnerable. "Why, she's just a young girl," I thought. She caught the look on my face, and explained. "I get a little tired of playing the severe school-marm."

Then she laughed a gay and exciting laugh which I joined in and we walked arm in arm to the door.

Right along, my studies were becoming easier for me. Spelling, in which I always had been poor, I began to excel in. I'll never forget one day when we had a spelling contest. Two students would choose up sides and then all the students would line up against opposite walls and try to spell each other down. As usual, I was the last to be chosen and stood at the bottom of the line. The word "lyre," the musical instrument, had been spelled wrong up and down both sides of the room. When it came to me, all eyes focused on me, reflecting assurance that I would miss it too. Without hesitating, I spelled it correctly.

"Right," called Miss Shipman loudly. "Frances, you may go to the head of the line." Everyone moved out of the way, in obvious surprise, as I marched to the head of the line, chin high and glowing inwardly.

My final triumph came on the last day of school when the grade cards were handed out. These grades showed the results of our final examination. Our eighth grade final examination papers were always sent away to the County Superintendent's office to be graded, and the marks were given by the Superintendent's office rather than by our own teachers. Those who had passed received their diplomas along with their grade cards. When they were being handed out, Miss Shipman announced, "I'd like the entire school to know that Frances Wright made the highest grades in her graduation class."

I was the last to be handed my diploma, and when I went up to receive it I searched for proper words to thank her, but my thoughts choked in my throat and I could not say a single thing. She took me by the arm and we walked out the door together. "I'm proud of you, you know," she said. "You got no more than you deserved, I assure you." That was the last I have ever seen of her.

No, I could not find the proper words to thank her then. And I still don't have words adequate to express my gratitude to her. But in my heart and memory, I have never ceased to pay tribute to the gracious hand she held out to me to help me along the way.

As years went by, I decided to put my memory of her on canvas. When the portrait was finished and I hung it in my gallery, her beautiful face so calm, so sweet, so inspiring, drew the eye of an admiring public and they asked, "Did you really have a teacher that lovely?" and I said, "Yes I did."

18

The Hay Balers

Carl and Annie lived in one shack after another, but they never did have a house that had more than three rooms.

The one Annie and Carl lived in now was on a farm, about six miles from our home, further up the Glaze River. They were sharecroppers on this farm and would received only a small portion of what they raised. This farm, with rich bottomland, was spread out in a long apron at the foot of heavily wooded hills. The shack they now lived in was the worst they had ever occupied. Not smaller nor more disreputable, but because it was built on low ground and shadowed by the hills, it reeked of musk and mildew and was a breeding place for flies, mosquitoes, and a myriad of other insects. The sun never seemed to reach it long enough to dry its timbers. Its unhealthy atmosphere had always made me shudder with revulsion, and I shuddered now as I approached it.

I was going there in answer to a pleading note from Annie that Carl's brother had brought that morning. It seemed Carl had arranged for the hay balers to come the day after tomorrow as they had a lot of hay to bale and the cutting couldn't be put off. Annie had gone to Toronto for supplies to feed the men, and on the way home her horse had thrown her, and in her fall she had broken her arm. Carl met me at the front gate.

"Am I ever glad to see you! Poor Annie. We took her to the doctor at Richland and got her arm set all right and got home, but she didn't sleep a wink last night, it hurt her so badly. The kids'll sure be glad to see ye."

He took the reins of Old Verdun's bridle, whom I had ridden. "I'll take him to the barn and unsaddled him for ye." He looked at the horse and frowned. "How come Old Verdun is all covered with lather and breathin' so hard?"

"I had to teach him a little lesson," I told him. "Every time I ride him he tries to throw me. Today I got me a stick and showed him who's boss."

"I'm afeered you're gonna git hurt one of these days."

"If I do, Old Verdun will pay for it," I said with spirit.

I waded through the chickens in the muddy yard and entered the dark, stifling interior of the bedroom. Annie lay on an unmade bed. She greeted me in a tearful voice.

"Howdy, Frances, I'm so glad you're here. Things are a mess. I was already behind in my housework. Got a big washin' piled up. Got so much to do I can't seem to keep up with it. Been tryin' to weed the garden, bug the 'taters, can a few blackberries. The baby's cuttin' teeth and is cranky as a bear and wants to nurse every five minutes. And Carl didn't know "til yesterday that the hay balers were coming. Gosh. Were gonna have twenty men to cook for three times a day, for five days, anyway. I just had to go to town and get a few staples. We were out of flour and sugar and coffee, and wanted some vanilla to make some cakes, and I needed a new oilcloth for the kitchen table, and some skeeter netting to cover the baby whilst she sleeps, 'cause the flies and skeeters are about to eat her up. And then comin' home, this thing had to happen." She pointed to her bandaged arm. Her lips trembled and the tears welled up in her eyes.

I glanced around the house. Things were indeed a mess. The iron beds were bare of linen, exposing dark straw ticks stained with bed-wetting spots. There was the usual broken windowpane with a pillow stuffed in it, and where there was glass, you couldn't see through for the flyspecks. The floor was covered with cakes of mud from muddy shoes. I've often wondered why the mud had to be so cantankerous to wait until it got into the house to fall off.

Someone had kicked over Carl's spittoon and tobacco juice lay splashed across the floor. One of the babies sat by the puddle, patting its hands in the mess. I gasped. Snatching it up, I took it into the kitchen to wash its hands. The kitchen table, the worktable, the washstand, and the stove were piled high with dirty dishes over which swarmed millions of flies. I was searching round for a washrag to wash the child's hands when Carl stuck his head in the kitchen door.

He must have read the disgust and anger in my face as I whirled around, because he inquired meekly, "Anything I can do to hep?"

"Ya-ah," I almost shouted. "Fetch me tubs and tubs of water." And I looked around, "There'd better be some soap around here or I'll really holler."

Annie, a face full of pain, followed me in. Her hair was matted. She had a dirty dress on, stockingless dirty legs and shoes without laces and without toes. My heart went out to her in sympathy. In her soft, gentle voice she said, "My arms almost quit hurtin' now, and I still have one hand, so guess I kin be of some hep."

"Nobody ought to have so much on their hands as you have. You need hep or ought to quit working in the fields and garden and just keep house and care for the children. Now, never you mind. If we all work together, we kin clean this place up in a hurry. You've jist got too much to do for one person."

I looked around for a place to start.

"If you'll hold the door open, I think I'll chase out a few flies." So I found a couple of dishtowels and began at the farthest corner, flapping the towels. I shooed a swarm of flies towards the door while Annie held back the screen door to let them out, and then closed it quickly so they wouldn't dodge back in. We went from room to room, repeating this performance. When we got back to the kitchen, the oldest child stood holding the screen door wide, just dawdling. Annie pleaded sweetly with him.

"Please, honey, don't hold the door open. You'll let all the flies in. Frances has gone to so much trouble to chase them out." He flashed her a beatific smile and just stood there.

"Shut the door!" I shouted, "Or I'll whip the tar out of you." He puckered up his face to bawl, but shut the door in a hurry. I glanced at Annie to see if she was going to resent my interference, but she only smiled.

"He's awful stubborn, ye know. I ain't been able to break him from dirtyin' his britches. Him or his sister either, and this washin' for three younguns is about to git me down. If I could only break him, it would help a lot."

I resolved silently that I would break both of them before I left there or know the reason why. But all I said to Annie was, "Maybe you ought to show them who's the biggest."

We started in on the dishes first. After Carl had brought enough water from the spring to fill all the vessels on the place and we had a wash boiler full on the stove to heat, he wanted to know what else he could do.

"Why don't you take the quilts out and hang them in the sun? And would you mind findin' something to plug up that rat hole behind the stove. I keep imagining I see eyes looking out at me and it makes me jittery all over." During all this I kept thinking our house was never like this. Our beds were always clean. Mother had always been a good manager and we children were quick to obey her. But Annie's children were entirely out of hand. They ran in and out and around, holding the doors open, letting the flies and chickens in. They would leap on the beds with their dirty feet, discard their pants when wet or dirty, and run around most of the time half-naked. They seemed to always be gnawing on something. Sometimes it was a half-eaten apple covered with dirt and flies—always it was some form of food covered with dirt and flies. They constantly demanded the attention of their mother. They would fall down and hurt themselves and she would stop everything to kiss them. Then they wanted to sit straddled of her hip and see what was in all the pots. And she would drop whatever she was doing to give them the demanded attention.

This display of maternal patience began to drive me to distraction. At last I could hold back no longer.

"I don't see how you ever get anything done with that big youngun on your hip, and with them undoin' everything you do as fast as you git it done."

"But they want to see what's in the pot." She said lamely.

I pushed them outside and hooked the screen door. They pressed their faces against it and screamed. I fixed the baby a pallet by the front door in the cool draft. She too was getting on my nerves, because Annie felt she had to answer her demand to nurse every few minutes. I gave her a crust of bread and said, "Lay there and behave so we kin get somethin' done around here."

Annie observed all this and said, "I guess I'm just too soft with 'em. They always manage to get ahead of me, somehow."

I was beginning to get a kick out of ordering her husband around and he obeying so meekly. My power lay in the fact that they needed me desperately, and so I began to crack the whip. "Bring me some more water. Carry in some wood. Go empty the slop bucket. Hang out these here clothes. You better dig a lot of "taters—'nough for all week. Don't bring those onions in here to peel. Clean 'em outside. No use bringing in dirt and carryin' it out again." Annie laughed and said, "He never has done any of that for me."

"Did you ever tell him to?" I asked.

We developed into a wonderful team. A neighbor girl came to help us get ready for the haybalers. By the evening of the next day, after working most of the night, we had washed, starched, and ironed all their clothes and bed linens. The beds were made up with clean sheets and Annie's pretty pillowcases trimmed with lace. There were clean embroidered scarves on the dresser and sewing machine. We had tacked up a piece of mosquito netting over the broken windowpane. The old black leatherette davenport in the living room, with its broken springs sticking out along with the cotton stuffing, we covered with a bright crazy-quilt that had been stored in Annie's trunk. We washed the windows, scrubbed the floors till they were spotless and polished the mirror on the dresser. We covered the kitchen table with the new oilcloth Annie had just bought. It had a bright red cherry pattern and added a cheerful note. I scrubbed the old oilcloth, cut it in two, and put it under the sheets on the beds. "It may leak a little, but it's better than nothin'," I said. All the lamps were cleaned and filled with coal oil, and their wicks trimmed, and their chimneys shining.

After the baking was done I took the children for a walk and brought back bouquets of wild flowers—bleeding hearts and fern for the dresser, wild roses for the sewing machine, black-eyed-Susans for the table. The kitchen was a sight to behold. Everything was polished and in its place. On the table, covered with a clean cloth, were four large three-layer cakes, stacks of mince, cherry and apple pies, loaves and loaves of home-made bread, and dishes of freshly churned butter and newly made clabber cheese. On the floor soaking in clean pots were cut-up chickens, fresh string beans, and new peas and potatoes.

The four of us were exhausted but triumphant. I looked at Annie. She had shampooed her hair and had made Carl strain the tadpoles out of the rain-barrel so that she would have clean soft water to do it. She looked fresh and young again. Her hair shone. She had on a pretty blue plaid dress, all starched and ironed, and a frilly apron trimmed with red rickrack. Gazing proudly around the rooms she said:

"Everything looks so nice I'm afraid to sit down. All we have to do now is bathe the children and put them to bed."

"Why don't you take a walk with Carl in the fresh air? I'll bathe them and put them to bed," I volunteered. She accepted my suggestion gratefully and Carl took her by the arm, saying, "You look mighty purty. Shyly they strolled out into the soft twilight, and I turned to the job still awaiting me.

The two older children had begun to jump up and down on the clean beds with their dirty black feet. They laughed and squealed as their feet flew in the air and they landed on their backs.

"Stop that this minute," I said, and grabbed each one by the arm and dragged them into the kitchen. There was a tub of cold water sitting by the back door which I had meant to warm for their baths. I wasn't about to wait. I plunged them into it, and they screamed at the shock.

"Now just you hush," I commanded. "Just remember that every time I catch you jumping on the beds I'm going to dump you into a tub of cold water." They looked at me to see if I meant it. Deciding that I did, they stood still and shivered while I finished bathing them. I dried their naked, clean, pink bodies, thinking, "They're so beautiful. I'd love to kiss them. But if I do, they will think I have given in and start to be naughty all over again."

"Now you sit here while I go get something for you to sleep in."

I found them each a clean shirt and on returning to the kitchen, I almost stepped into a pile in the middle of the floor. Pointing to it, I said, "Who did that?"

They both began to giggle.

"He did," she said, and pointed to her brother.

I took them by their shoulders and glared into their faces. "If either of you ever do that again I'll rub your noses in it and spank you until you can't sit down for a week. Now don't you wet the bed tonight, either; you both know better. I don't like being wet on in the middle of the night. Do you hear me? I mean every bit of it."

Wailing, they ran and climbed into bed. I cleaned up the mess of the floor, threw the bath water out the back door, and glanced around the kitchen to see if there was anything else that had been left undone.

At the sight of all that food I shuddered, remembering things about its preparation. We had sifted cups of weevils out of the flour; fished a drowned mouse out of the clabbered milk; drained flies, dog ticks, and hairs out of the fresh milk; made the cakes with rancid lard, scraped maggots off the ham, and peeled pecks of worm-eaten apples. I nearly put a rotten egg and one with a half-formed chicken in it into the cake. I remembered the green flies that had swarmed about the chicken's entrails when we had cleaned them out in the yard—I had grown up with this sort of thing but suddenly it nauseated me. I rushed outside, leaned against a tree, and retched.

In every ridge home you would find the same decrepit furniture, the same sparing use of water. The pumps were usually in the barn lots to be handy for the cows, making them seem more important than the women. There were the same flies, the same low-grade staples, the same absence of refrigeration, of proper clothes and linens, and utensils with which to work. The same old brooms worn down to their handles. The same lye soap rose in gray scum on the water. The same chickens hovered around the door picking at the garbage as it was thrown out.

And the same weary women fought these conditions without spirit because they knew they were whipped. I pictured myself as a married woman under these circumstances. Would I do any better? After all, physically I wasn't as strong as Annie because I knew my chest had been weakened by my childhood illness. I was aware of a constant nagging pain in my chest and of how short-winded I was. I wondered how long I could bear up under Annie's burdens, in addition to having a new baby every year.

But what really frightened me was the sense of futility, of the failure the lives of these farm women represented. I wanted not only a happy family life, a nice home, money to spend for pleasures, but fulfillment of my inner self. I owed it to myself to bring out and use whatever was in me instead of letting it die in the drudgery and repression of our hill way of life.

"I'd rather die than face this kind of future," I said to the night around me.

The hay-baling crew, twenty of them, descended in force next morning at 5:30. But Annie and I were up long before that, frying side meat, making biscuits, gravy, oatmeal, and frying apples. We were through with breakfast dishes and had the house straight by nine. Annie remarked, "I have never seen anybody work as fast as you did, Frances."

"Well, I always figure that if I hurry through my work, I'll have more time to rest."

She laughed at me as if I weren't very bright. "I don't figure that way myself. Seems like the more you git done the more you have to do."

"I guess you're right, 'cause now we've got to hurry to get another meal ready by noon. But I'll be darned if I'll keep this up all my life. I don't aim to spend my life starting another meal up just as soon as I've finished with the dishes from the one before."

But there was no way out of it that day, so we went on preparing food and more food. The orgy of eating went on for five days. The men came in smelling of sweat. When they rolled up their dirt-stained sleeves to wash their hands, they exposed the dirty long underwear which they wore all summer. Hollering and laughing at each other, they descended on our carefully prepared food and left the table in ruins, with only the bones for us to pick and another mess to clean up.

Another neighbor girl came and helped the last three days, enabling Annie and me to be free for a few hours in the afternoon. Carl noticed us as we sat on the porch.

"If you've got so much time on your hands, I wish you'd mount the horses and give us a little help by dragging a few shocks of hay. We're a little behind."

So our rest period was spent working in the hot sun, with me raging inwardly. A stalwart young fellow pulled his horse up beside mine.

"Yer shore a swell cook," he said. "Yer purty too," he grinned and shifted the cud of tobacco in his mouth to spit.

"Thanks," I answered ungraciously. I almost bit my tongue to keep from saying, "I may be a good cook, but I'll be darned if I'll spend my life cooking for a clodhopper like you." And I whirled my horse away.

The few hours I was able to spend in bed were miserable, what with the mosquitoes, and all of us sleeping in one room—I with the two oldest children. They kicked like mules and cried out at intervals. I was disturbed by the noise of the baby nursing frequently and Carl's snoring like a buzz saw. When the last day came to an end, I was so weary I could hardly drag my feet. Even though it was almost dark, I saddled Old Verdun and headed for home. Even Old Verdun seemed dejected as we forded the Glaze and proceeded slowly along the road.

Of course, Carl and Annie thanked me profusely. Carl said, "We don't know what we'd done without you. You can bet your life we'll see that you get material for a new print dress the next time we go to the store."

"Ya-ah," I reflected. "I'll get material for a new dress that'll cost a dollar and twenty-five cents for my week's work. And the hay balers will have a few bucks in their britches for fishing tackle and shotgun shells. And the tons of hay that we slaved so hard over will be eaten by contented cows owned by rich bottomlanders so that the women will have more work to do taking care of the milk and churning the butter, so their families can have more fly-blown food to eat.

"But poor Annie will get nothing for her labors. She probably won't even get material for a pretty dress.

"And next year the whole performance will be repeated, and the only difference will be Annie will have another baby." I ground my teeth, "I'll not be here."

19

The Hills Close In

Time passed, and while I was not happy, life was not unbearable. Inevitably I began to look about me for other interests.

When I turned fifteen everyone was talking about the new high school at Brumley and wondering if it would benefit the children in our area. The district schoolteachers were starting to urge the benefits of a higher education, holding out to the young people visions of a fuller life.

When I first heard about the new school, I was happier than I had been for months. I had no doubt that I would somehow find a way to attend. I discussed the possibility with other girls my age who had graduated at the same time I had. It boiled down to the fact that while Brumley was only eight miles away, it was at least a three-hour ride by horseback over rough country roads. This meant I would have to rise by 4:30 in the morning, prepare my breakfast and a lunch, do the chores, and catch and saddle my horse before I could even start for school. Class started at 9:00. Although classes were dismissed at four, I couldn't possibly be home before seven, and I would still have the evening chores to do and dinner to prepare. That meant I would be on the go from 4:30 in the morning until 10:00 at night, with only six hours to rest. On Saturdays and Sundays, I would have to devote every minute to cleaning house and doing the laundry. Very importantly, I did not have enough clothes to stand the wear and tear of six hours a day in the saddle. Dejectedly, I decided that as far as I was concerned, the school might as well be twenty miles away. The Georges were able to afford to send their children to Richland, to a larger school, where they had nice places to board within walking distance of the school. Flo Pemberton, a rugged strong girl, decided she was going to Brumley or bust, even if she had to ride a mule. And that is what she did.

In my case the situation was made worse than hopeless by the high tuition required and the cost of the books. Flo, sturdy as she was, could only attend about half the time, because of bad weather, even with her parents helping by doing her chores and preparing her meals. She was very proud of herself, however, and she had every right to be. She became engrossed in her school activities and insisted that I go with her to the school play so that she could show me what she had been talking about. She had me so excited at the prospect that I wouldn't have missed it for anything.

I pressed my best dress, put on my precious shoes, and caught Old Verdun and saddled him, and met Flo at her house.

I enjoyed the play thoroughly. Afterwards, Flo and I toured the building and the gymnasium, and I was impressed. When we started home I found that quite a group of young people had come to the play on horseback and I noticed that the boys and girls were pairing off. Flo rode past me laughing, talking gaily to the young fellow who rode beside her.

My old enemy Hank rode up beside me and I noticed how spruced up he was in contrast to the way he used to look when he sat beside me in school. He grinned, and said, "Do you mind if I ride home with you?"

"I don't mind," I answered, afraid to say no. I glanced shyly as him as we rode along, appraising him fully. He was very well built now, and he sat his horse easily. His blond hair was slicked down and he was clean, and cut a handsome figure. In spite of how nice he looked, I decided I hated him, but still he was a boy and I was a girl. I was very confused. We had very little to say to each other. My Old Verdun was in a skittish mood and it took all my strength and skill to hold him back. He shied at every other horse we saw. Finally I asked the boy beside me if he would break off a long switch for me so that I might whip him into behaving. He got me a thick branch. Old Verdun saw it and began to act meek. He didn't fool me. This was one of his tricks, to walk quietly along, then suddenly leap to the side of the road in an attempt to unseat me.

We rode along for quite a spell, with Hank on my left. Flo and her friend were out of sight ahead of us, and another noisy couple whom I didn't know were immediately behind, but were falling back. Suddenly I became embarrassingly aware that the couple behind us were laughing, squealing and carrying on in a manner which left little to the imagination.

I was aware that Hank knew what was going on. He rode closer to me. I was horribly embarrassed. My heart started to pound, and I began to be afraid. If he made advances, I should not know what to do to resist him or defend myself.

To cover my confusion, I began to chatter and talk. Hank paid no attention. Instead he grasped my arm in a hard grip and swung me half around in the saddle. "How about a little kiss. How about it? Let's you and me go in the bushes." I tried to be calm. "Would it matter if I said I don't want to?"

"No," he said, and grabbed at me again.

Without an instants hesitation I brought the switch down with all my strength across his face. I heard him gasp in surprise as I leaned forward in the saddle and hit Old Verdun. He took off like a streak of lightening.

I passed Flo and her companion in a flash. She called out, "Hey! Where you goin' in such a hurry?"

"Home!" I cried, and sped on. The little wooden bridge where Old Verdun had always shied, he took in a long clean leap, while I rode as if I were a part of him. Glancing anxiously behind, I could not hear above his pounding hoofs if anyone was following. "Come on, giddap, hurry, faster, I know you can outrun anything in this country if you try," I begged.

At last he began to tire. We came to Dean's Creek and I pulled him up under a sycamore tree and stopped to listen. Apparently I was not pursued, as I could hear nothing but his loud breathing and the pounding of my heart, and the loud croaking of the frogs, "Jugarum, jugarum, jugarum." I looked up at the white limbs of the sycamore spread above me and the limbs seemed to swim and waver around, and then I suddenly felt ill. I laid my head on the saddle horn and breathed deeply.

It had been a narrow escape. But I had to face the question: From whom? From Hank? Or from me? If he had been gentle and kind I don't know what I would have done. I think my panic was due to my realizing that this was the way one was trapped—by ones own instincts. It didn't occur to me then that I had humiliated a man in a region where men are used to having their own way.

A month or so later a pie supper was held at Rainwater School two miles beyond Toronto. Flo Pemberton and her little sister Chloe, who was twelve, and I went together. I went to their house and we made chocolate pies, one for each of us to take, and had fun making boxes to put them in, trimming the boxes with pretty crepe paper and flowers. After the usual battle to saddle Old Verdun was over, we started out. Flo and Chloe both riding their old gray mare. I looked at their mare and said, "Gosh, looks like she's about ready to have a colt."

"She is," Flo agreed. "Any minute. Jist so it don't happen tonight. Let's keep our fingers crossed."

"Maybe," I suggested, "it would be safer for Chloe to ride behind me. I don't want her to have a colt on the way."

"Yeah, maybe so."

So Chloe climbed down and I fixed her a pad from a piece of old quilt behind my saddle, and helped her up.

The little schoolhouse where the pie supper was held was crowded and stuffy, but everyone seemed to be having a grand time. I saw it was my pie going up for sale and heard the auctioneer say, "How much do I hear for this purty thing all done up in a yaller box with flowers all over the top?"

"Twenty cents."

"Who'll bid thirty? Thirty, forty, sixty, I hear. Who'll bid seventy?" Then I noticed that Hank was bidding on my box.

"A dollar," he shouted. The auctioneer chanted, "Once, twice, three times, and sold to the young gentleman over thar."

My heart quickened as he marched up and paid for my pie. I knew for a certainty that somehow he had found out it was mine. I burned in silent rage. When the men were searching out the owners of the pies they had purchased, he came over to me with a look of triumph. I knew very well that men loved the pursuit of a spirited girl; that even though he hadn't brought me to the ground before, he hadn't given up and would try again. I stood up haughtily.

"You bought the pie and paid for it," I said. "Now eat it all by yourself. I don't crave your company."

People around us stared. His face became scarlet. I gave him a long and scornful stare and turned to Chloe, who was eating with a jolly fat old man.

"When you're ready to go home, I'll be waitin' for you where Old Verdun is hitched."

I paraded out with my head high and climbed into the saddle thinking, "I guess I'm in for trouble now. But I don't care. No country jake is goin' to get ahead of me."

Hank rushed out and when he saw me he started gathering up small rocks and filling his pockets.

"I'll fix you," he snarled. "I was crazy about you. I'll make you sorry now for making such a fool out of me, you wild heifer."

I was getting frightened and kept one eye on the lighted doorway for Chloe. She didn't keep me long.

"Come on," I pleaded. "Hurry, let's get out of here." She put her foot in the stirrup, and I gave her my hand and pulled her up behind me. In the same instant I whirled my horse around toward home. It was then that Hank began to pelt us with stones. The horse went crazy with fear. He reared and nearly fell backwards, snorting, and bucking and kicking and prancing while I fought to control him.

"I hope you break your goddamned neck," Hank yelled.

My horse started to run at break-neck speed towards home. The road led over a weird rocky bald thicket with thorn trees that tore at our clothes and flesh. Then down the long hill he raced and plunged into the Glaze, where the water rose and drenched us to the skin. Then across the treacherous gravel bar and up the muddy banks where he slipped and skidded but still fought on. His speed was not abated as he raced the next four miles through the woods and over the hills to within sight of Chloe's house, where two of Chloe's cousins caught up with us, took the reins from my hands, tied them to their own saddle horns, then rode on each side of us the rest of the way home with Old Verdun bucking and snorting between them. It was a terrifying experience and I still don't know how we kept from being killed.

I hoped my troubles with that young man were over, but they had only begun.

In about two weeks Paul came unexpectedly from a painting job he was doing in St. Louis. He greeted me with a dark face, his lips in a grim straight line. He didn't say much, only that painting had slowed up a bit and he reckoned he'd come home and do a little hunting. He tramped around the house nervously, his hands in his pockets, looking at everything, but never once looking me straight in the eye. The he got down his gun and began to clean and load it. I knew something was wrong, but decided his girl had probably thrown him over, so I didn't question him but chattered on hoping to cheer him up.

"I'm sure glad you came home. We got about thirty chickens big enough to sell, and you kin help me take them to Toronto." He was unenthused at this news. In fact, he was downright grim.

"I got to see a feller tomorrow," he said and squinted along the sight of his gun. "And when I do I may shoot him."

The next morning we caught the chickens, loaded them into the wagon, and started out along our muddy lane for Toronto. I noticed Paul had put his gun in the back of the wagon. When he saw me looking at it, he explained.

"We might scare up somethin'. Ya never can tell."

I looked at Old Verdon's back and remarked, "That durn fool horse is goin' to kill somebody someday. Why, he nearly broke my neck twice lately. Scared Chloe Pemberton and me half to death."

Then I laughed and told in detail my two experiences with Hank. Paul looked at me in astonishment and kept saying, "Is that a fact? Are you sure that's all that happened?"

"Why sure, I'm sure. Wasn't that enough? I could have got killed, you know, I said with spirit."

A look of vast relief flowed over his face. He suddenly seemed very happy. He began to whistle, urging the horses to a trot, and then sang snatches of popular songs. I meditated on the strangeness of men's behavior.

In Toronto we marketed the chickens, purchased a Vienna sausage, soda crackers, yellow cheese, assorted candy, and two bottles of grape soda.

"We'll have us a picnic," said Paul. On the way home we pulled up in the cool shade of a native sycamore and crawled into the back of the wagon and spread out our feast. Paul talked about his work and I wanted to know all about Jim and Sybil, Nellie and Goldie, and if they were all getting rich. Jim was working at the lime kiln in Dykie where he was soon to have the accident that would lose him an eye. Paul bit into a hunk of cheese.

"Na-ah," he said. "They're no better off there than they were here. They live about the same way. They jist don't get paid enough money, $45.00 a month, I hear tell. Why that ain't enough to raise a family. And the customs and habits of the people around there is about the same as here."

"Well, I hope they don't come back," I said. "At least they're near enough to St. Louis so that they could go there and look for work if they had to."

"Work's pretty scarce," Paul said.

The next morning, to my surprise, he got ready to leave. I followed him about. His excuse for going' so soon was, "Looks like the weathers clearin' up a bit. My boss may be needin' me. There's a big job coming up and we've just been waitin' for nice weather to paint."

He left without saying a word about what had been on his mind, only cautioning me shyly to be careful. I said I would, not knowing what he wanted me to be careful about.

A week passed, and I received a letter from Jim's wife, Sybil. I sat down on the bank by the mailbox and opened it. This is what it said:

"Dear Frances: Paul and Jim were sure glad to find out you hadn't been raped and it was all just a pack of lies. Paul was all set to kill Hank and sure had his dander up when he left here. Imagine, that stinkin' feller braggin' about takin' you in the brush the night of the pie supper. Things shore do get around fast. Imagine us hearin' it way down here so soon. It must have been spread all over the country in no time. My brother Orville told Jim, and Jim told Paul and Paul swore he'd kill the son-of-a-gun. He meant it too. Jim sure was worried. I was, too. But guess there's no sense of worrying about you. You kin take care of yourself. We all got a kick out of the way you whacked Hank with a stick."

I read on in disbelief and finished the letter in a state of shock.

So I was being talked about all over the country. I just couldn't believe it. I felt as if a hand were closing around my heart.

Clutching the letter I ran as fast as my bare feet would carry me to the Pemberton's. Flo and Chloe were washing clothes on a board, bending over tubs in their backyard. They stopped, wiped their hands on their skirts, and took the letter I handed them.

"I wish you'd just read that," I panted. "Do you reckon Sybil is exaggeratin' about all that talk?"

"Oh no," they assured me. "Its the honest truth."

And they told me in detail all the things they themselves had heard. How so-and-so told so-and-so all about it. I stared at them round-eyed. I simply couldn't imagine all those people whom I had regarded as my friends saying such terrible things about me. It was past understanding. I wrung my hands and wailed.

"Why, oh why, Chloe, didn't you say something to defend me? You were there. You know it's a lie. You saw everything that happened that night."

"I started to," she shrugged, "But they jist wouldn't believe me. They all said, "Must be somethin' to it, 'cause 'where there's smoke, there's bound to be fire'."

Then I realized that they didn't understand the full significance of what this meant to me and how deeply and irreparably I was hurt.

I snatched the letter from them, running madly for home. At the top of the hill the pain in my chest was more than I could bear, and I threw myself down under a tree to rest. My mind kept racing around in circles, and I became more and more horrified as my imagination went to work. I could visualize the faces of my neighbors as they leaned on their rakes, or talked across the fence, or hovered outside the store at Toronto, whispering to each other what Flo and Chloe had just disclosed to me.

"Howdy thar. Did you hear tell how Hank took Frances Wright out in the brush, and…? Girls can't get by acting like that. Boys maybe. But not girls, She'll have to pay for it and serves her right. She ought to be horse-whipped and tarred and feathered. Maybe that'd teach her a thing or two."

"Why, oh why, did this have to happen to me," I moaned. "I could kill Hank for that. I wish Paul had blown his head off." I beat the ground with my fists.

"What can I do? I'll go to each one and explain that it's a lie, made up to get back at me for what I did to him." Then I discarded that idea. I could imagine of the look of disbelief on their faces as they said, "Where there's smoke, there's fire." I wondered if I dared stand up in church and cry out my story, demanding that those without sin be the first to cast a stone. But I knew that I didn't have the courage to face them that way. No woman stood up in church and talked. I wondered if the minister could possibly help me. Then I remembered the kind young man who had preached Mother's funeral had left our community, and as yet no one had replaced him. And even if there were another minister, he would probably only preach a sermon about an adulteress, and I cringed at the thought.

But what could I do? I felt that as long as I lived I could never hold my head up in this community. There was not one person to whom I could go, tell my troubles, and talk openly and frankly, who would offer me sympathy and belief.

I decided to kill myself. I reasoned somehow that the act would be a punishment to them. I imagined I could see them gathered around my coffin, sorry for me now that it was too late.

I rose and walked slowly home, still numb with shock. There really did seem to be only the one way out. I kept thinking, "I've got nothing to live for anyway. The future holds nothing for me. Like Father said, 'I wouldn't never amount to nothin' no-how'."

It was dark when I reached the house. Father was away, and Garsy, I guessed, was in the caves listening to the men talk about me. I entered the dark interior of the house and felt my way to the front room. Without lighting a lamp, I took Paul's shotgun and went out to the porch. I felt along the barrel. Then I set it down. I simply couldn't do it. I felt I had to keep moving. I started towards Dean's Creek. Past the walnut trees I wandered. Past the wild cherry trees, and then through the bottom fields. I stopped on the bank of a large pool which reflected the sky and its million stars like a mirror. The moon was up now, and white fluffy clouds floated across it, sometimes obscuring it and tinting the edges of the clouds with gold.

"There's no use jumping in the creek," I reasoned. "I'd only swim out." I lay down on my stomach on a large rock, hanging out over the pool and stared into the water, dimly conscious of the night sounds around me and the fireflies that sparkled erratically.

I lay there for hours. I must have been exhausted for I finally slept. The sky lightened and the sun began to rise. A raccoon came down to the edge of the water and washed his hands; I then washed my face in the pool and turned wearily toward home. I was too tired to think about it anymore. I decided I'd just stay away from everybody until I could figure out a way to get out of the hills.

But I was frightened, frightened of the day now and its people, as well as of the night.

20

The Ghost With a Wet Tongue

Three years had gone by since Mother's death and loneliness was a part of my existence. I think of that time as a period of waiting. Two crises were approaching.

The first came one night in the fall. Annie had asked me to come and stay the day with her to take care of her small children. She was having an auction to dispose of her household goods. Her husband, Carl, had given up trying to make a living as a sharecropper on a ridge farm and had taken a job in a tremendous dairy at Crescent, Missouri, about forty miles from St. Louis, where Nellie and Arly had gone the year before. So he had left her to sell everything they could not take along. Though he was going to a job that only paid forty-five dollars a month, at least of this they could be sure. However, they were bettering their lot very little.

It was an agonizingly long day for me. As I saw Annie's possessions go one by one, I felt more and more forlorn. It was almost dark by the time everything was sold and Annie and the children were ready to leave. They were to spend the night with some neighbors who would take them to the railroad station in Richland, 12 miles away, the next morning.

I walked with Annie and the children to the neighbor's house and lingered long, saying repeated good-byes. When I finally left to go home, I stepped out into a night that was black as a pit. A soft rain had begun to fall. When I saw how dark it was, I wanted to turn back and ask them to let me spend the night. But in my present frame of mind I couldn't bring myself to ask for anything. So I decided I would just have to feel my way home. It was almost impossible for me to get lost. I had only to follow the rail fence through the woods where I knew and remembered every tree along the way, and then when I came to a gate, I would simply turn right, up the hill to our house, altogether about two miles. But it was not an easy journey. I walked with my hands out in front of me, feeling the path with my hands and feet. There was not a breath of wind and the night was still except for the gentle falling of the rain and the rustle of my shuffling feet.

I had gone quite a distance when I heard something moving in the leaves behind me. I froze in my tracks, listened, but heard nothing more. I decided I had only imagined it, and proceeded slowly on my way. Again I heard the sound behind me and again I stopped to listen. When I stood still I could not hear a thing. I began to think of all the things that might be there in the woods behind me, even of the ghost Jim used to declare lived in these woods. When I heard the noise once more, my heart began to throb in my throat.

Now I was positive I was not alone. Fear gripped me and I started to run. Once I gave in to terror, it took complete possession of me. I started screaming until the night seemed to be filled with cries from every direction, echoing and reechoing through the woods. In my frantic flight branches clawed at me and scratched me, but I didn't feel them. All the time the thing behind me kept pace. Finally I ran squarely into a tree, knocking myself flat on my back. I lay sobbing in hysteria, expecting I don't know what to come and finish me off.

Nothing happened. At last, too exhausted to fight, I gained my voice and sobbed, "Come and get me whoever you are." I heard steps approaching slowly in the blackness and I awaited my fate. Suddenly the awful thing was upon me with four feet. A long wet tongue licked all over my face and arms. I reached up and felt a pointed canine nose.

I was filled with astonishment. Then I knew. It was Annie's and Carl's dog. I remembered how all day, sensing as dogs do, the uprooting of their home, he had looked as forlorn and sad as I had felt, and how, when she left her empty house, Annie had scolded him and sent him back. She didn't know what else to do with him. He had apparently followed us to the neighbors and then had followed me, hesitating when I hesitated, no doubt fearing he was not wanted.

I was wild with relief. I threw my arms around him and petted him and he wiggled all over with delight. Then I began to laugh. I laughed at how funny he must have looked sneaking along behind me. I laughed at the thing I had imagined, only to have it turn out to be a small harmless dog. I laughed at myself for being such a coward.

It came to me that if there was nothing more in the world to fear than a small frightened dog, I need not be afraid. Wasn't I a grown girl now? What was there to be afraid of? What else could happen to me that hadn't happened already? Suddenly I felt indestructible, and through me surged an exalted feeling of strength and freedom. I squatted in the wet leaves and cuddled my new friend, and repeated over and over as it were something I must not forget, "I'll never be afraid again. I'll never be afraid again."

No more shrinking and sniveling, I resolved. I was fed up with weeping and self-pity. No more would I run away from people and things. All at once I remembered the advice that Cousin Laura had given me the evening after Mother died.

"Frances, don't try to run away. It will do no good. Wait until you can go forth with your chin high."

So, rested and with renewed strength, I started homeward. The dog, my dog now, trotted in the path ahead of me.

I have never ceased to marvel at the fact that when you win back your courage, things seem to go better. For instance, the next day Paul came home and we laughed and cried and talked. He told me he had a teachers certificate and was going to teach at the district school this year. He suggested that I go to school with him and through the eighth grade again, if only to have something to do other than the drudgery of housework and chores. This was a happy idea and the prospect began to occupy my mind with more wholesome thoughts.

Paul was good for me. He purchased groceries with his own money, so that once more I was well fed. That added to my feeling of well being. He helped me with the chores and even the washing, carrying the water needed from the well. He slowed his stride to match my shorter one so I could keep up with him on our way to school. In school he made my lessons easy, reminding me that I needn't work too hard as I already had my diploma. He took me hunting and fishing and made these excursions a lot of fun.

Then he decided that he and I would start a project for next summer. We would buy an incubator and turn the home place into a chicken farm. He ordered the incubator and we began to plan a big scale affair.

His kindness and consideration must have had some effect on Father, whose general behavior began to change. Father took to helping with the chores. He repaired some of the fences, and even talked of planting again in the spring. Paul's attitude seemed to have an effect on Garsy, too, and that somber young man spent less and less time in the caves.

Another thing happened that winter to promote better relationships in the house. Garsy took down with the flu and was quite ill for a time. Paul and I nursed him. Paul had to be at school in the daytime, so I stayed home, took Garsy's meals to him, made him cough syrup, and rubbed his back and chest with turpentine and lard. We didn't have much to say, but there were times when he said, "Thanks," or "That tastes good," or smiled at me—something he had never done since Mother died. He was a long while recuperating, and during that period he would make his own bed, sweep the floors, and do a few things around the house, such as building fires, and carrying out the ashes. By spring he began to look better and then disappeared. We supposed he had gone back to the caves. Several days later he came home to announce that he had been to Lebanon and taken a job painting. So he got his things and left, and only Father, Paul, and I remained on the farm.

Paul gave me money from his modest salary to buy new material for dresses. Again, I attempted to sew for myself. This time I did quite well.

That winter I lived in a sort of a hush. I was waiting, perhaps, for the answer to the question, "Is the farm to be my future?"

I would be sixteen in April. I knew all about how hill girls were trapped into becoming hill wives. Or was my lot to be that of an old maid taking care of an aging father?

I knew the answer would have to be soon. There were some handsome young fellers thereabout.

The second crisis developed slowly. In spite of Father's changed manner toward me, I was sure his plans for me were basically the same. In his mind I knew I was destined to be Mother's successor as household drudge and farm manager. Nellie and Annie were married. Ruth was gone. Now Goldie had followed Annie to Crescent and had married a young farmer there. She was only sixteen and our high hopes for the genius of the family vanished. That left only me, the logical person to keep the house and farm going.

At the end of five months of school, Paul went off to Kirkwood to work. He promised he would send me what money I needed to keep the poultry project going. Father left again.

The incubator finally arrived. I was deeply excited. This might be the means of my escape. It held one hundred and twenty-four eggs and was most efficient looking with its burner, glass door, and thermometer. I read the directions carefully and set the incubator by my bed so I could watch it day and night. I purchased eggs from a neighbor who had what was reputed to be a sturdy breed of chickens. I would awake in the night many times to see if the burner was lit, and would get up and feel inside the incubator to make sure the eggs were not too warm or too cold. Every morning I turned them over gently as a mother hen would do. When they started to hatch I spent hours at the little window watching the wet chicks fight their way out of the shells and stagger on uncertain feet, to become as fluffy as powder puffs when dry. Often I would reach in and help them a little to get free from their shells. To watch this miracle occur before my very eyes always was an exciting experience.

Out of the hundred and twenty-four eggs, a hundred and ten chicks hatched. A certain amount of loss was to be expected, and I was elated that after three weeks there were still ninety left. The danger period seemed to be over and they were well on their way. In the daytime I put the chicks in a pen out in the yard to sun. I was careful to keep their drinking water clean and to see that they had fresh cornbread and milk. At night I put them in a washtub with new straw on the bottom, then brought them into the kitchen and covered them with a thin cloth to keep them warm. They were growing so large now they were trying to hop out of the tub, so I planned to fix up a brooder for them in the chicken yard. If I were so fortunate as to raise ninety chickens, we should be able to net about fifty dollars on their sale. Optimistically I figured that a hundred and twenty-four chickens could be hatched every two weeks. By the end of summer we could realize a considerable sum. Literally, I was counting my chickens before they hatched.

One morning I came to the kitchen as usual to check on my brood. I noticed that the room seemed very quiet. The chickens generally were peeping noisily with hunger in the morning. My heart stood still. I snatched the cover off the tub and found that every one of them was dead. A rat or weasel had got in during the night and had slit the throats of every one of them. I buried them in the peach orchard and meditated bitterly on the blows that life seemed to deal me. But I didn't weep over things any more. I gritted my teeth and went about the task of preventing another such catastrophe. I circled the house inch by inch and with rocks and dirt blocked all holes by which a weasel or rat might get in to destroy my next brood. Paul wrote and encouraging letter saying that it was a bad start, but not to let it throw me, and sent money for two more hatchings.

My spirits rose again, but somehow not to the height of elation Ruth and I had shared when we tried to run away. I was certain now that I could make enough money, and that it was only a matter of time before I could head out into the world on my own and perhaps study art and make something of myself.

Then I heard from Ruth and Goldie that they planned to come home for two weeks. With their arrival, life became great fun, the first real fun in years. We had loads to talk about. They told me of all the friends they had made. Goldie talked constantly about her new husband and the baby she was expecting, and their plans for making a home. I listened eagerly.

The three of us put in a nice garden, and even though food and money were scarce, with the help of some of my young chickens, we managed to get by. Goldie spent hours going to and from the mailbox waiting for letters and sending her own. Ruth planted a large patch of sweet corn, worked in the garden and canned everything she could possibly find to put in a jar. I hovered over my chickens like a mother hen. Evenings we would sit in the twilight on the porch and talk and plan and dream.

Gradually it came over me that the things they dreamed were not what I wanted for myself. I had ambitions. I wanted to make something more of myself. I wanted fulfillment as a woman, but I reasoned that if I could develop into more of a person myself, I could ask more from life than just being a housewife.

I listened to their eager planning with growing concern—not only for them, but for myself if I were unable to find my way out. It would be Mother's life all over again. But what was the answer?

Although I had no idea as to whether I would ever make my escape from the farm, still in one respect I felt fortunate. Now I saw clearly that the way my brothers and sisters were living was not the way I wanted to live. I also saw that the snare into which they had fallen had been love and marriage to boys and girls of the hill culture. These young people had no knowledge of the world outside, sought no broader horizons than their parents before them, and struggled for no status. While I knew and liked many young folks my age, I was resolved that I would not be trapped by such pitfalls; that the bearing of children, housework, and grubbing in the fields was not nor ever would be enough to make me happy.

Garsy was soon to marry Jim's wife's sister and take up farming again. Annie's and Nellie's husbands had been sharecroppers. Jim, who had gone to work in a cement plant, was still there, but unhappy, biding his time to return to a farm. Burdened by a fast growing family, he was finding he had no time for his engineering correspondence course. Also, to his disappointment, he found that his living conditions were no better than he had in our hills, and with a large family and his inability to cope with a world he knew nothing of, his thoughts ever turned back to where he grew up. Goldie married a farm boy after her first year of high school. Now Goldie was pregnant, trapped like her sisters and living under conditions no better than theirs. Even though she had been an outstanding pupil that one year and had won a gold medal for oratory, to Father's and Paul's disappointment, she had given up what seemed to be brilliant future to marry a poor country boy. Paul, who tried the hardest to better himself and who had even gone to Teachers College, was drawn back to the hills as if by a magnet, and was now dating a country girl. Ruth, although working far away from home, had a boy from our neck of the woods following her, trying to woo her back to our hills.

Thus the web was spun—what Mother had feared would happen. Those fears had made their imprint on me and made me cautious and watchful, and now, though unarmed, at least I was warned. My brothers and sisters had married children of ridge farmers because in them were the reflections of what was in themselves. They spoke the same language. They understood each other's poverty and hardships, their way of life, their culture. They were compatible. These were the children they had been brought up with. With them they felt at home, as I had felt more at home with poor little Pearl than with rich bottomland girls. They would not have known what to do with a fine house or a large productive farm. They could cope with poverty better than with wealth.

But what of me? I was no different. I knew only poverty and hardship. I had the Ozark twang. The idioms of the hillbilly were mine. I hadn't the faintest idea how to run a nice home. I was as bashful, ignorant, and as inhibited as the worst. But in me had been planted seeds of discontent, that grew and flowered. Change to me was not a thing to be abhorred as it is abhorred back there, but a thing to run toward and embrace eagerly whether for better or worse. Perhaps I was lucky because I was the youngest, for I had the example of the rest set before me. I knew if I allowed myself to fall in love with a country boy, I would be as bound as my brothers and sisters. My lot would be to labor and breed and make my Lord and Master happy.

21

Escape

I remember every detail of that last summer on the farm. One morning, one of our remaining cows was missing at milking time, which meant I had to search for her in the pastures and woods. I did not mind these quiet excursions. I knew every cowpath on the farm, and I walked confidently, deep in my thoughts, keeping one eye open for the cow. I had not even noticed that my dog, whom I had named Skip, was with me this morning. In fact, I hadn't thought of him at all. I walked along in underbrush higher than my head. At length I though I might better turn back or my clothes would soon be wet all over from the dew. I paused a moment, undecided what to do next. Then I heard a hissing sound and looked down to discover a deadly poisonous copperhead snake coiled in the path in front of me, almost under my feet. I stood motionless, gripped in terror, not daring to move. Suddenly Skip leaped past my legs, almost upsetting me, grabbed the snake in his mouth, shook it vigorously, and flung it further along the path. Before it could get away, he pounced upon it again and worried it until it fell lifelessly from his mouth. I sat down in a clear space, my legs weak. Skip came wagging back to me for approval and I stroked his head declaring to him that he was the best friend in the world.

Then I noticed a small gash on his nose and knew the snake had bitten him. The lost cow was forgotten as I gathered him up and hurried home, fearful that in saving my life, he had lost his. Before we reached the house, his head had begun to swell. I didn't know what to do other than to slit the cut a little deeper to make it bleed, and to fix him a comfortable bed on the porch, and drench his feverish body with cold water. He lay there in agony for three days, his head and body swollen at least twice their normal size, and his poor eyes entirely swollen shut. I hovered over him every minute I could, dropping water down his throat and bathing his poor distorted body. At last he began to recover and was able to stand on wobbly legs and wag his tail a little.

As he got better and the swelling went down, his skin lay in folds around his head. He was the most comical looking thing I ever saw, and I think he realized it, too, for every time I would laugh at him, he would roll his eyes, making his face still more grotesque, and the corners of his mouth would turn up as if he were laughing with me.

With what spirit I could summon, I went about my daily tasks trying not to dwell too much on my problems.

Father came home at long intervals. He would simply arrive, well dressed and well fed. Little by little he exhibited a better humor. I asked nothing of him now. If he were in a good mood and he wanted to talk, I listened. By now I was a fair cook and manager, as well as a pretty good housekeeper, and this obviously pleased him. Sometimes he played his banjo and sang with me his sole audience. These rare moments were precious to me.

There were few words between us, although I still seemed to be a puzzle he could not quite solve. He never ceased to be shocked when I expressed an opinion on matters considered to be beyond a woman's sphere. And he couldn't quite comprehend how I would flare up in anger, then forget it quickly and bear no grudge whatever. His way was never to discuss anything openly; and if he was angry at someone, to carry his grudge in silence and never forgive.

He still would go off without notice, leaving me alone on the farm for months without any money. For months I would see no one but the fowl and the animals.

The strangeness of my situation was that the struggle between him and me had now developed into a struggle within myself. Sometimes my heart would leap at the thought of escape from this dreary lonely place. At least I could be myself. I could work and buy nice things, and above all, have my art.

At other times my conscience troubled me. I was a hill girl, brought up to accept farm life and everything that went with it. I had joined the same church and gone to the same school as the others. Mother had accepted as her lot the privilege of slaving for the man and the children she loved. None of our neighbors seemed to question the rightness of the system. I began to be afraid of the guilt which might follow me if I broke from this accepted pattern.

I stopped thinking. Instead I drew and drew. I drew pictures every minute I had to spare and on every scrap of paper I could find. I must have drawn pictures on the blank pages of every book in the house. I became so desperate for subjects, I even used a dead grasshopper for a model.

One day in the middle of August, I decided to help myself to Father's paints, easel and canvas, and brave his wrath if he found out. I took the precious paint box with its tubes of beautiful colors out of the trunk where it had lain untouched the four years since Mother's death. So I set up my materials under a lilac bush and decided to paint the large hickory nut tree, and the ramshackle barn it sheltered. I painted steadily until it was so dark I could hardly see the canvas. Then I did my chores by the light of a lantern. The next morning I was up at sunrise to continue what I hoped would be a thing of beauty. The day rolled by swiftly and the sun was sinking again when I heard footsteps behind me and a long shadow fell across the canvas. I knew in an instant it was Father. I stiffened and waited for whatever he had to say.

To my surprise he stood cocking his head and squinting at my picture. Then without a word about my work he made an astonishing statement. He said it quietly, almost humbly.

"I made arrangements for you to go to high school in Eugene."

At his words I was too stunned to turn my head for I could not believe my ears. I closed my eyes and prayed silently, "Dear God, please let it be true. Only help me to escape these hills and I will make my own heaven."

Father broke the silence.

"Looks like you're goin' to be a better artist than your Father. I'm glad one of the youguns took after me."

It was a gracious compliment from him. A compliment I had waited a lifetime for. My heart overflowed with gladness and love for him. I leaped up, threw my arms around his neck, and planted a kiss in the middle of his bristly red mustache, and for the first time in four years I saw a smile hover around his mouth. My mind was spinning with questions, but I only managed to voice one of them. "When do we leave?"

"In the morning," he said. "You can go and stay with my niece, Della Brinkley, in Eugene until I finish a little house I've started there. Its a cute little house. I think you will like it. I'm building it just for you. We won't take the furniture with us. We can come back for it when the house is finished.

That meant I had no time to do anything but pack my few belongings.

It was a simple phrase to be so fateful; go to high school in Eugene. Almost as short as a jury's verdict. Its real significance was that I would have Father to front for me. Instead of sneaking off as a fugitive, headed for almost certain disaster, I would have respectability. Being introduced as his daughter would command the protection and the help of the very people who might otherwise show little mercy to an ignorant farm girl. I shudder now to think what might have happened if Ruth and I had managed to reach St. Louis, or if later I had run away alone. Our traditions and taboos made it unthinkable that a girl would tramp unescorted on a highway. The nearest way would have been by our farm-to-market road from Brumley to Richland. We could have stood there a week without so much as a wagon passing by.

If we had been able to get to St. Louis or Springfield or Kansas City, to this day I do not know what might have happened to us. We had never seen a streetcar, or paved streets, or house numbers. We didn't know how to use a telephone for neither one of us had ever talked on one. We knew nothing of hotels and could not have afforded one for more than a day or two. Of course, we were young and bouncy and felt sure we could find work before our money was gone. What we did not realize was that the future would have been no brighter than before.

Now the future was suddenly brilliant.

Ruth had told me wonderful things about Eugene. It had a population of 262 people. She said there were homes there filled with pretty things, even carpets. That parents went to dances with their young folks and liked to see them have a good time. That the school was large and nice and all girls were given an equal chance to participate in sports. That our cousin, Della Brinkley, was a lovely and broad-minded woman, a leader in the Christian Church where everyone, including the women, spoke out freely, and even socials were held in the church. What a wonderful place it must be.

Ruth had told me that we had cousins who not not only went through high school, but some of them went on to college. The girls had silk underwear and a different dress for each day in the week. Perhaps if I just got near such things and learned about them, I could somehow attain them for myself.

That evening I made a last tour of the farm. I visited the well and remembered all the people who had come there for refreshment, and I seemed to hear Mother's mischievous voice saying, "The tramp preacher is here again." I walked through the fields, barren now of everything but weeds. I walked along the meadow path with Skip trotting behind me, saying goodbye to all the secret places I loved. Once I knelt and threw my arms around him and cried out in great confusion, "Skip, I do want to go, but why do I feel so sad about leaving?" I knew that this was the end, that I would perhaps never return. I passed the huge apple tree and seemed to hear Goldie say, "Let's build a play house." I walked through the quiet woods and heard many voices, and all the while I wondered what the future held for me. Whatever it held, I faced it gladly now.

Back in the house, I started to collect my personal belongings. When I had packed my clothes, my suitcase was not filled, so I looked around for something that I especially wanted that would be small enough to go in it. I decided to take the beautiful bisque china doll, the last gift Mother had given me, and wrapped it carefully among my things. In the closet in the kitchen was a blue milk-glass butter dish that had been given to Mother as a wedding present. I took that, too, for I remembered that she loved it. I went through the trunk upstairs, searching for some special item for a keepsake. I came upon the leather picture folder containing a tin-type picture of Mother when she was a child, and one of Father at sixteen, and Annie's and Nellie's wedding pictures. In the back of the folder was a card bordered with forget-me-nots. On it was this message in beautiful script:

"May joy be forever near thee." It seemed as if this message was now for me.

Then I climbed on a chair, took Mother's plain gold wedding ring from the nail where it had hung all these years and tied it on a string and hung it around my neck. I was in bed when it occurred to me that I should not be able to take Skip with me if I was to live in someone else's house. I got up, tiptoed out into the dark and whistled softly. He came running. I picked him up, took him upstairs and laid him on the foot of my bed, where he cuddled down and lay still, wagging his tail as if he knew that this was our last time together.

I slept not a wink that night, almost sick with joy, sorrow, anticipation, and dread of what the outer world might hold for me. Before daybreak I stole out of the house with Skip at my heels and ran the full mile to Glover's Chapel and crawled through the fence surrounding the graveyard, and knelt by Mother's sunken weed-covered grave. I was a big girl now and realized that this might be the last time I would visit her. I also realized that I had come to the end of something, and that today was the beginning of something else. The sun came up, making the dew-drenched landscape look bright and glistening. I rose and said, as I had so long ago, "Goodbye, Mommy," and turned towards home.

The wagon was ready at the gate. I closed all the windows in the house and latched the door, and then ran back because I had forgotten to put out water for Skip and the chickens. I had climbed up beside Father and tried not to look back as the wagon started up the hill. But I had to have one backward look. Then I saw my dog Skip, running desperately back and forth behind the yard fence, scratching at the gate, whining and barking frantically after me. "Can't I take him? I cried. He's been my only friend." Father nodded yes. I jumped down, gathered him up in my arms and climbed back into the wagon. He waggled happily and licked my chin.

With mixed emotions in my heart, I leaned back against the wagon seat, wrapped my arms about my dog, and let my body sway with the jolting of the wagon.

22

My Irish Rose

The iron rims of the wagon wheels slammed and banged against the rutted red clay of the lane. To the left of us was a large meadow fenced in by split railed fence; the meadow was awash in goldenrod waiving in a soft breeze like a bright gold ocean down a long hill we banged along, Father holding on to the brake to slow the wagon down. Then across Dean's Creek, the horses stopped to drink and I hung my feet over the tailgate of the wagon and dipped them in the cold stream. Minnows gathered around to nibble at my toes and I thought of how I might someday long to come back to the stream again. I thought of how I had waded it on icy mornings on my way to school, of how I was baptized in its cleansing waters and then I thought of the time I had forded it after a raging storm with Mr. Willoughby on a gallant horse. I then remembered I was swimming in this beautiful stream when I received the news of my mothers death. I put this thought aside with an ache in my heart.

Off we went down the long dusty valley road, past the bridge I had leaped over on my horse the night I felt so threatened by my childhood enemy. There were several miles to go, winding around the valley; we passed one fine farm house, white with gingerbread trim, and another that was a shack so ancient it was only standing on one leg.

With every mile I breathed a new breath of freedom. More and more I was filled with excitement and adventure.

Then there was the town of Brumley, with a huge mercantile store, church, school, and a post office. There were quite a few people gathered around the store. Some were on horseback, some in wagons and buggies.

To my utter delight my brother Paul was standing by a neat little car; he explained he would take us the rest of the way to Eugene. Father spotted Garsy in the crowd, who said he would take the team and the wagon back to the farm.

My brother Garsy looked so good with a fresh haircut, dressed in his Sunday best and Paul explained to me that my eldest brother was now in love with the young very pretty sister of my brother Jim's wife. They were to marry; I was very happy for him.

People gathered around my father, shaking his hand, slapping him on the back and calling him Uncle John and talking about him painting their houses.

A woman with a huge slat-bonnet and an apron trimmed in rickrack asked me, "Are you Aunt Lilly's girl?" When I said, "Yes," she said, "She was the purtiest woman in these parts." She wanted to know where we were going, and I told her I was going to Eugene to live and attend high school, and she said that was "a fur piece"; I said, "I don't know, I've never been there."

Father, Paul and I and Skip crowded into the little car; driving up a long hill we came to another town called Ulman. The town was full of small houses all painted white; on the right was a tall pretentious home where my mother, as a young girl, had worked as a maid.

On we whirled seemingly with the speed of the wind, down and down to a vast river valley. There were trees and tall bluffs on each side of the road that met a swinging bridge across the Osage River. The car rolled onto the swinging bridge and I looked down on a glistening river winding to the horizon. I was enthralled by its beauty. Seeing the reflection of the bluffs in the water, I declared I would paint these reflections some day, and I did. Across the river we approached the town of Tuscumbia, my father's birthplace. This was where he was born and raised, where he had painted houses, paddle-wheel riverboats and signs for all of the stores. He had also helped establish a newspaper in Tuscumbia; it was really a small town populated by the Wright family. This was where Paul, Goldie and Ruth had attended high school; I wondered but I didn't ask why I wasn't going to go to school there. We went through this beautiful little town and I wished I could have stayed.

Ten miles further on we came to the little town of Eugene. Eugene was a little railroad town where a train came through about twice a day. There was a church, a barbershop, a large general store, and a teeny tiny store perched along-side the street that would become a part of my daily life, and I would learn to love it.

Up a gentle sloping street lined with maple trees, we stopped at a beautiful white house and got out of the car; this was our destination. I was ecstatic, "Was I to live in this beautiful home?" Beside an inviting gate stood a woman about my father's age; she was a very plain woman of medium height, hair pulled back in a bun, with the sweetest smile I had ever seen. She held out her arms, kissed my father, and called him Uncle John. And then turned to me and asked, "Is this my little cousin, Francie? We are so glad to have you!" Surely I had arrived in paradise.

Della Brinkley, my fathers niece, was my first cousin and she was my fathers age. Della put her arm around me and led me into the house. Grandly furnished it was, with a piano and carpeting woven with a cabbage rose design. A table was set with white linen and our dinner was waiting for us. There were large pieces of ham, sweet potatoes, home made bread and stalks of celery, a vegetable I had never seen before. There were canned fruits and relishes to complete the meal. This truly was paradise. Later, we toured the yard, the orchard and a spotless outhouse. My cousin showed us the cellar, full of canned fruits and vegetables; I couldn't believe it all. Paul left for his new job near St. Louis—he would have a long night's drive ahead of him. My father told Della that he only had to put the roof on a house down the hill that he was building for him and me, and it was understood that I would stay with cousin Della until the house was finished, which would be several months.

At bedtime after settling Skip on a bed by the front door, Cousin Della showed me a large cabinet in the living room. She rolled the cabinet out from the wall, unfolded it, and lo, it became my bed! A comfy feather mattress, soft pillows and a pretty handmade quilt on top beckoned me; when she tucked me in she leaned over and gave me a goodnight kiss and said, "I'm so glad I talked Uncle John into bringing you here. It must have been awful over there on the hill all by yourself. At that moment I finally knew why my father had had a change of heart, and taken me away from the farm. This angel had intervened on my behalf. She had opened her heart and home to me and I fell in love with her. Della said, "Goodnight, tomorrow we will visit the high school."

The next day while on the two-mile walk to the high school, we stopped to see the house my father was building. It stood on a small plot of land 'neath a huge oak tree. The house had one large room down stairs with two bay windows and there was a small room upstairs; the problem was there was no stairway. I would in the future, when the house was finished, have to go out the front door, circle around back, climb onto the bay window roof and into the bedroom door. I asked, "Father where is the kitchen?" He said, "Oh, I plan on a lean-to on the north side big enough for a stove, a table and chairs." By the front door there was a beautiful collection of rocks, I asked what they were for. Father told me he planned on building a fireplace. I said, "It will have to have a tall chimney." He said, "I don't plan on a chimney." With pride he showed me a beautiful mantle he had carved. So we were to have a fireplace with a beautiful mantle and no chimney.

Months later I almost killed myself trying to get to the upper room without a stairway, and because father liked to make unusual things he said, "How about if I build you an elevator? So, he cut a hole in the upper room floor above the main room window. He built a platform big enough to stand on, that was moved up and down by a rope over a pulley in the ceiling upstairs. The elevator was efficient but not pretty. My cousin Della hated it. She tried it once and threatened never to speak to my father ever again, after it flew upstairs with her and threw her on the bed with her petticoats over her head. Father had a terrible time coaxing her down, as she was afraid she might be thrown out the window by this crazy machine.

My father's inventiveness couldn't be quelled. He started digging a cellar under the house; since it was almost solid rock it was very hard work. He dug a room about six feet by eight feet before the walls started to leak. He had hit a spring, so we had running water; thus, he had to dig a drain for the water to run down the hill. One day with energy to spare it seemed, he moved the stove down to the cellar hoping to cook near the running water. Within three days the stove was covered with rust.

Happily, at that first viewing of our new home I did not anticipate that this house would become the town joke. In those days I was so utterly full of joy with my new life that none of this bothered me. And later I learned to love the big sunny room with the bay windows and window seats, and the useless rock fireplace and pretty mantle. Father painted the walls a warm orchid and stenciled a border around the ceiling in a lacy black and white pattern. However, the elevator never did quite enhance the room. The house was neatly constructed with square corners and nicely fitted doors. On this first day though, Cousin Della and I were anxious to get on our way to the schoolhouse.

We went up a long sloping meadow covered with tall grasses now drying in the late August sun. We came to a beautiful Antebellum home. Cousin Della wanted me to meet its occupants, as they would be my close neighbors. Ever kind and thoughtful, she said, "This old couple might appreciate a little visit on your way to and from school. I was soon to learn to call them Aunt Nancy and Uncle Hugh Miller. Aunt Nancy had a goiter on her throat as large as a cabbage; she lay on a couch in the front room too frail to stand up. Uncle Hugh was a tall shadow of a man dressed as though he might be on his way to church. Later I realized that this was the way he dressed every day. I fell in love with this sweet old couple and made a point to stop everyday and share the school gossip; it was such fun to hear Aunt Nancy laugh at my exaggerated stories.

On down the road Della and I continued walking towards the schoolhouse. There it stood on top of the hill overlooking the small town. It was a square ugly building of red brick; however, the front doors were wide and inviting and the windows were large and sunny. The downstairs consisted of several rooms for the lower grades. Up a wide stairway were the high school classrooms. There were a lot of young people everywhere registering for classes, as school was to start the next day. In one large corner room, we were told that this would be the freshman classroom, where I would study.

Standing around the large desk by the blackboard were four people in conference. Della introduced me to them: "This is your cousin, Professor Cal Thompson." He was tall and thin—almost "Lincolnesque." He said, "Is this Uncle John's youngest?" It seemed everyone knew my father. Cousin Cal had the kindest eyes, and I noticed his long legs were encased in shiny blue serge pants that may have been pressed too many times.

Miss Bivens was plain, very straight-backed, and her hair recently "marcelled." I was to know her as a very dedicated math teacher; she expected you to learn and you did. No one ever failed Miss Biven's math classes. The next teacher was a man lately over from England; he had sandy hair and a very sober countenance. I was to spend a lot of time trying to get him to smile, just once. The last teacher of the group was a rather pretty woman named Lena Spalding; another cousin, she was all business. I learned she was the manager and organizer and very innovative planner for all the high school activities. From the very first she took hold of me and I knew I had a new and fun bossy big sister.

While the group continued to converse I leaned against the blackboard, took up the chalk and scribbled a tiny scene; Della turned to the others and laughed, "She's just like her father." Lena said, "It's in the family." I came to know that Lena was very artistic with all kinds of arts and crafts.

While Della registered me, I wandered off down a long hall that led to a balcony that was full of a large number of boys and girls my age and older. As I emerged from the hall onto the balcony, a very beautiful girl walked up to me with a wide smile and an arm load of books and said, "You're Frances aren't you? I'm Omega Spalding, a close neighbor; come on I'll introduce you to everybody." And I looked into the eyes of the dearest friend I would ever know.

From that first meeting we were soul mates. There was nothing shy or bashful about Omega—there needn't be for she was the most beautiful and popular girl in town. I found out that she had studied the piano since she was six years old. Her hands flew over the keys like a virtuoso, while she literally danced from one end of the piano bench to the other. From that first meeting on, we were hardly ever separated. After the introductions she said, "Hey, I'll take you and Mrs. Brinkley home in my car. I couldn't believe my new friend had her own car, as Della and I climbed into Omega's little Flivver with its top down. We sailed towards home, I looked back at the school; it looked big and warm and I thought, "It's mine and I'm going to love everyday I come here."

We dropped Cousin Della off at her house and Omega told me she had something to show me; her father had just bought her a little store that she could manage and call her very own. The small store had shelves lined with canned peaches, salmon and pork and beans; there was an icebox for cold soda pop and for storing bologna and bacon. There were crackers and bread and large jars of pickles on a shelf behind the counter. By the ancient cash register there were candy bars and gum for sale. Omega handed me a bottle of orange soda pop and while we sipped, she said, "If you could help me with the store, I could give you some groceries." I hugged her and our deal was closed.

The next day was the first day of school. Cousin Della woke me up early. She had warmed water on the stove that she had brought in from the back porch pump. I washed my face and combed my hair in front of the little mirror on the wall by the back door. I had only one outfit that I thought was suitable to wear to school. It was a white broadcloth shirt that my brother Paul had outgrown, and from a pair of old gray tweed knickers he had left on the farm, I had made a neat straight skirt. This along with my black patent leather pumps was to be my uniform for my high school years. I washed it out every night and ironed the garments dry every morning. No one ever remarked about me wearing the same outfit everyday for those years. Within two months Skip and I moved into my father's house and my classes were into full swing. The hours after school for the most part I spent with Omega in her store where I was given enough groceries to live on. My father was gone most of the time as he had always been—visiting with his cronies or painting. Omega and I were inseparable: she would often spend the night with me and sometimes I would spend the night at her house where she would play the piano until we were both drunk on the music.

On weekends we would attend the church where Cousin Della directed and supervised all the activities. Occasionally, an ordained minister was brought in to preach. Cousin Della taught Sunday school, and all ages attended, especially most of my high school classmates. I was surprised at their enthusiastic participation. I enjoyed these open discussions and how they even joined in saying the prayers. This was uninhibited freedom of speech that I was not used to in our church in the country where only men dominated the pulpit. After church Omega and I gathered up candy bars and soda pop from her little store, and we got in her little car and sped along the back roads at the fast speed of fifteen miles an hour; dust flying we laughed and sang popular songs of the day, like "My Blue Heaven, Carolina Moon and Stormy Weather." We would find a tree and in the shade, then picnic and gossip about our teachers and classmates and everybody else in town. I felt so privileged to have a girlfriend who was the only girl in town who had a car; as a matter of fact there were very few automobiles at all in the little town of Eugene. This little town had only one telephone that was in a small booth in the heart of town. Electricity had yet to come to this village, nor did anyone have running water. Omega and I felt wild and free as the birds while we sped along in her little car.

One day in our "hide away" in the woods, I told her about my four years on the farm when I was mostly alone. She seemed very quiet and I turned and looked at her and the tears were rolling down her cheeks. This beautiful girl, loved and pampered by her parents, adored by the whole town, was able to shed tears for me. I was not used to such love.

As the soft balmy autumn days passed, our classes fell into a pattern. My first class in the mornings was with "Mr. English"; I had given him this nickname. This sober man taught what were to be my most fabulous subjects: Socrates, Plato, The Hanging Gardens, and The Great Fountains and the most incredible stories of art that the world has ever known—Michael Angelo painting the Sistine Chapel came to life before our eyes. Day by day we wandered through the ancient stories and were enthralled.

Miss Bivens taught math in the second period class of the day. Everybody hated math but nobody hated Miss Bivens. She was like a performer on a stage. She stood in front of the blackboard and attacked it with such vigor that the chalked screeched on the board. We all learned math because our lives depended on it! The last period of the day was with my cousin, Professor Cal, who taught geometry, government and geography. The soft sunny afternoons made us sleepy and we longed to pillow our heads on the open books and snooze the afternoon away. Professor Cal would have none of this, he would bring out his violin and play Humoresque and many of the old "classics" and my favorite, Listen to the Mocking Bird. His long slim fingers could alternate with the bow and make the sounds of the birds in the trees trilling all of their notes. These recitals woke us up and we would all soon be tapping our feet to the rhythm of the music. I fell in love with this multi-talented man.

Cousin Lena handled our bouts with literature, science and nature. With her we explored mountains rivers and streams. She was like Mother Nature to me, always exciting, taking us on long field trips and walks in the woods. We had to learn every plant and every tree, through its seed, blossom and fruitation. Lena was proud when I drew pictures of our nature studies; she never let us have a dull day. Soon she was coaching basketball and volleyball and planning on our teams to compete with teams from other towns. At competition time off we all went in a big truck, Lena leading us in song. To me she played the big sister. She gave me a basketball uniform, which was a white middy blouse and black bloomers and of course I had to have her high-top tennis shoes to go with the outfit. They were a little big but that was fine with me. I wore this outfit in our first tournament in Tuscumbia. The Tuscumbia group looked down on us mostly because their town had a courthouse, newspaper, a much larger high school, and Anchor Milling Company. We beat the socks off of them in our first game!

Sometimes Lena spent the night with me when my father was away, and would prepare biscuits and oatmeal for our breakfast the next morning.

Lena arranged for a field trip for the freshman class to visit the capitol building in Jefferson City, which was forty miles from Eugene. We all went together in that same big truck. The capitol building, a small replica of the one in Washington D.C., stood imposing, white and pristine looking down on the Missouri River. The rotunda walls and ceiling were decorated with murals by Missouri's famous artist, Thomas Hart Benton. I was awed by the beauty of the rotunda and the artwork. The murals were so colorful, so full of distance and atmosphere, that I was almost transposed out of time and place. The others moved on but I stood transfixed before all of the beauty. That night after we went home, I went outside and put my arms around the big old oak tree, and asked the stars above, "Will I ever be able to paint like that?"

Halloween was an excuse for Lena's inventiveness. This twenty-four-year-old college graduate schoolteacher planned our Halloween party. She dressed us all in ghosts' and goblins' and witches' costumes and pushed us out the door while telling us to go have fun. It was a dark night and we decided to do "great damage" to the town. First we booed and made crazy noises and got all the dogs to barking. We banged on screen doors and then ran, we mischievously pushed over a few outhouses, and ended up at the railroad station where a huge fire was burning in a big iron stove. We cuddled up on benches by the fire, warming our feet and telling ghost stories. Beginning to get tired and sleepy, we decided we better go home. In the street as we wandered through town, to our amazement, stood a large Billy goat, hauntingly white in the dark night. I guess we blinded him with our one flashlight. We asked each other what mischief we could do with a goat? Someone suggested that we put him in the large vacant room over a big store that had an outside stairway and then he would make noises that would scare the owner the next morning. Pulling pushing and shoving we managed to get him up the stairway and in the door. I was huffing and puffing, pushing him with all my strength on the rump. We couldn't wait to hear what the owners would say the next morning, when they heard the racket upstairs.

I thought no more about our escapade until I got out of school the next day. I was walking across the schoolyard headed for home when I was suddenly confronted by "Mr. Billy Goat," himself. I held out my hand maybe to pet him and to be friendly, but he seemed to recognize me and glared at me with the most malevolent eyes I had ever seen. He snorted, lowered his head and began to paw the earth. Terrorized, I turned to flee from this raging animal. My fear and fleeing was his invitation to charge at me. I ran as fast as my legs would carry me with my hair flying, feeling his hot breath on my heels. My heart was in my throat and I thought I couldn't out run him; I was afraid to look back for fear he was gaining on me. Everybody in the schoolyard was screaming and laughing. At some point he gave up the chase, but I was so scared that I kept on running until I got home! I thought, "Never again will I pick on a billy goat on Halloween." The next day you can believe the boys at school used this wild chase as an excuse to tease. They called me, "The Goat Girl"; not offended, I laughed with them.

Omega and I managed to think of something to do every weekend. Her little store didn't keep us very busy, so on Saturdays sometimes, we would go to Jefferson City and see a matinee. Omega always paid my way since I had no money other than an occasional dollar bill for my school supplies sent to me from my sister Ruth, who worked as a housekeeper somewhere near Iberia Missouri. These excursions were my first encounters with a movie screen. We saw Fay Ray in Wings, King Kong and All's Quiet on the Western Front. Other times Omega would spend the night with me and at dinnertime we feasted on canned peaches, pork 'n' beans and bologna and soda pop of course. All this came from my friend's little store.

Father was hardly ever at home these days, but one night when he was there, Omega and I giggled and laughed so much in the upstairs room, he banged on the ceiling and shouted at us to be quiet. We were so glad when he wasn't home; we could practice our dances in the yard under the big oak tree. We danced the Charleston, the Foxtrot and the Can-Can, high kicks and all.

Cousin Della still chaperoned me at every town function that I attended. Patient and dear, she was always there to protect me; I felt loved and comforted. Della had an older son, who was married and had two children that I adored. I took them for walks to gather walnuts from under the Walnut trees, and often cuddled them in my lap and told them stories of Peter Rabbit in the Cabbage Patch. Della's son owned the only bank in town. I hardly ever saw him, but one day when I was playing with his children in a pile of leaves that I had raked up in Della's yard, He said, "Frances if you ever need any money, just come to the bank and I will give you what you need." But I never did; I had my pride, but I knew I would never forget that gracious offer.

At Christmas time the entire population of Eugene gathered at the church to watch the little angels perform the traditional Christmas pageantry. Omega and I sang "O Little Town of Bethlehem," accompanied by her lovely piano playing. Everyone came up to us after the program and said our song was beautiful. There were dozens of presents under the shimmering Christmas tree that was as high as the ceiling and was decorated with paper chains and popcorn garlands. I received a very pretty handmade dust cap and a box of delicate linen hankies.

There was to be a dance at the Town Hall during the Christmas Holidays. There would be banjo players, and of course, Professor Cal and his violin.

I told Omega and Lena that I couldn't attend the dance for I had nothing to wear. This was a wonderful excuse for them to play "dress-up," and loan me some of their "best," because I mustn't miss out on the dance; we all loved to dance, so I agreed to their plans.

We gathered at Omega's home where Lena and Omega had put armloads of clothes on Omega's bed for me to try on. They first pulled a pair of silk hose from the pile of clothes and lectured me on how to keep the seams straight. The hose were to be worn with the silk panties and a ruffled petticoat that was included in the collection. Then Omega insisted that I try on something I had never worn before: a lacy brassiere. Now here was a problem that sent both of them into hysterics, since nature had not endowed me with a very large bustline. Laughing and giggling they tried to make it fit, for it was several sizes too large. Laughing wildly they pinned and tucked, but it just wouldn't do. Afraid that they had hurt my feelings, they both assured me that with my eighteen-inch waist, curly hair and beautiful blue eyes, I needn't worry about my bust. How flattered I was! I fell in love with a red wool dress that sported a black velvet Peter pan collar and a wide black patent leather belt. The girls were having so much fun, but the earrings they hung on my ears did not meet with Cousin Della's approval; I took them off without a word.

The Town Hall was large and ugly but had a fine dance floor. By the time we got there it was crowded and noisy and the music seemed to raise the roof. Cousin Della sat primly on the bench that lined the wall, along with the other Mothers, and watched me with a twinkle in her eye. All the young people danced whether they had a partner or not; even the little tots got out on the floor and danced. Omega and I did the Charleston and almost danced everyone off the floor. Lena said, "You girls are really a scream."

Cousin Della was patting her foot to the rhythm of the music when Professor Cal pulled her out onto the dance floor and swung her into a Waltz. There were the two roll-models of the town dancing beautifully together.

The Winter months drug on as they always do; then Spring came and the hills were in bloom with Dogwood and Redbud and we studied hard for our last exams.

I had gotten better acquainted with my classmates and I made Uncle Hugh and Aunt Nancy laugh when I described some of them. There was Garland, who was the most beautiful young man in school and knew it. If the teacher left the room for a few minutes he would race up and down between the rows of desks kissing the girls. We clumped him on the head with our books and swore we would tell the teacher, but we never did. Then there was the short handsome lad that sat in front of me: he had black wavy hair, seeming to drip with grease, that he combed all the time with a little fine-tooth comb he kept in his breast pocket. Since his head was directly in front of me, the temptation was just too great. Every little bit I would reach and muss up his hair. He would glare angrily around the room not sure who the culprit was, and take out his little black comb and comb his hair again.

There was a girl with close-cropped hair, a perky nose and a bustline better proportioned than mine. She had a large collection of very pretty sweaters and wore a different one every day. I thought she was a very cute girl and the boys called her "Whistle Bait."

Towards the front of the room sat a very nice boy who helped the teacher keep the blackboard clean, sharpened my pencils and was courteous and helpful to everyone He seemed to follow me always with his eyes. At Christmas he had given me a bottle of perfume, which was the most foul smelling stuff that I had ever smelled. I told Aunt Nancy, "If I wore it I would scare all the skunks out of town," the odor was so revolting.

There was a small boy in our class who looked like he belonged in the first grade. He was exceptionally bright and made the best grades in school. He was quiet and uncommunicative. He was later to become a published writer.

I also told Aunt Nancy and Uncle Hugh how difficult geometry was for all of us. The last exam that we had had, everyone had failed the test. Professor Cal was so disappointed; he tore up all our papers and threw them in the trash, saying to us, "If you failed, it's my failure also. Let's start on that lesson and do it again." We were all so moved by this that we studied harder in order not to disappoint him again.

Cousin Lena had been inviting me to come spend the night with her and especially wanted me to meet her Grandma who was history incarnate. Grandma Kate had been bed-ridden for years; now she lay propped on pillows, the Bible in her hands. She was over a hundred years old and had read the Bible twenty-eight times without glasses. She was utterly delighted to see me and immediately launched into the history of our family.

Lord Baltimore had sponsored the first colonization of Catholics in America; another ancestor had established the first "Church of the Colonies" in Winterhaven, near Boston. And another ancestor had written a book of poetry in the seventeenth century.

She told us stories of the Civil War. One of our family, a very young soldier, full of anxiety for his pregnant wife who was about to give birth, went "AWOL" to go be at her side, and as he was swimming the river his Captain shot and killed him.

Proudly, Grandma Kate recited the tale of her grandmother who had ridden alone on horseback from Tuscumbia, Missouri, to somewhere in Texas to visit her husband who was a soldier in the Mexican American War. During this horrible war another tyrannical captain threatened to hang one of our family on the courthouse steps for a crime he hadn't committed. The soldier's mother pushed thru the crowd with a long-barreled gun aimed at the captain's heart. It took no time at all for the captain to untie the rope and let the lad go.

Another ancestor, a friend of Lincoln and a large slave-owner, was persuaded by Lincoln to free his slaves. This was the man that I had heard of before, who had a team of Reindeer; when he hitched this team to his fancy surrey and drove thru the town of Springfield, Illinois, people gathered and pointed at the strange sight and laughed and laughed.

Grandma Kate reminded us that we were all distant relatives of General Lee although our people had sided with the "North." After the Civil War the "Bushwhackers" raided the countryside, robbing and stealing; Grandma Kate remembered that the family had hidden their money in a wormy hole in an apple tree. Grandma wanted to continue her stories of the family history, but she became weary; her eyes closed and she went to sleep. We kissed her on her forehead and tiptoed out of the room.

Lena and I laid down on Lena's huge feather bed and she told me of her years away at college and how she had studied art. The next morning we had a very large breakfast. Lena's sisters and mother had gotten up at daylight and killed chickens to fry. We also had fried apples and potatoes and big bowls of gravy. Lena walked me the three miles home and remarked repeatedly, "I told you that you would love Grandma and her stories."

"Oh Lena, I could have listened to her for hours!"

Spring came quickly full of bloom, and summer came after, rich and warm and sweet. One day Lena showed up at my door with a box of paints and a couple of canvases under her arm, she said, "I'm in the mood to paint, would you like to paint along with me?" Would I like to paint along with her? I was ecstatic! We propped our canvases on the dresser and on the mantle. For palettes, we found some roof shingles in the yard. Joyfully we squeezed colors on the palettes and happily went to work. Lena was painting a still life, from memory, of her garden in bloom. I chose to paint trees—my favorite subject. Quietly we worked for a while; finally I stood back to look at my canvas and it was a mess and I began to cry a flood of tears. I said, "I don't know what I'm doing; I haven't worked enough with oils and I'm just wasting the paint and the canvas." Angrily I took my brush and wiped half the paint off.

Lena put her arms around me to comfort me. "You are just beginning to learn," she said. "Your talent is like a gift that has to be unwrapped and handled carefully like the treasure it is. First you must say to yourself, 'I want my picture to make a statement.' Is it spring, summer, fall, or winter? Is it morning, noon, or night? You have to bounce your light and colors around to say what you want them to say. Your trees need to tell you how old they are and what kind of life they have led. Are they young or old and twisted, have they withstood lightening, wind and rain? Is the bark damaged in places by animals feeding or the ax of a lumberman? A tree does not stand alone, as a rule. To look large it must have smaller ones near it and maybe it's roots crawling around a rock. If you want the trunk to look rounded, the light should come strongly from one side and reflected lights from the other. Take your palette knife and rake it in the bark."

She instructed, and talked on. "From every painting you paint, you will learn something on your own. You will not only learn how, you will learn why, and one day perhaps you will paint something so beautiful, maybe by divine accident and you will say to yourself, 'At last I know what I am doing and I can make it happen,' then you will know a great joy and you will know that all of your effort has not been in vain. Just smooth out your paint and let's start over again. Remember this: if you are an artist you have to paint!" I smiled, picked up my brush and started over.

In the heat of the summer, on a Sunday afternoon, a group of us girls went for a walk along the railroad tracks. We came to the mouth of a dark tunnel that we knew ran under a hill for a mile or so. Dare we try to walk thru? It might be dangerous but an exciting thing to do, considering there was very little space between the track and the walls of the tunnel. One girl lit a cigarette, passed it around and even thought I don't think any of us had ever smoked before, with much laughing and choking we all tried a few puffs. Omega said, "Those things are awful! They'll make your teeth yellow and give you wrinkles!" We gave up on the puffing but decided to take the lit cigarettes into the dark so that we could see. We were hardly a few yards into the tunnel when we heard the train whistle. The loud noise scared us half to death and we raced back to the opening; safe outside, we all huddled together as the train went roaring by. We swore none of us would ever tell about our scary escapade!

That summer I was asked by a distant cousin, who had a strawberry patch and needed help canning, to come and help. I was pleased; they had a nice county home and a nice family of four boys around my age. We picked and stemmed and washed berries and washed jars for three days non-stop. We worked so hard, the juice stained my arms up to my elbows, and I ate so many strawberries that I thought surely they would come out of my ears. As I remember, we canned about one hundred and fifty quarts of berries. On the fourth day I trudged wearily home with two jars of strawberries, one under each arm; this was my pay. I thought I might not like strawberries ever again.

Eugene was a family oriented town: most activities centered around the church, the school and the train station. There were "Ice cream socials" and "Fish frys"—with corn on the cob, catfish, coleslaw and of course, apple pie There was always one Country Fair during the summer, with no Ferris wheel or merry-go-round, just a dance pavilion and lots of food, with all the women competing for prizes in cake and pie baking.

Sometimes there would be an auction, where everything imaginable was sold. There might be anything from crock churns to horse collars; fruit jars to someone's prize bull.

On Sundays, folks would gather, young and old, at the ballpark, where they would play ball while on-lookers cheered from the rickety old bleachers. At one of these games the joys of this summer came to a tragic end. Margarite, one of my classmates, a beautiful girl, with long blond hair, was at bat; suddenly she collapsed on the ball field. Our town doctor was fetched and it was decided that she had Polio, a very dangerous and contagious disease that could quite possibly infect the whole town; however, Margarite was the only victim. She was taken to her parent's home, where she laid at death's door for months, while the saddened town-folks sent up prayers for her.

In late August the big doors of the school opened again. Students crowded in. The only ones missing were last year's graduates, and Margarite, of course. Her empty seat brought tears to all of our eyes. In the cooler months, surprisingly, she began to recover. And when the Holidays came along she was brought to school once, in her wheelchair, with half of her body paralyzed. Smiling sweetly, she greeted us all and we were so happy to see her.

After the Holidays, Professor Cal decided that we better do something to erase the gloom in our classroom. To our surprise, one day he announced that he had plans to give a play at the end of the school year. The name of the play was "My Irish Rose," a comedy-drama in three acts.

The High School Auditorium, a huge basement room under the building normally used for basketball games, would be used for the theater. We were to build a stage and arrange for a curtain. Chairs and benches for seating would be borrowed from the church.

The big exciting question was: "Who would be chosen to play the different parts in the play?" We waited anxiously for copies of the play to arrive. The day they arrived, several were handed around the rooms to the students. I had not hoped or dreamed that I might have a part in the play; hurriedly, I scanned the cast of characters. As my eyes followed down the list of characters, I was amazed to see my name following "The Irish Rose," the leading character in the play. I believe my heart stopped, and this was the most exciting moment of my young life.

From that moment on for the next few months the script hardly left my hands. It was a lot for me to memorize. Everyone seemed happy for me and helped me with my lines. I even took the script home to be with me by the dim light from the oil lamp. I would study my lines for hours. I even enlisted Aunt Nancy, to her delight, to help me to rehearse. Of course, other studies and activities had to come in between.

Meanwhile in the basement room of the schoolhouse there was lots of noise of hammering and sawing as the stage was being constructed; even the basketball and volleyball games were put aside for this project.

Then Cousin Lena decided that I had to have a beautiful gown for the performance. She and I would design and make it ourselves. She bought the material with her own money, as I had none. She purchased yards and yards of white voile for our creation. The bodice was to be fitted, with a low neckline and puffed sleeves. With Lena's ever-ready imagination to be called upon, she created a spectacular skirt; for the hemline we laid the material on the bed, and painted a scalloped hem with clear glue and sprinkled on silver sparkles that clung to the glue. We then cut the fabric, following the edge of the scallops—and lo and behold—there was a beautiful sweep of skirt that would reach to the floor. For the waistline we had a wide blue satin ribbon to be tied in a large bow in the back. At the throat we planned for me to have a white rose on a black velvet ribbon. Then, to my amazement, Lena brought out a pair of fabric pumps and painted them with silver paint. Our "Rose" would be a vision in this costume! And she certainly needed to be beautifully dressed, for in the theme of the play there were plots, counter-plots and vicious gossip, with flirty girls all vying for the hero's attention, and all contriving to keep Rose and her lover apart.

Finally the stage was finished and somebody's parlor was robbed, for the time being, of furniture for the "set". Pictures were hung and Omega and I covered our eyes and held our breath while her piano was brought down the steps. She was contributing her most precious possession to the show.

It was announced that we would stay after school for the rehearsal the first couple of days; there was pandemonium. All the upper classmen gathered on the stage, eager to help with their own notions about what should be happening; laughing and clowning around, they contributed their own lines and everyone became a director. Finally Lena and Professor Cal said, "This won't do. Would everyone that's not part of the cast please leave the stage." Pushing and shoving the rest finally lined up in the audience chairs, still over-zealous. Miss Bevins, who had been watching from the back row, marched up the isle, folded her arms across her chest and glared at the culprits. They all slunk quietly down in their seats.

The second day things still continued to go wrong. The "landowner" came on stage huffing and puffing with his fly undone; this set the actors into gales of laughter. I experimented with my first lipstick and consequently I made red lip-prints on my lover's face. In my first attempt at fainting, I fell so hard on the boards that I saw stars. While the other actors were helping me up, I thought, "I've just got to do this a little more slowly and a little more gracefully."

We began to work on one of the girls, the gossipy character in the play, who was made very buxom with lots of padding on the stomach and bust. During rehearsal, while speaking her lines, she became over-enthused and accidentally stepped backwards and fell off the stage with her skirts over her head and all her padding out of place. The boys scrambled around, trying to help her, laughing all the while—which made her furious.

Our school-ground pet, a big yellow dog, wandered onto the stage one afternoon, enthusing and drooling and wagging his tail as he greeted everyone. With pulling and coaxing, he was finally dragged off the stage after his wagging tail had knocked all the props down; of course, he had had to be rewarded along the way with a few sweet treats.

One of our youngest cast member's voice was changing, so it was either too high or too low. Then came the worst part of the whole rehearsal, our sad attempts at the Irish dialect. My own dialect left a lot to be desired. My Ozark twang, to my embarrassment, sent everybody into gales of laughter. Taking pity on me, "Mr. English" decided to coach me. He and I were doing fine until Professor Cal stopped the lessons as he attempted to teach us all the "Kerry" dance. Gracefully he waved his arms, swayed his body and twirled on his toes. The sight of his long skinny legs, swinging arms and tapping feet, suddenly sent Mr. "English," who always wore the countenance of a funeral director, into spasms of laughter that he couldn't seem to get under control. None of us had ever seen him laugh; now he was doubling over, holding his stomach, turning beet-red in the face and roaring. Someone rushed to get him a glass of water, fearful he would be overcome.

Days and days of rehearsal passed and at last the important evening arrived! Omega, at the piano, began to play the sweet romantic music of "My Wild Irish Rose"; we took our places and the curtain rose.

The Auditorium was crowded with people; there were folks even standing shoulder to shoulder along the walls and huddled together on the stairway. The crowd became quiet and "the play was the thing."

Suddenly all of us on the stage transformed ourselves into the characters of the people we were to portray, we were no longer our real selves—we became the living, breathing, fighting, and loving people of the Irish Isle across the sea.

Time passed, differences were resolved, and at long last, Mr. Fitzgerald, in his "morning coat" and Rose in her flowing gown, came together in a passionate kiss and embrace!

The lights dimmed, the music swelled to the sweet notes of the "Last Rose of Summer," The curtain fell—to loud applause and a standing ovation—and we all joined hands to take our curtain calls. We were all so very proud that we hadn't flubbed a line or missed a cue!

Professor Cal handed me a large bouquet of flowers, hugged and kissed me on the cheek and said, "You will be another 'Sarah Bernhardt'." I took this as a compliment, having no idea who she was.

I looked across the crowd and saw my Father; I had not known he would be there. He looked proud and pleased. I hoped my Mother—in Paradise—was just as proud.

The Beginning

About the Author

Francesca Wright, who studied art at Washington University and helped found the New Mexico Arts League, is a gifted artist with over a thousand original oil paintings in private and corporate collections worldwide. While painting and writing, she created two award winning restaurants and designed and built seven unique homes.

978-0-595-38959-9
0-595-38959-7

Printed in the United States
122195LV00002B/155/A